Blood Relations

Blood Relations

Chosen Families in *Buffy the Vampire Slayer* and *Angel*

Jes Battis

McFarland & Company, Inc., Publishers
Jefferson, North Carolina, and London

LIBRARY OF CONGRESS CATALOGUING-IN-PUBLICATION DATA

Battis, Jes, 1979–
Blood relations : chosen families in Buffy the vampire slayer and Angel / Jes Battis.
p. cm.
Includes bibliographical references and index.

ISBN 0-7864-2172-X (softcover : 50# alkaline paper) ∞

1. Buffy, the vampire slayer (Television program). 2. Angel (Television program : 1999–). I. Title.
PN1992.77.B84B38 2005 2005012763
791.45'72 — dc22

British Library cataloguing data are available

Manufactured in the United States of America

McFarland & Company, Inc., Publishers
Box 611, Jefferson, North Carolina 28640
www.mcfarlandpub.com

For my parents

Acknowledgments

Thanks foremost to David Lavery and Rhonda Wilcox, for giving me the positive feedback and encouragement necessary to undertake this project.

Thanks to the following people for support and scholarly advice: my doctoral supervisor, Peter Dickinson; Nancy Earle, Tanya Krzywinska, Lorna Jowett, Viv Burr, Elizabeth Rambo, Rebecca Beirne.

Thanks to my friends and peers for ongoing emotional support (including, when necessary, dragging me out of the office and into the sunlight): Matt, Cec, Jef, Kerri, Hannah, Marty, Jamie, Ben, Lisa, Ken, Karen, Tara, Jessica, Nancy, Jasmine, Dorritta, and Jason.

Thanks to wonderful and carefully maintained websites like *Much Ado About Buffy the Vampire Slayer*, and *The Buffyverse Dialogue Database*, for allowing me to search for vital quotes.

Thanks to Joss, and the *Buffy* and *Angel* cast and crew, for all the fabulous stories.

Contents

Preface

I include this preface as a brief introduction to the core characters within *Buffy the Vampire Slayer* and *Angel* that this book will address. For those readers not intimately familiar with both shows, the following character sketches should prove helpful. They represent, basically, a more orderly recollection of the dozens of conversations that I've had about *Buffy* with friends who don't know anything about the show, or defenses of my research that I've had to construct when I was introduced at parties as "Jes, who's writing a book on *Buffy the Vampire Slayer.*" Nobody has neutral opinions about either show. Often, I've found myself saying things like, "No, I really don't think Buffy is a feminist icon," or, "actually, Television Studies represents a thriving critical discipline" to people who know very little about *Buffy* in particular, or the study of popular culture in general. I wrote this book partly as an exploration of the idea of "family" as it shifts between both shows, and partly as a celebration of what are, I think, two of the most amazing and emotionally resonant programs on television.

I have tried to include as much vital information about each character as possible without summarizing any episodes or spoiling any plots. I have also, of course, saved the most fascinating details for later. This is what's called a hook. I didn't invent it, but I have no qualms about using it. There's an angry witch, a vengeance demon, a one-eyed carpenter, a vampire slayer, two British guys, a brilliant physicist, a karaoke-singing demon, a vampire with a soul, and a very peculiar immortal with blue hair. Did I mention the British guys?

The characters that this book directly addresses have extended biographies, while the characters that it touches on peripherally have somewhat shorter entries. I have also included a few terms that might require explanation.

Angel: a vampire, once known as Angelus, who murdered hundreds of people before being cursed with a soul. Now, in an attempt to pay for his past crimes, Angel runs a detective agency in L.A. He and Buffy have a doomed relationship that can never come to fruition because of his curse. Angelus is Angel's vampire alter-ego, his psychological shadow always threatening to break free. Angelus is also a smoker. Angel survived for some time in abject poverty, feeding off animal blood, until he was enlisted by the Powers-That-Be to watch and protect Buffy. He was turned into a vampire by Darla, with whom he eventually has a son, Connor. Angel's friends call him cheap, although he considers himself "thrifty." His favorite color is black.

Anya: a former vengeance demon who, as a result of having her mystical amulet broken by Giles, becomes human. Vengeance demons, as their name implies, enact vengeance (or "retributive justice") on evildoers. Anya's specialty, when she was a demon, was visiting creative and agonizing punishments on men who were unfaithful. After she becomes human, Anya gets involved romantically with Xander. Her sense of comic timing is surpassed only by her literal view of the world, which often translates into inappropriate statements and confusing questions. Anya was a vengeance demon for a 1100-years, and has only been human for about four years, so she still has a pretty steep learning curve to contend with. Like Cordelia, she often says the one thing that everyone needs to hear, but no one *wants* to hear. She has a terrible phobia of bunnies and, centuries ago, transformed her husband Olaf into a troll. She now owns and manages the *Magic Box*, the magical-supply store that Giles purchased after its original owner was killed by a demon. As it is located in Sunnydale, California, a nexus for supernatural activity, the *Magic Box* does booming business.

Buffy: Buffy Summers is a vampire slayer, which means that she is a prophesied warrior who must battle vampires, demons and other unpleasant creatures in order to keep the world safe from the forces of darkness. Buffy's real problem is that she keeps getting romantically entangled with those forces of darkness. She falls in love with Angel, a vampire with a soul (there's only two in the whole world), but they can never be happy together because of Angel's curse, which causes him to become evil if he ever experiences "one moment of true happiness." Buffy is fiercely protective of her extended family, the Scooby Gang, and is visually the opposite of what most people think a prophesied warrior should look like. Her signature move is the delivery of a great pun before slaying a vampire. She has died twice, and was buried once. She originally operated beneath the guidance of the Watcher's Council, a collection of mostly middle-aged white British men who monitor Slayers, but she eventually rejected them and decided to work without "official" supervision. She has worked, if briefly, as a construction worker, a store clerk, a fast-food employee and a high school counselor. She has a phobia of puppets.

Connor: Angel's son, who ends up getting sent to a Hell-dimension as an infant, and subsequently returns as an angry teenager. Connor, like most teenage boys, resents his father for just about everything. He sinks Angel to the bottom of the ocean as punishment, but Angel escapes and, wisely, decides to give Connor some space. Connor falls in love with Cordelia, but their relationship is cut short when she gets pregnant and gives birth to an evil life-sucking god. Eventually, Angel strikes a mystical deal to have Connor's memories erased, and places him within a normal family so that he can experience a happy and harm-free life.

Cordelia: an actress-turned–vampire hunter who grew up in Sunnydale with Buffy and then moved to L.A. Cordelia was an abrasive, popularity-obsessed, witheringly critical teenager who made most people's lives miserable at Sunnydale High (before it blew up, which is another story). When she moved to L.A. to pursue a doomed acting career, she reconnected with Angel, and helped him to form the Angel Investigations crew. Eventually, Cordelia was given debilitating visions from the Powers-That-Be which allowed her to see people in danger, but which also caused her physical and psychological trauma. Over the course of *Angel*, Cordelia grows into a warm, protective and compassionate mothering force.

Dawn: Buffy's little sister, who is actually a mystical energy force called "the Key" which melts dimensional walls. Dawn is implanted into Buffy's life by a group of monks who are trying to safeguard the Key. Buffy and the Scoobies accept her as a member of their family regardless, and she becomes an effective vampire slayer in her own right, although not before acting as an endangered prop for several seasons. Dawn's first kiss turns out to be with a vampire, which is probably a bad omen.

Faith: another vampire slayer, and Buffy's opposite in more ways than one. Faith is originally assigned as Wesley's "charge," but she abandons the Watcher's Council and sets off on her own. Buffy is initially drawn to Faith's amoral philosophies, her instrumentalizing of slayer-power, and her sexual freedom. But she eventually opposes Faith, and the two become enemies.

Fred (Winifred Burkle): a brilliant young physicist who, as a result of an experiment gone wrong, was trapped in another dimension for five years. Angel rescues her, and she subsequently ends up joining his crew. Fred is socially awkward, but very smart, and eventually becomes a vocal and energetic member of Angel Investigations. She specializes in particle-supersymmetry, but occasionally builds crossbows and catapults as well. When Fred's body is taken over by a demonic force, she dies and is "resurrected" as Illyria, a pureblooded demon with only some of Fred's memories.

Giles: a former Watcher and member of the Watcher's Council who ends up losing his job and becoming a shopkeeper. Giles is Buffy's assigned Watcher, which means that it's his job to train her in combat techniques, demonic lore and, sometimes, vaguely Eastern spirituality. Giles becomes a kind of surrogate father to Buffy, and a paternal presence among the rest of the Scooby Gang. He falls in love just once, with a cyber-pagan computer-science teacher named Jenny Calendar, but Angelus (evil Angel) kills her. Giles tends to be the voice of reason among the Scoobies, when he isn't getting knocked out, tortured or kidnapped. He drives a Citroën, enjoys listening to *The Very Best of Cream* and was known as "Ripper" in his younger days because he was a rebellious and defiant warlock. He has since calmed down, and abandoned the use of magic in favor of selling magical artifacts. Once, under the influence of powerful magic, he slept with Buffy's mother. He divides his time between Sunnydale and London.

Gunn: vampire hunter who joins Angel's crew after his sister is killed and turned into a vampire. Gunn is first coded as the brawn of the group, but he evolves into a powerful communicator and litigator. He falls in love with Fred, but their relationship is rocky and short-lived. Gunn is the only central character of color in *Angel* (aside from Lorne, who is green), and his poor background and gang-related history make him a troubling character, especially when we consider that an all-white staff of writers crafted him. The only other people of color in the two series are peripheral at best. Principle

Wood, whose Slayer mother was killed by Spike, isn't introduced until Season 7, and doesn't ever seem to achieve dynamic characterization; the unfortunate Kendra, who precedes Faith as a vampire slayer, is killed after two episodes; and, among the potential slayers, there is Rona, whose vocal resistance to Buffy's rules is routinely silenced by white characters (like Dawn), and Chao-Ahn, whose Asian ancestry seems to have been used as a joke by the writers. I discuss racial marginalization in both shows throughout the book.

Lorne: a green-skinned empath demon who can read people's emotions by listening to them sing karaoke. Lorne is a bit of a Fred Astaire throwback, wearing a lot of silk bathrobes, but his ambivalence around fighting doesn't stop him from acting as a critical source of information for the Investigations crew. He also baby-sits for free, and speaks several different languages, including one composed entirely of clicks and whistles. His singing voice can shatter glass and cause people to lose consciousness. His favorite drink is a Sea Breeze.

Riley: a Psychology T.A. by day and covert government agent by night, Riley Finn works for an organization called The Initiative which captures and studies vampires, among other creatures. Riley falls in love with Buffy, but soon begins to feel outclassed by her in terms of strength and ability. Eventually the two split up, and Riley leaves to fight demons in South America.

Slayer: a prophesied hunter of vampires and demons, always a female, who protects the world from the forces of evil. There can, originally, only be one Slayer at a time. When Buffy dies (briefly), Kendra is "called"; when Kendra dies, Faith replaces her, and becomes a more permanent fixture. Slayers are supposed to abide by the rules set forth by the Watcher's Council, though neither Faith nor Buffy tend to listen to those rules.

Spike: a leather-clad vampire who has killed two Slayers in his time, and who falls in love with Buffy. Spike has a tough exterior, but he cares immensely for Buffy and for Dawn, her little sister. He smokes drinks, and plays kitten poker. Deciding that he wants to change, Spike journeys into the desert in search of his lost soul. What he finds is more than anyone bargained for. He does end up saving the world, but only through the help of a magical artifact that, in his own words, makes him look like Elizabeth Taylor. He has peroxide-blonde hair, a penchant for punk music and a history of writing terrible poetry.

Watcher's Council: a London-based organization that controls and monitors Slayers. They have access to the most advanced demon lore in the world, and guard their information jealously. They subject Buffy to a battery of traditional tests before she rejects them outright and decides to work on her own. Both Giles and Wesley are former Watchers who were officially stripped of their position due to perceived incompetence and mismanagement of their Slayers.

Wesley: a younger Watcher who begins his career as a by-the-book scholar, and attempts to usurp Giles's position in Sunnydale. Wesley was assigned to watch Faith, a rogue Slayer who ends up kidnapping and torturing him. Wesley moves to L.A. to become, in his own words, a "rogue demon hunter," and joins the crew of Angel Investigations. He begins his tenure there as a demon expert, but eventually transitions into an accomplished fighter and strategist. Wesley develops a romantic interest in Fred, but she prefers to date Gunn instead. When the two finally do get together, Fred is consumed by a millennia-old demonic force and transforms into Illyria.

Willow: A high school friend of Buffy's, Willow begins the show as an awkward and socially inept nerd, and ends it as one of the most formidable witches in the world. She has a fascination with computers, and her penchant for crafting simple charms eventually manifests itself into a magic-addiction that endangers Willow and the rest of the Scoobies. After a few failed heterosexual romances, Willow meets Tara, another witch, and falls in love with her — a relationship cut brutally short when Tara is killed by a stray bullet meant for Buffy. Luckily, Willow finds love again with Kennedy the vampire slayer, who also has a tongue ring. Willow hates *M. Butterfly*, loves dolphins and often uses memory charms to give her friends amnesia. She is a brilliant student who could have attended any ivy league university, but chose instead to go to UC Sunnydale with Buffy.

Wolfram & Hart: an evil law firm with offices in Los Angeles, Venice, New York and London (as well as in with a few other hostile dimensions). Wolfram & Hart begins as Angel's main adversary, dogging his efforts and attempting to capture and study him. They are concerned by his supposed role in an ancient prophecy, which dictates that he will avert a coming apocalypse that they would like to see go off without a hitch. Later, Angel ends up working *for* Wolfram & Hart, although that's a long story.

Xander: Willow's childhood friend, who gets terrible grades, works a string of unremarkable jobs and (just once) works as an exotic dancer to pay for car repairs. Xander is a wisecracking perennial virgin whose first sexual experience ends up being with Faith (shortly before she tries to kill him). Xander is the character who coins the phrase "Scooby Gang" when talking about Buffy and company, referring to the cast of *Scooby Doo*, who also fought supernatural forces. He eventually falls in love with, and attempts to marry, Anya, only to leave her at the altar because he's afraid of being a terrible father and husband. Xander's levity and wit are all designed to conceal his powerful sense of protectiveness and attachment to his friends, and he even manages to stop Willow from destroying the world by reminding her of kindergarten. It is Xander's job to see people as they are, and remind them of who they used to be. Eventually, he loses his depth perception, but still retains some carpentry skills.

It is not necessary to understand all of the nuanced connections between these characters, nor to remember every bit of dialogue that they've spoken over a collective 12 seasons worth of televisual narrative. What is important to remember is that they all interact, in various ways, as a family, and this family both depends upon and rejects conventional notions of the nuclear family. Both *Buffy* and *Angel*, as shows, revolve around radical conceptions of family, and depend for their coherence on the establishment of non-traditional families that admit vampires, demons, witches, werewolves and other bizarre characters without censuring them for their peculiarities. The key signifier for being a member of these alternative families is loyalty, not heredity.

I argue, in the following chapters, that these characters would not be so enduring or engaging if not for their critical family connections. Their most involved struggles occur not within the graveyard, but around the dinner table, just as the most challenging adversarial forces that they must face end up being the matter of everyday life, rather than demons or vampires. It's being alive, not undead, that remains the hardest negotiation for Buffy, and family is what makes that process possible. Just as a whole extended family of fans have grown up around both shows, so has a close-knit family of academics emerged to criticize and discuss them.

I hope you will see aspects of your own families within these radical and unconventional ones. I certainly do. Everyone's family is, after all, just a little bit strange, a little bit unearthly. We may not all have demons for relatives, but we do all experience "family" as a contingent and personal idea that doesn't necessarily translate into discourses of universality. Deep down, we've all suspected that our parents might be from another dimension, or that our siblings might be demons put on Earth to torture us. In *Buffy* and *Angel*, these fantastic motifs are given life, but they are given an elegant, particular, and fully formed life that doesn't depend upon science fiction tropes. These "unreal" families seem, at times, more real than our own.

In the end, what remains important is not what a family looks like, but if it *works*. I leave you to decide whether or not the radical families in *Buffy* and *Angel* work, and to what extent they are, like our own families, simply collections of fallible human beings who love, challenge, support and infuriate each other, and who can't really imagine living any other way.

Introduction

Any critical study of a television program — but especially the critical study of a television program as ambiguous and double-voiced as *Buffy the Vampire Slayer*— invokes an uneasy combination of enthusiasm and ire within the academic community. Texts like Lavery and Wilcox's *What's at Stake* (Rowman and Littlefield, 2002) and Kaveney's *Reading the Vampire Slayer* (IB Tauris, 2002), while attempting to legitimate the show by discussing it through the time-honored scholarly essay format, have also been met with a certain amount of Parnassian disdain from the halls of the academy. After all, giving *Buffy* the full theoretical treatment via deconstructionist analysis does not, by itself, grant the show any sort of agency. It only raises the argument that such analysis can be applied to any "text." And this is, of course, the root of all fear within textual studies: that the sanctity of literary analysis will be diluted, thinned, rendered hollow and threadbare, as a result of being stretched endlessly over the gaping field of popular culture. Derrida does *The Flinstones.* Kristeva looks at *The Sopranos.* Where can we stop? What is the breaking point? How radically have we mutated and distended Barthes' use of "text"[1] to signify anything legible, watchable, consumable?

Does *Buffy* truly represent the edge, the end, the vanishing point, of scholarly analysis? And if so — why? How can this show, this hour-long serial about a pert, blonde-haired Valley girl and her gang of evil-fighting comrades, be a cultural vortex threatening to devour the ivory foundations of the academic world? Or, more importantly: Why does that world seem suddenly divided into those who wish *Buffy* would just go away, and those who eagerly organize panels, articles, special issues and anthologies in order to deconstruct everything from gender to capitalism within the program? If anything, increased scholarship around *Buffy* has proven that there is no line between those who dissect the show and those who rapaciously consume it. The professors are also the fans; and although this dynamic exists, fundamentally, within most teacher/text relationships, it is hybridized within television studies. Scholars of *Pride and Prejudice*, after all, are not on pins and needles waiting for the next installment of Austen's text. To study a serial is to admit, even as the article or book chapter or conference paper is being written, that everything could change next week. Televisual texts — especially ongoing ones — are capable of disproving all our careful research with a single episode.

Buffy is now finished. Officially. The seven-season story arc has finally come to an end, and the program is no more, nor is its younger sibling, *Angel.* Joss Whedon, the creator of both shows, has continually expressed an interest in turning his attention to movies, which means that there will probably not be a *Buffy Returns* or *Slayer: The Next Generation*. And it also means that, while previous studies have explored the *Buffy* phenomenon as an unfolding text, we now have the opportunity to discuss the "finished" product. The question is: Why should we? The inscription on Buffy's gravestone is simple: "She saved the world. A lot." Perhaps the program should leave a similar epigram behind: "It confused academics. A lot."

But, just as Buffy's friends — her surrogate family — cannot lay her aside (or to rest), neither can academics lay the program aside. Derrida warns us that the most seductive texts, the most powerful texts, are those which have no edge.[2] *Buffy* is a text without an edge — a text that has been transformed, remediated through endless marketing and merchandising, reimagined through fanfiction that spans the gap between the hauntingly erotic and the patently ridiculous. It is powerful, unclassifiable and — quite possibly — one of the most wildly implausible and absurd shows ever to occupy televisual space.

What, then, gives it agency? What makes people watch? What strategy, like a hypnotic suggestion, evokes such passionate response within the spectator? Why the conferences, the books, the articles, the commentaries, the syllabi? *Should* we, in fact, slay *Buffy*? Should we forget about it, turn our attention to more "legitimate" media studies — like rhetoric in television, or experimental cinema? What would it mean if we did? What would we be foreclosing? What would we be authorizing?[3]

Let me posit, briefly, my first experience of the show. This is not designed to be a testimonial, but rather to trace my interest in the program, and by extension, my interest in the many universes created by Joss Whedon. What struck me as I watched the first season was *Buffy*'s unique narrative structure. Like most hour-long serials—*Star Trek* or *Dallas*, for example—it was basically a novel in episodic installments that resembled miniature chapters. Unlike most serials, it called that structure into question. The foreshadowing, the acerbic pop culture references and the play of cinematic language—all present in the very first episode, and evolving throughout the season—marked *Buffy* as a program that was ready and willing to address its own existence *as* a televisual text, and to challenge that existence. It was, I began to conclude, a kind of postmodern novel. And that thought—the idea that a genre-crossing television program might stand in for a novel, and that, indeed, televisual texts were swiftly becoming simulacra of the formerly privileged novel—fired my real interest in *Buffy*, and led to the first early conceptions of this scholarly investigation.

As the aptly named *Blood, Text and Fears* conference—the first international symposium on *Buffy the Vampire Slayer*, held at the University of East Anglia (October 19–20, 2002)—suggests, *Buffy* is an evocative web of overlapping stories that could easily form a set of weighty novels in Tolkienesque tradition. Over seven seasons, with 22 episodic "chapters" per season, it is possible to develop an abiding love and attachment to these characters; they are layered and nuanced through endless action and dialogue that a standard novel could not reasonably sustain between its covers. *Buffy*'s story moves across differing textual sites (from adult fanfiction to youth-oriented novels), televisual sites (spinoffs like *Angel*, which very quickly became a separate text in its own right), merchandising sites (computer/console games, toys, CDs, glossy magazines and other material phenomena), erotic sites (spectacular consumption of the actors' bodies) and the hybridization and intersection of all four of these unstable narrative spaces. It is a hypertext novel, in the tradition of Shelly Jackson's *Patchwork Girl*,[4] through which fan(tastic) desires can be realized through constant textual remediation.

Recent academic treatments of *Buffy*, and to a lesser extent *Angel*, have concentrated on aligning the show with specific theoretical traditions in order to discuss its position as a cultural text. *What's at Stake, Reading the Vampire Slayer, Monsters and Metaphors* (forthcoming; Chris Weimer, ed.) and *Buffy the Vampire Slayer and Philosophy* (Open Court, 2003; James B. South, ed.) all span the range of discussion, from canonical to transgressive, offering thoughtful and engaging essays on the show's critical applicability. Wilcox and Lavery's online journal *Slayage* has also provided a wealth of scholarship on the show, exploring themes from technology and research to—a personal favorite of mine — Spike's "hybridized gender."[5] *Buffy* has already engaged more academic focus and debate than any other hour-long serial program in the history of television studies, and much of that scholarship seeks, through citation of critical theory, to inscribe the show with an *agency* that will justify its enshrinement in academic discourse. Conferences on Shakespeare do not require further legitimation; conferences on the misadventures of a Californian twentysomething — who slays vampires while delivering an inexhaustible barrage of puns and sarcasm — are not so easy to classify as "serious" sites of textual interpretation.

I do not intend to offer another collection of scholarly essays. Work on *Buffy*, in that format, has been done already, and done well. Nor do I intend to plead the show's case chapter by chapter, hoping to sketch out diagrams of social applicability with explorations like "Buffy and Market Capital" or "How Buffy Saved Feminism." What interests me primarily about *Buffy* and *Angel* is that, if they are indeed postmodern novels, then their unconventional narrative structures intersect and collide around the unstable notion of *family*. Buffy and Angel — the shows' eponymous characters — both construct core family units that have nothing to do with heredity or biology. In actuality, both characters are far removed from their biological families. Aside from Buffy's mother and her "sister" Dawn, we experience her extended family as an absence; of course, Angel killed his family two centuries ago. But, in lieu of what might be deemed as the "failure" of heredity, both characters become fiercely interlinked with *surrogate* families. Buffy has the "Scooby Gang" (Willow, Xander, Dawn and, to a lesser extent, Giles, Spike and Anya) and Angel has the "crew" of *Angel Investigations* (Cordelia, Gunn, Fred, Wesley and Lorne/the Host) who are employees in name only. These groups are not simply support structures for the archetypal hero (and Buffy and Angel both queer conceptions of classical and contemporary heroism) but rather the psychic, spiritual and corporeal essence of the "heroes" themselves.

Buffy and Angel both depend enormously, if not exclusively, upon their queer families — and I deploy the term "queer" to signify multiple and overlapping forms of ambivalence: physical, sexual, psychic, philosophical, mystical and moral. Let us turn, then, to the cast of characters. At a summative glance, we have: Willow, who is herself a queer witch; Xander, whose "handyman" persona is constantly being challenged by his perceived effeminacy and ambivalent status as the "heart" of the group; Dawn, who is not human at all, and whose blood unleashes the ultimate queering of physical and dimensional boundaries; Anya, who vacillates between wreaking demonic vengeance and attempting to simulate normative human romance (with connubial bliss as her eventual goal); Giles, the problematic father figure who defies the "rules" of the spectator; Spike, the masculine/feminine "rebel" who moves easily from broken-hearted tears to brutal physical assaults; and of course Buffy herself, who constantly blurs the performative boundaries between prophesied warrior, sexualized woman and irresponsible twentysomething.

Angel gives us a similar panoply of colliding identities: Cordelia, who is simultaneously a maternal force, a voice of unflinching truth and the embodiment of shallow materialism; Fred, whose time spent in a hostile dimension forces her to mediate intellectual brilliance with highly queer notions of social interaction; Gunn, the masculinized fighter who is consistently out-fought, out-planned and out-matched by the women in his life; Wesley, the younger (and, many would argue, far more ineffectual) version of Giles, who constantly becomes a site for moral and psychological debate; Lorne, the sexually ambivalent "Host" who wears silk bathrobes and practices empathy through karaoke; and Angel, the vampire whose soul remains a locus of total ambiguity, and whose eroticism is over-emphasized by his perfectly gelled hair and long flowing trenchcoats.

These "core" groups are, essentially, composed of social exiles. They represent not an invasion of the center by its margins, but a call to the immateriality and ambivalence of the "center" itself. The characters of *Buffy* and *Angel*, in true Stein-like fashion, "act like there is no center."[6] They sometimes casually, sometimes deliberately challenge the safe and heteronormative boundaries that constitute most performed televisual "families."

Buffy is, of course, not the first televisual text to introduce the image of the "chosen" family — the surrogate sphere of friends who sometimes succeed, and sometimes fail, to recuperate ideals that the characters' biological families cannot properly transmit. Shows like *Friends, Felicity* and *Sex and the City* (wherein the biological family is a barely felt absence, totally subsumed by the bonds that link the four female characters) all present variations, or queerings, of the normative families proposed by past shows like *Family Ties, Growing Pains* and *The Cosby Show*. The action (in every sense of the word) that occurs in Buffy's vast, inherited three-floor house, we must say, is radically different from what was discussed in the living room of the Seavers (*Growing Pains*), or the dining room of the Keatons (*Family Ties*). Alex P. Keaton concerned himself with stock options, not vampire slaying (unless we want to say that he was slaying the shadows of "Reaganomics," which would require a different sort of analysis).

If this book is to query *Buffy's* (de)positioning as a queer serial, a nomadic text or a postmodern "novel" (with all of the ironic inscriptions implied by such a classification), then its entry point must be "family." It is the deeply ambivalent — but entirely unavoidable — thread that both stitches and sunders the many complex narrative traceries within *Buffy*-the-text. Is *Buffy*, then, a Deleuzian rhizome? An assemblage with no points, only lines, and each one interconnected? Or, more specifically, does *Buffy* represent what Deleuze might call the "family-becoming,"[7] the family rhizome whose territoriality is constantly being queered into a "state" that is both chaos and synergy?

Once again, we run the risk of theorizing the show into a legible corner — of granting it a legitimacy that becomes a totality. *Well, yes, of course we understand that text: Derrida, or Baudrillard, or Deleuze, or Foucault have allowed us to exhume its secret critical depths.* But the Foucaultian archaeologist in all of us, despite her best intentions, can offer nothing but a framing device for these volatile narratives. Like unstable isotopes, they shift, distend, confound and penetrate any critical apparatus meant to contain them.

Yet, *Buffy* is not a subversive free-for-all that attempts to de-hinge all normative and hegemonic structures (and my grave pronunciation of this "fact" will no doubt cause skeptics to roll their eyes). In many ways, the show reiterates a time-honored heroic narrative: the prophesied figure who must evolve, and ultimately sacrifice something, to defeat a formless and negative power. The obvious change is *Buffy*'s reinscription of this hero as a young girl — Buffy herself— and the commemoration not of her Beowulf-like deeds, but of her many attempts to negotiate a "normal" life between the margins of the monstrous (teenage adolescence, vampires and demons and the hyperreal blur that the combination must inevitably become). This narrative is, at first, built upon the classic heterosexual love-and-lack relationship: Buffy and Angel, whose love for each other is, predictably, frustrated by the monumental forces which seek to drive them apart. Her companions — Willow, the loveless intellectual, and Xander, the hapless (and perennially uncool) virgin — are, upon cursory examination, familiar staples of the serial genre. But things are not exactly as they appear.

For the show does not coalesce around a master-narrative (what Buffy herself might call an *über*-narrative), nor does it celebrate the positive growth of its principle characters — including the formation of long-awaited romances. *Buffy* instead focuses on the ambivalent social interactions that constitute the materiality of its family — the Scoobies. Their name is borrowed from another familiar group of social outcasts — the cartoon protagonists of *Scooby Doo*— who blundered their way through solving paranormal crimes while retaining their own comedic implausibility as "heroes."

Unlike the X-Men or the Fantastic Four, who fought the forces of evil by cooperating with existing social structures (which tried to render them invisible) while at the same time using their extraordinary powers, the Scoobies continually found themselves thrown into situations where "something was fishy."

They meddled when and where it suited them, utilizing a mixture of critical deduction (Velma), bravado (Fred), subterfuge (Daphne) and wild incompetence (Scooby and Shaggy) to subvert adult criminal schemes—which were often exposed as being simply mercantile rather than supernatural. Moreover, they cohered as a group not *despite* their individual exile status, but *because* of it.

Like *Buffy*, *Scooby Doo* required the audience to accept certain crucial points of absurdity or impossibility—a talking dog, for instance, as well as a protagonist (Shaggy) who many have postulated was perpetually stoned—for its narrative to make sense. More than a suspension of disbelief, in serial television, this acceptance of human fallibility (or inconsistency) becomes a condition for watching. To love the characters of *Scooby Doo*, viewers must not simply ignore their absurd elements, but appreciate and identify with them on some level. To love the modernized Scoobies of *Buffy the Vampire Slayer*, viewers must internalize—not exoticize—the dark, violent and, at times, ridiculous world that serves as their milieu. However, while the original Scoobies could never evolve or explore their own distinct character traits (confined as they were by the cartoon genre of that era), *Buffy's* Scooby Gang has exploded the equally cartoonish typologies that its characters originally inhabited in the show's pilot episode.

In "Welcome to the Hellmouth" (1.01), we are introduced to an array of familiar high-school stereotypes: the awkward and plainly dressed academic (Willow); the wise-cracking goofball who hides his sexual insecurity with humor (Xander); the sardonic and sexy prom queen (Cordelia); the long-suffering authority figure (Giles); and, finally, the hip-but-vulnerable girl—a transfer student, no less—who hides a dark secret (Buffy herself). This is, at first glance, nothing but *Beverly Hills 90210* with a much higher casualty rate. But, as the show itself continually illustrates, surface-level observation is not enough. What makes these characters engaging from the moment they appear on screen is not their individual narratives, but the dialogue that results from the uneasy collision of those narratives. When Xander observes that "the dead rose—we should at least have an assembly" ("The Harvest," 1.02), or Willow clarifies her problem with boys by stating that "when I'm with a boy I like, it's hard for me to say anything cool, or, or witty, or at all. I — I can usually make a few vowel sounds, and then I have to go away" (1.01), there is an irony at play here that typical high-school-survival stories lack.

What they're saying isn't radically *smarter* (read: the elevated, quasi-academic banter of *Dawson's Creek*), but there is an equally absurd and technical language being deployed: the language of demons, vampires and other mystical horrors. These characters seem at once to acknowledge the wild impossibility of *both* their worlds — high school on the one hand, vampire-slaying on the other — and thus, through sarcasm and citation, they undercut both narratives. Vampires, *Buffy* proposes, are no more ridiculous, no more implausible and no more insurmountable than the experience of adolescence itself. Thus, what may disarm us most about these characters is that they *don't* philosophize — they don't ask deep epistemological questions, or wax eloquent about their romantic instabilities.

This is because, in *Buffy*, the banal and the horrific occur in such close proximity to each other so as to become indistinguishable. Xander's first visible romantic rejection of Willow is a result of him being possessed by an animal spirit ("The Pack," 1.06); Buffy's post-coital betrayal at the hands of Angel occurs when he transforms into Angelus, his soulless vampiric persona ("Innocence," 1.14); Giles is first drawn to Jenny Calendar when they abjure a demon by means of an online cyber–Pagan ritual ("I Robot," You Jane," 1.08). The quotidian blends with the grotesque, creating an impossible space where every position is equally ungraspable, equally absurd. How can Willow complain about relationships when she's exploring the darkest aspects of witchcraft and, by extension, her own psyche? How can Buffy afford to be irresponsible when her debt to humanity has already been prophesized? How can Xander worry about his own "failed" masculinity, and his various sexual insecurities, when he's thrust every night into potentially fatal situations without magic, slayer-strength or even the most rudimentary self-defense skills to protect him?

What audiences come to love about "the Scooby gang" is not their superpowers, not their Herculean accomplishments, but rather, their brave (and often frustrated) attempts to maintain normalcy within a world that constantly horrifies them. An iconic example of this occurs in the episode "Family" (5.06), when Tara must choose between her biological family, and the more flexible notion of "family" that Buffy and Willow offer her. The choice, at first, seems obvious: Tara's father is a brutal misogynist and her siblings both despise and fear her. But Tara is being asked to abandon everything she has ever known, in exchange for comfort from a group of people she has only just met. Tara's next word, her next gesture, is the knife-point upon which the entire episode rests.

Thus, with the ambivalence that makes this show so critically fascinating, an apparently climactic battle scene (between the Scoobies and a pack of demons, aided unwittingly by Tara herself) is followed, and eclipsed, by the quiet, wrenching power of Tara's choice to walk away from her "real" family. The episode ends not with a swordfight or a spectacular display of magic, but with a return to absolute normalcy: Tara's own birthday party, which occurs right on schedule. Absolute normalcy, that is, except for the lasting image of Willow and Tara embraced, and floating, several feet off the ground. "Best birthday," Tara says, as she is lifted by magical means into the air—and no one notices. Or, perhaps everyone notices, but not a word is said. Not even the slightest erring glance is thrown in their direction. Are the inhabitants of Sunnydale so brainwashed by supernatural forces that they can't, or won't, pay attention to a couple who are magically levitating in their midst? Or is the show creating yet another impossible moment—an unstable unity of the mystical and the mundane, wherein both categories blur, bleed, lose their knowability and become merely shadows of each other?

"*We* are her blood kin," Tara's father exclaims, after Buffy has forcefully demonstrated that he will not be dragging Tara out against her will. "Who the hell are you?" Her reply—"We're family"—nicely crystallizes the motif of surrogacy and choice that weaves its way throughout the show, and also the point of entry that this investigation will observe. *Family*. Both *Buffy* and *Angel*, if they can be said to embody any "theme" other than media deconstruction, are shows about the production, maintenance and disruption of families—families we're born with, families we choose and families we stumble upon. I have, in this introduction, focused primarily on *Buffy* because it is the more familiar—or, to be grammatically perverse, the more *familial*—show of the two. Although both programs inform, mediate and in many ways constitute each other, *Buffy* has received more critical attention. And, as a result of its recent finale, *Buffy* can now be observed from beginning to end, whereas *Angel* is still very much in progress. But this investigation does intend to treat both shows, exploring the ways in which they mesh with, and diverge from, each other, as well as the contested ideal of *family* around which they both orbit.

Why family? There are, after all, many tropes that *Buffy* and *Angel* focus upon as narrative texts: blood, addiction, consumption, power, knowledge, sexuality, individuation, visibility ... the catalogue could extend in all directions, eventually surpassing the discursive edges of both "texts" and colliding with the larger symbolic forces that make them legible. Why not vampirism as a metaphor of consumption anxiety? Why not the "slayer prophecy" as feminist empowerment? The short answer is that these themes have already been combed through, already been given serious academic treatment through articles or conference discussion. The longer, more ambivalent answer, is that *family*— I believe — is a master narrative from which these other ideas extend. Family is the equation that both of the shows' pilot episodes open with — the discovery and assemblage of a core group — and the support system that emerges, again and again, for these characters to fall back on. It is the sense of belonging that these exiles achieve, and the omega-power that not only infuses, but makes possible, their efforts to push back apocalypse.

But neither *Buffy* nor *Angel* conveys anything close to a normative definition of family. Indeed, as texts, they depend precisely upon the *queering* of family-systems in order to maintain symbolic integrity. Are Buffy and Angel themselves the heads, the patriarchs and matriarchs, of their individual families? Such an assumption would negate the considerable steering power of Giles and Cordelia, who both act as cohesive parent figures, and who both often have to dispense the crucial advice that nobody wants to hear. Are Willow and Xander brother and sister? Buffy calls Xander "big brother" in the magical-realist-cum-dadaist "Restless" (4.22), but this naming is pejorative, or at the very least incomplete, when we consider the complex romantic feelings that Xander has felt for Buffy in the past. Similarly, Xander's rescuing of Willow in "Grave" (6.22), although it may resemble the duty of a "big brother," is symbolically shadowed by his claim to love Willow in all of her contestable forms — and even if she does, indeed, destroy the world. (This will be explored further in Chapter One. The same readings can be applied to the Cordelia-Angel relationship, or even the Spike-Angel relationship (for they were, at one time, family). And this panoply of readings is made visible by the sheer volume of revisionist fan-fiction that surrounds *Buffy* and *Angel*. These families seem to present endless opportunities for imaginary revision and redaction.

A brief discussion of Family Studies as a discipline, and how it applies to this investigation, might be appropriate here. "Family" as a term has, depending upon historical and geographic factors, referred to a variety of different systems, models and ideas. At times, nation-states have possessed quite clear guidelines for what a family should be. In Quebec between 1940–50, for example, public policy around the mother's role as a bastion of French-Canadian culture remained prominent. This was similar to the responsibility of middle-class parents to raise democratic citizens — what Meg Luxton calls "capable workers for a meritocracy" — in post-war Britain (1997, 165). Most nation-states, but especially the United States and Great Britain, have a long and colorful history of state intervention within the "private" affairs of the family. Moen and Schorr define these interventions as part of a "family policy," which has historically been designed as a "widely agreed on set of objectives for families, toward the realization of which the state ... deliberately shapes programs and policies" (Moen and Schorr, 795).

In many cases, family policy has evolved into a national ideology called "familialism," which Lynn Haney defines as "[being] usually associated with patrimonialism ... familial states merged family lineage and political authority; they were regimes in which actual familial norms and principles constituted the political structure and elite" (2003, 4). Familial states were state-models which exhibited a sort of symbiotic relationship between governmentality and the family, in that the state attempted to mold the family for political reasons while at the same time implementing a state systematization that both resembled and valorized aspects of the patrimonial family. Examples of this were evident in the Chilean popular fronts of 1938–48, wherein prohibition campaigns, regular home-visits by social workers and the financial privileging (in the form of government compensation) of married women over single mothers all "assured ... that recreational practices would articulate and propagate a vision of a disciplined and collaborative sportsman-citizen" (Rosemblatt, 131) while increasingly forcing women into the role of reproductive non-workers.

Historically, Western-centered models of the family have also been used as vehicles for justifiable imperialism and military action — mostly manifesting itself in the west's "duty" to protect, or re-educate, what it sees as morally circumspect, deficient or endangered families. This can be as general as Gayatri Spivak's famous statement detailing the west's need to "protect brown women from brown men" (Spivak, 297). It has also had more politically specific examples, such as Britain's restructuring of families in Colonial Africa in order to install a system of primogeniture — a system whose "de-laboring" of African woman created massive disruptions within existing systems of home-centered agricultural exchange (Brantley, 140); or, Britain's public linking of Egyptian family practices with polygamy and the "production of unsound motherhood" at the turn of the century, in order to "legitimize the occupation of Egypt and construct a pseudo-colonial state" from 1882–1922 (Haney, 8).

Given the fluctuating nature of the family — which has been fluid at some times, and incredibly rigid at others, depending upon the global political climate as well as regional particularities — the practice of studying the family has been fraught with conflict since its inception. That "inception" is, of course, difficult to pinpoint. Plato began talking about the family in *The Republic*, and, centuries later, Hobbes and Locke both debated its moral and contractual significance. The nineteenth century, with its explosion of regulatory measurement and classification techniques, probably marked the most widespread global scrutiny of family systems and their relationship to national and civic development. Everything from the sexualization of citizens along axes of normality and perversion — developed by the scientist August Comte, among others — to the specific modeling of classrooms and department stores, produced families that policed themselves in order to resemble a state-specific ideal (Rose, 39, 45). And it was the philosopher Hegel who first intimately connected the strength of the (nuclear) family with the efficacy of the nation, claiming that the family was the "ethical root of the state ... [and contains] an objective universality in a substantial unity ... it is within the state that the family is first developed into civil society" (Hegel, 155).

Although quantitative methods for analyzing the family emerged, as we have seen, in and around the nineteenth century, Family Studies did not begin to resemble its present-day incarnation as an institutional discipline until the 1940s. Kingsley Davis was one of the first scholars to situate the family within a capitalist model, arguing for its satist function as a site for the continual reproduction of labor in 1948. After the Second World War, discussions of the family became increasingly preoccupied with classification and quantitative methods, relying upon sociological systems-theory to analyze an essential "family core." Talcott Parsons introduced the model of the "isolated nuclear family" in 1964, which he claimed to be the only version that did "not conflict with the requirements of an industrial economy" (Cheale, 5).

The first serious challenges to this systematized family theory came from feminist–Marxist quarters, with scholars like Jessie Bernard insisting that marital experience was different for men and women, creating what were essentially "two marriages" within each household — a divisive atmosphere marked by unequal power differentials and gender-influenced reportage (Bernard, 1972), which complemented Arlie Hochschild's subsequent work on the domestic division of labor in her book *The Second Shift* (1989). Bernard was followed by Heidi Hartmann, who advocated for the replacement of the family as "social agent" model with a more flexible and inclusive model of the "family as a location" for various competing forces and overlapping roles, as well as an inscription site for nationalist ideologies (Hartmann, 1981). Later, the work of Pauline Boss would reconceptualize the family as a site of overlapping crises rather than a fortress of systematized order, and more recent feminist scholars like Lynn Haney, Meg Luxton and Suzanne Peters have continued to trouble static conceptualizations of the family, pushing for more critical dialogue on women's unpaid labor, child support and daycare concerns, and equal financial compensation for unmarried mothers.

In analyzing the role of state policy on queer families, Valerie Lehr asserts that "gays and lesbians, because we remain deeply dependent on external communities to raise children who will become part of our communities, are in a unique position to understand the importance of reframing political discussion ... yet [we have to be] able and willing to question central institutional structures, rather than to seek equality by acting virtually normal enough to fit in with only minimal change" (Lehr, 176). This brings us more or less to the contemporary appearance of debates within Family Studies as a discipline — that is, the tension between families who appear "virtually normal," in Lehr's words, and families who disrupt patriarchal and institutionalized models by queering, in various ways, the nuclear-family model. The families in *Buffy* and *Angel*, as we will see, belong to this latter category.

This particular "look" will query the notion of family as it begins, evolves and mutates across the narrative lines of both shows. It will position each show as a text that relies upon the trope of family, but also relies upon the disruption of that trope in order to find a living space. These characters endure because they know that they are part of a family, but also because they know that "family" is a signifier to be enlarged, distended and ultimately exploded as it attempts to contain them. They recreate the discursive experience of "family" from episode to episode, transforming it into a lived (and living) story rather than a static system. When Tara is rejected by her own family, the Scoobies extend theirs to include her; when Dawn's legitimacy as Buffy's sister is challenged, and eventually deemed false, Buffy simply rewords "sister" so that it continues to encompass Dawn. Nothing changes. Rather than surrendering to the normative (and, as the show implies, patristic) powers of language, Buffy alters the language so that it more suitably describes her own visible reality. She remakes the world, one word at a time.

Let us re-frame, then, the idea that this introduction opens with: the various negotiations, all of which hinge upon family, that the characters of *Buffy* and *Angel* undertake in order to find their place in the world; even, or especially, when that "place" becomes an impossibility. These groups — these families — are weighed down by the impossible task of reconciling their "normal" lives with the various forms of monstrosity that threaten to invade them on a daily basis. Yet at the same time they are drawn to that monstrosity, finding both shelter and solace in the unmapped borderlands between the binary fictions of "human" and "monster." They fight what they desire, embrace what repels them, and are continually forced to live through this paradox, with all of its tragicomic elements.

To spearhead such an investigation, we must cite *Buffy* and *Angel* as televisual texts which gain critical power and narrative embodiment through a variety of different forms. They are open-ended stories, complete with their own conventions, gaps and linguistic strategies, then further mediated by the screen (and director's gaze). They are visual representations, whose imagery is double-coded with semantic "values" that often conflict, or even negate, each other. Finally, they are forces, phenomena or even "theories" — and why *not* Buffy Theory? — which can be mapped across spaces (fansites and fanfic), disciplines (academic readings and revisions) and media extensions (novels, computer and console games, posters, figurines, etc.). Along the way, *family* as a concept yields, splits, is rendered unrecognizable to itself, becomes a palimpsest to be scraped over and retold endlessly. This book is its own retelling — it offers up stories about stories, versions of versions, peculiar reflections of the shadows cast by that idea of family within both shows. "I want to see how it ends," Spike says in the final episode "Chosen" (7.22) — his last words before dissolving into ash and fire (although we know that visible death holds little narrative finality within either show). This book wants to see where family ends. Or if.

Each chapter treats a character or group of characters in general, then foregrounds that critical snapshot against the larger theme of family: how they complicate, constitute or even negate the various families that they claim access to. To discuss the Scoobies as a real dynamic rather than aids or peripherals to Buffy, we will work our way *towards* Buffy rather than beginning with her. The same system will be used to position Angel. Chapter One, will begin with Willow's ambivalent characterization — evolving from the girl in need of constant rescuing, to the only woman (aside from Glory, who was never really human; and, of course, Willow's brief transformation into Goddess-form in "Chosen" nicely complicates this) capable of defeating Buffy herself. Chapter Two will shift the lens to Xander — the "heart" of the group, whose conflicted masculinity is belied, even recuperated, by his power to hold the family (*his* family?) together, come Hellmouth or high-water. Next, we will treat Buffy, exploring all of the various foreclosures she must make in order to be a "hero," and how that status is constantly challenged, remediated and (de)authorized.

Chapter Four, will examine the fathering roles of Giles and Wesley as Watchers, as well as the conflictual father/son relationship of Angel and Connor. Chapter Five, will treat Cordelia and Fred as characters who become strange and ambivalent mothers, both producing "children" that are ultimately threatening. Chapter Six will conclude with a discussion of *Buffy, Angel* and the academy, examining the differing roles as "closed" and "open" family systems that rely upon each other, even as they repel each other. The book will close with an epilogue that is at once a non-ending, a retrospective, a critical musing on the future and a final intrusion by the author.

Rather than proposing yet another collection of critical essays, this investigation tells a story of sorts. It is a story about *Buffy* and *Angel*; about how these shows tell stories; about how the stories themselves explode the confines of serial television, hovering close to orality, being retold through episodic variation, through academic investigation, and through fan intervention. It is a story told by someone who loves *Buffy* and *Angel*, but who also sees them as cultural instruments through which to explore the blending together/bleeding together of power, sexuality and family as it is mapped across visual and narrative spaces. As you read it, do not resist the urge to change; to retell; to cut; to alter words or worlds. Fill in the gaps, scribble over the implausibilities and find your own story. The final episode of *Buffy* ends with a question—"What do we do now?"—and so should this book. How do we read "family" in these texts? How do we proceed?

CHAPTER ONE

"She's Not All Grown Yet": Willow Rosenberg as Hybrid, Hero and Middle Child of the Scooby Family

> "Who can I become in such a world where the meanings and limits of the subject are set out in advance for me? By what norms am I constrained as I begin to ask what I may become?"
>
> —Judith Butler, "Doing Justice to Someone" (621)

> "Willow doesn't live here any more."
>
> —Willow, "Grave" (6.22)

Buffy the Vampire Slayer is a program that teases, explores and sometimes violates the liminal space between social ideals that are themselves constructions. It needs to be addressed as a complex and ambiguous work of fiction that explores the decay of "normal" as it intersects with the fantastic and the grotesque.[1] It is monstrous bodies in *Buffy* which hold the most ambiguity, the most danger; and when the principle characters (some of whom *are* "monsters") collide with this erratic and subversive lack of positioning, the veracity of "normal" becomes as untenable as that of "monstrous." It is not the non-humanity of *Buffy*'s characters that makes them so intriguing, but rather the ways in which their bodies, psyches and — in the case of Angel and Spike — their "souls" become sites for the intersection of everything that we think is human with everything that seems not to be. This tension finds its most prevalent expression within both shows' construction of non-conventional families: families of vampires, families that include non-humans, and families whose cohesion — a cohesion rooted in difference, and even queerness, rather than predictability — subverts any simple application of a good vs. evil binary by audiences or critics.

As our entry point into the shifting space of family within *Buffy* and *Angel*, this first chapter aims not at deconstructing Buffy herself — the archetypal figure who embodies every televisual feminine caricature from Bridget Jones (cinematic, admittedly) to Xena — but rather Willow. Like Xander and the rest of the Scoobies, Willow is often overshadowed by Buffy; unlike Xander, she has — at times — *eclipsed* Buffy, forging a significant narrative of her own. While Buffy experiences, more or less, the same essential conflicts (Slayer versus teenager, prophecy versus normality) until Season 5, Willow is torn between a multitude of competing identities: shy academic; computer expert; budding witch ("budding" being a signifier commonly ascribed to Willow's magical studies, which holds all kinds of double-voiced meaning when connected to her name[2]); ingénue; agent of the apocalypse; and, finally, a guilt-stricken "reformed" addict. Unlike Buffy, who is the satellite around which her surrogate family of Scoobies revolve, Willow has lingered on the outer edges, and proven herself to be a chaotic force more powerful than the Slayer, the Watchers or any other instrument of authority within the show's diagesis.

Willow is, therefore, the dangerous middle child of the Scooby Family. Entering *Buffy*'s narrative as a confidante and potential sister-surrogate to Buffy, she quickly becomes a powerful force of knowledge and ambition, unfettered by Giles' moral compass or Xander's inarticulate fear. She is romantically sidelined for much of Seasons 1 and 2, watching the melodrama between Buffy and Angel play out, but lacking any significant erotic attachment save for the inaccessible (and unwitting) Xander. Upon discovering that Xander and Cordelia are engaged in their own enmity-fueled love affair, Willow's reaction fairly bristles with the rage of a thwarted sibling. When Xander protests, "Look, I was gonna tell you," Willow demands, "Gee, what stopped you? Could it be shame?" ("Innocence," 2.14).

Her disgust here is aimed not just at Xander's transgression (for he is the self-described "treasurer" of the "we-hate-Cordelia fanclub" [2.14]), but at her own complete lack of romantic fulfillment. Even when she later falls in love with Oz, Willow obsessively scrutinizes the relationships around her, and sabotages her own courtship by transgressing with Xander. Like an unsatisfied sibling, she wants everything that she cannot have — everything that, as she perceives it, her family members already possess. And, as we shall see, the lengths to which Willow goes to achieve power and subjecthood within her own family will radically spin her narrative into newer — and unquestionably darker — places.

The title of this chapter was taken from the episode "Restless," wherein Willow describes the nameless kitten (referred to only as Miss Kitty, or Kitty Fantastico) that she and Tara have adopted as being "not all grown yet" ("Restless," 4.22).[3] Willow, like all of *Buffy*'s characters, is still very much in a state of evolution. But her growing pains are of particular importance, for they identify her as a hybrid character within which several of the show's most resounding ambivalences converge, overlap and shadow each other.

Let us begin at the end — the end of Season 6, as Willow is about to invoke apocalypse. "On the first day of kindergarten," Xander reminds her in "Grave," the season finale, "you cried because you broke the yellow crayon, and you were too afraid to tell anyone" (6.22). This childhood Willow (further described by Xander, the ironic communicator, as "crayon-breaky Willow") bears little resemblance to the black-eyed figure of violent energy that he is addressing. Their confrontation ends not with an epic battle, but with a speech act — a declaration of love — that forces Willow to re-access her own humanity, and sees her crumpled against Xander's uncertain body, weeping, as her black hair reverts to its previous shade of orange. This is not, as it may seem, the safe containment of the Gothic, or the triumph of normativity over the abject 'other.' Willow must still learn how "not to be evil," as Anya calls it, and her insecurities, like those of Xander and Buffy, remain very much in the foreground of the show's narrative ("Same Time, Same Place," 7.03). Like Season 4, which ended with a dream rather than a battle (as well as a battle within a dream), and Season 5, wherein the defeat of Glory was overshadowed by Buffy's death, Season 6 ends with a question: Who is Willow, and what shall become of her? How can she reconcile the oppositional binaries of her character, which Xander so aptly terms as "crayon-breaky Willow" and "scary-veiny Willow?" Is there any space left for her between these poles, and if so, is it a space that she wants to occupy?

Willow's transition from the show's passive "information system,"[4] to an instrument of chaos who seeks to vitiate the bonds that join her own family together, can be traced from the end of Season 2. In "Becoming Pt II," the audience sees a weak, bedridden Willow suddenly snap into a trance, and begin chanting a powerful spell in ancient Romanian ("Becoming II" 2.22). Injured after an attack which was supposed to kill her, Willow instead experiences a moment of naked and frightening power, during which a voice — not her own, but one that the audience will come to know much better as the story progresses — intones Angel's curse with the ease and facility of an expert linguist.[5] It is she who reunites Angel with his soul, thereby making Buffy's task of killing him all the more difficult, and shadowing her apparent victory — the world, after all is saved — with the clear expression of betrayal on Angel's face as he disappears into the void. The enormity of this destructive act is never fully articulated until an episode five seasons later, when Buffy is forced to remind Xander of the impossible choice that, more than anything, propelled her from childhood to adolescence ("Selfless," 7.05).[6]

It is valid to observe that a character's shift from good to evil (usually rounded out by a return to good) on the show is sometimes clearly marked. As Krzywinska notes, "'bad' Willow's black lipstick and leather, or Angel's smoking and cruel laughter, indicate their changed personas" (181). This of course refers to Willow's transformation in the episode "Dopplegangland," when the "good" Willow meets her other-dimensional shadow, an emboldened, violent and pan-sexual vampire (3.16). The "bad" Willow, as Krzywinska suggests, is negatively coded by her sultry appearance. She is nothing like the impish Darla, whose vampirism is subverted by her blonde hair, wispy voice and hyper-feminine clothes (one outfit, that of a preparatory schoolgirl, being probably the most disturbing when aligned with Buffy's own age and status as a high school student). When Willow is at the height of her destructive powers, she is similarly re-coded, given black hair, black eyes and a kind of dark power-suit that makes her appear strangely businesslike.

But the audience does not have to look too deeply in order to see the gaps in this binaristic transformation, for Willow's outer "darkness," like Angel's vampire-face, still contains remnants of the physical beauty that preceded it. Angel is still very much attractive as a vampire — not a loathsome creature like the Count Orlock of F.W. Murnau's film *Nosferatu*— and Willow is simply Willow with black hair and different clothes. Xander recognizes this easily, and thus addresses not the black-eyed Willow, but the old Willow whose face is still visible underneath. It must also be remembered that both of these characters perpetrated significant cruelties while still appearing very human. Angel's speech to Buffy after they have sex for the first time — a callous dismissal of her as a lover — is made more disturbing because he retains his human face,[7] just as Willow's multiple betrayals and violations of her relationship with Tara happen long before her physical metamorphosis. The shift between good and evil is not so smooth; for Willow, finding normalcy after her brush with apocalypse merely re-emphasizes the exile status that she has struggled with since the show's first episode.

Like all serial shows, *Buffy* relies upon the concept of sameness. Unlike most serials, it constantly calls this sameness into question, challenging its own programmed structure as a media vehicle that must obey certain popular themes — it may obey them, but not transparently, and not without visual and narrative resistance. Umberto Eco's description of the serial as a constant narrative that gives the illusion of change, and within which "the secondary characters must give the impression that [their] new story is different from the preceding ones, while in fact the narrative scheme does not change" (Eco, "Limits," 86), is both applicable to and resisted by *Buffy*. Repetition gives a show emotional currency with its audience, for by rehashing the same scenarios, it "consoles us (the consumer), because it rewards our ability to foresee: we are happy because we discover our own ability to guess what will happen" (86). And in this sense *Buffy* conforms to Eco's model, for every season presents us with the same core group of characters (Buffy, Willow and Xander) who are visited by alternating supporters (Anya, Oz, Riley), detractors (Adam, Glory and the First Evil) and ambivalent characters like Spike, who straddle the line between protagonist/antagonist in ways that continually disrupt the audience's perceptions.

Every season culminates in a new disaster, which is averted by some means, thereby saving the world (or the universe). The core group changes, both mentally and physically, but the characteristics that they first brought to the show — Willow's childlike and insecure grasp of the world, Buffy's protectiveness and defiance of authority, and Xander's wise-cracking which masks his powerful sense of loyalty and optimism — all remain untouched. The audience loves these characters because they are the same, they are predictable, they are "their" people. Like the safe spaces within *Buffy*'s diagesis — the Bronze,[8] the Magic Box (before its destruction) and above all, Buffy's massive three-story house with its warm decor and bright, cheery kitchen, and enduring status as what Lorna Jowett calls "the site for much of the show's representation of both the real and the alternative family" (Jowett, 3) — the characters themselves represent security to the audience. Their static lives seem superior to the reversals and exigencies of the "real" world.

However, *Buffy*'s narrative also demonstrates marked changes that derail story arcs and surprise audiences — changes that are not overwhelmingly positive. When Angel talks about leaving Sunnydale (and thus, the show), he really does *leave*. The formative, heterosexual romance upon which the show was originally built is suddenly absent, and Angel's replacement — Riley — is coded as a failed love-choice almost from the beginning of his courtship with Buffy. Similarly, the death of Tara is cruel and permanent — Willow can never see her again, never contact her through some mystical proxy, and Amber Benson (the actor who plays Tara) does not make another appearance on the show. In lieu of these events, Eco's claim that all serials depend upon this principle of monotony, and that "the era of electronics ... [has produced] a return to the continuum ... the Regular" (Eco, *Apocalypse*, 96), does not address *Buffy*'s willingness to sever relationships, eliminate characters and frustrate its viewing audience with new story arcs that may not be so easy to digest.

Buffy's characters do change, evolve and, most often, flow between varying identities. The audience sees, for example, Xander's retreat into the useful, effective "handyman" persona after leaving Anya; they see Willow's struggle to negotiate a life without reckless magic, and without Tara; they *see* these transformations, like wrinkled skin, waning beauty, and are sometimes horrified, sometimes pleased by the mutability of their beloved characters. And this suggests that there is no clear distinction between Eco's "critical spectator," his *experienced* reader, and his naive or semantic reader (93–94). An academic, despite her ability to locate and articulate this phenomenon, is no better equipped to subvert or avoid it than the casual viewer. Every audience member, regardless of their critical interest in a given program, desires the unchangeable, and is simultaneously repulsed by it. That is the paradox of the viewer. They cannot be happy unless a program is both static and dynamic.

And if *Buffy*'s characters are looking back, returning the gaze of the audience with a frustrating gaze of their own, then it is Willow's black eyes that disarm onlookers the most. For, as Giles admonishes her after she capriciously describes Buffy's resurrection, "of everyone here ... you were the one I trusted most to respect the forces of nature" ("Flooded," 6.04). Shy Willow, outsider Willow—even sexualized Willow—is the character that the audience finds most easily recognizable, for she is the character most clearly "named" and positioned by her friends and family. Unlike Buffy's tryst with Spike, which is but one more perverse development in her ongoing flirtation with the dark powers that she allegedly subverts, Willow's abuse of magic challenges the audience to renegotiate their perceptions of "Willow ... she of the level head," as Buffy calls her ("Smashed," 6.09). Her awkwardness, paired with her great erudition and technological efficiency, makes her a delightfully stable character whose subsequent slide into deviancy (that is, a deviation from viewing expectations) thus becomes all the more pronounced.

Because she serves as both an information system, and as a repository of mystical power, her transition from ally to adversary is all the more threatening. It is Willow's magic that enables Buffy to fight cybernetic Adam via the enjoining spell; and the result of this spell, most fittingly, is a hybrid—Buffy united with the spirit of every Slayer, as well as the spirit of her family—whose power comes from a "source" that Adam "cannot grasp" because he is a cybernetic (metal/flesh) rather than a *psychic* (body/mind) hybrid.[9] That same magic is the only weapon capable of weakening Glory, and the only power against which Buffy's own strength cannot contend. Willow has proven herself to be Buffy's surrogate sister, the twin to Xander's "big brother" identity that Buffy herself hints at in "Restless" (4.22). Yet she is also the sole force capable of defeating the Slayer — capable, as well, of annihilating her family, and with them the world.

To find the real Willow, which may or may not be "like a tragedy," as Anya suggests, is to collide with a hybrid identity that deforms the text of *Buffy* itself. For Willow is still growing, still waiting for her redemptive moment. Buffy has her dive; Xander can say proudly that "I saved the world with my mouth" ("Same Time, Same Place," 7.03); even Spike chose to be ensouled,[10] although recent episodes have deconstructed this act as one of profound ambiguity and negative consequences. But Willow has yet to make a sacrifice. She has lost a great deal, but not yet *given* anything away — save for choosing to stay in Sunnydale for "Buffy's sake" rather than attending a major university, although this may very well be to fulfill her need for definition through the Slayer. Willow, unlike Buffy and Xander — who, despite their occasionally rash choices, still remain legible to the audience — is involved in a more complex negotiation of identity. She is the middle-child of the Scoobies, vacillating between Xander's immaturity and Buffy's hyper-responsibility.

Her vast power allows her to act out the Slayer's darkest fantasies[11] of violence and immolation — rather than saving the world, she can literally destroy it — and her childlike petulance allows her to become totally infatuated with a love object (Tara), while at the same time manipulating and controlling her in order to sustain the most pleasurable and anxiety-free scenario. She can, in effect, do what Xander and Buffy long to do, knowing that their affection for her will remain unchanged. Even when she is poised to extinguish all life on Earth, Xander simply tells her, "I know you're about to do something apocalyptically evil and stupid, and hey — I still want to hang. You're Willow" ("Grave," 6.22).

She is "Willow" not because she, or the audience, knows precisely who Willow *is*, but because Xander and Buffy have *told* her who she is. They have constructed a Willow who is always available, always ready with an innovative solution: the same Willow that Xander addresses, in "Becoming Pt. I," when he asks, "How am I gonna pass trig, you know? And who am I gonna call every night … and talk about everything we did all day? You're my best friend" ("Buffy," 2.21). She is Xander's best friend, and Buffy's best friend, and "she of the level head." But beneath that amicable façade lies an ambivalent, dangerous character, given form and em(bodied) purely by the perceptions of others, whose pain, confusion and psychic turmoil allow her to access what Giles calls "a place of rage and power" ("Grave," 6.22).

Her body — metamorphosing from healthy, to addicted, to destructive, and then back again — becomes a living signifier for the anguish that she feels.[12] She is the archive of Buffy's doubt, of Xander's foolishness, and she can hold all of this because she lacks corporeality. Or rather, she is inscribed with it to the point of excess — given a sexy doppelganger who actually licks her (thus, Willow licks "herself") — but fails to maintain her own body without making the radical foreclosures needed to satisfy her friends' expectations. Nearly every significant event in the show involving Willow suggests this, making her body less and less clear, until all that's left is the "costume" that Buffy summarily rips away.[13] And, as this chapter is bent upon the interrogation of Willow as an incomplete — and, therefore, potentially transgressive — subject, I will now address more specific scenes which illustrate Willow's lack of embodiment. I will further discuss her positioning (or de/positioning) as an exile, and her ability to destabilize not just the familial unit of the Scoobies, but the discursive fabric of the program itself.

Let us return for a moment to Eco, who suggests that "there are serial works that establish an explicit agreement with the critical reader and thus ... challenge him to acknowledge the innovative aspects of the text" (Eco, *Apocalypse*, 92). In accordance with this theory, *Buffy* "double-codes" many of its scenes, using a combination of foreshadowing and subtextual references that the more discerning reader can access. Such is the case with Willow, whose conflicts are explored as early as Season 3, when she comes face to face with her doppelganger. Upon meeting this simulation of herself, Willow is horrified to observe that "I'm so evil and ... skanky! And I think I'm kinda gay" ("Dopplegangland," 3.16). When Buffy assures her that one's 'vampire self' has nothing to do with one's "real" identity, Angel interrupts her containment of this evil with a highly ambiguous: "Well, actually...." It is thus made clear that "bad" Willow is shaped and informed by "good" Willow, and vice versa. Fittingly, then, Willow is not a static body, but rather a system of good and evil, capable of being dominated by either force. Like the double-voiced "death is your gift," which the first Slayer pronounces to Buffy, Willow's engagement with her dark self is neither helpful nor oppositional, but needs to be decoded.

This decoding occurs most prominently in dreams, which are powerful and didactic within *Buffy*. The two Slayers who exist in a kind of intimate opposition with each other — Buffy and Faith — can communicate peacefully, and meaningfully, only through dreams. Buffy's dreams are often prophetic, and in the episode "Restless," any demarcation that may have previously existed between the "real" world and the dream world is smudged away. If, as McLuhan says, "the movie camera is a means of rolling up the daylight world on a spool ... [and] the movie projector unrolls the spool and recreates the daylight world as a dark dream world" (290), then dreaming in *Buffy*'s televisual universe is a deepening of shadow, a more subterranean layer beneath the already simulated "real." The dream is the equivalent of the dark cinema for these characters, where their fears move and whisper just outside the light, and all that they considered stable suddenly takes on a new reflection.

"Restless" begins with Willow's dream, and the audience is at first not sure why. But it soon becomes clear that the disorienting imagery, tinged with violence, in Willow's dream world will influence and inform the content that follows. Unlike Xander, Buffy and Giles' dreams, which begin weirdly or comically, Willow's dream begins with a scene of physical intimacy — Willow is painting Greek characters on Tara's naked back as she lies with her head down, looking pensive. The Greek is an invocation to Aphrodite, translated in part as "I beg you, don't overcome my spirit with pain and care, mistress" (Bowman 2; Lattimore, trans., 515).[14] This is an oracular statement, since Willow's love for Tara, juxtaposed against her love for magic, will drive the conflict that precipitates her addiction and subsequent flight from reality. Tara expresses worry over not having found "her name," and Willow's interruption — "Miss Kitty?" — provides only one possible subject. It is still unclear just whose "name" Tara is talking about, but as the episode progresses, it becomes more evident that the character who fears being seen — being *named*— the most is Willow herself.

And Willow's answer to Tara's fear, "she's not all grown yet," only further emphasizes her lack of positioning. Willow, unlike Tara, is not all grown yet. Her corporeality is as fluid as her dream world, and thus, the only talismanic character traits that she brings to her own dream — asking questions, doing homework and transmitting information (via the Greek characters) — are the ones with which she has been most keenly inscribed by her friends. Buffy, Xander and Giles each have moments, however slight, during which they recognize that they are in a dream, but Willow tries to enforce order upon each scene—"This drama class is just ... I think they're really not doing things in the proper way, and now I'm in a play and my whole family's out there" ("Restless," 4.22)—even after Tara observes, "You don't understand yet, do you?"

What Willow does not understand is that she is not simply hiding from the first Slayer, but from the fear that her constructed identity may have no substance beneath it. With the kind of disorienting meta-criticism that *Buffy* is famous for, Willow, a character in a TV show, fears that she may be nothing more than a character in a play, and that her costume will not protect her from the scrying gaze of her friends. And, although she tries to contain this fear, pressing on with a sense of normalcy by delivering a book report on that staple of high school curricula "The Lion, the Witch and the Wardrobe," the phantasmal figure of the first Slayer still attacks her.

Willow's death at the hands of the First Slayer is far more visually exotic, and symbolically charged, than the other Scoobies. Xander's heart is ripped out, and Giles is scalped—both grisly demises—but the attack itself is a clear act of violence and organic invasion, since both characters have body parts forcibly removed. Willow, as she is mauled by the Slayer, actually transforms. Her skin becomes yellowish, almost reptilian, and her eyes change. She becomes not herself, and not the first Slayer, but a strange hybrid of the two—a demonic entity whose birth leaves the "real" Willow gasping on the couch, as if being strangled. Buffy—now a character in Xander's dream—see this and calls her a "big faker" ("Restless," 4.22), but it's unclear exactly what she's faking, or rather, which "Willow" is the fake.

What the audience expects from Willow is the slightly awkward, hyper-intelligent and intrinsically loyal friend that they have come to know. But her choices—and they *are* distinct choices, not the maneuverings of fate—within the last three seasons of the show seriously displace and disrupt these expectations. Her relationship with Tara, and consequent abandonment of Oz as a romantic interest, is probably the most dramatic character shift experienced by any of the Scoobies. Surprisingly, this relationship has received a great deal of popular discussion and criticism among fansites and magazines, but little academic attention.

The most prevalent critical reading of the Willow-Tara relationship is one wherein magic and lesbian sexuality are conflated. "Lesbian" may just as easily stand in for "witch," since both are socially othered identities, and Willow's sexual experiences are closely linked, and at times synonymous, with her magical ones (Winslade, 7).

Despite the fact that magic is coded as feminine within the show, Willow is not intentionally accessing a grand, feminine *spiritus mundi*. On the contrary, her scathing description of UC Sunnydale's Wiccan Group—"Blah blah Gaia. Blah blah moon ... menstrual life force power thingy" ("Hush," 4.10)—leads the audience to believe that she has no particular desire for feminine empowerment through Wicca. Unlike Tara, who holds intricate and reverent knowledge of the variegated mythologies which underpin the show's pseudo-Gardnerian type of magic, Willow's relationship with her power is visceral and emotional. Magic brings her closer to Tara, and closer to what she believes is an authentic identity. It becomes for her not, as Krzywinska suggests, a "witchcraft [that] is practical and not linked to any environmental issues or spiritual matters" (Krzywinska, 188), but rather a unity of sexual and elemental power that is every bit as primal as the Slayer's strength. And just as Buffy uses this preternatural strength to engage in a mutually masochistic relationship with Spike, so does Willow use magic to experience heightened forms of physical intimacy with Tara. Magic is not merely conflated with sexuality in the show, but contiguous with it, emerging from the same organic drives.

Willow's relationship with Tara, like her relationship with Oz, only further demonstrates her dis(embodiment) as a subject whose mentality and materiality is fragmented. She begins by desiring Xander, whose physical and emotional proximity to her—as a primary member of her support system—combined with his romantic disinterest for her, makes him an object charged with true *eros*, or lack. In calling *eros* a "verb," Anne Carson states that "the symbol of eros ... [is] in the space across which desire reaches"—that space being what necessarily separates lovers (Carson, 25). Absence itself, then, is what creates specifically *erotic* love in the classical sense—and, given the Greek characters being gently inscribed upon Tara's back in "Restless," it is clear that certain classical conceptions of love and sexuality are important to this story arc.

As with Buffy's later intense attachment to Riley, which Xander describes as being "right in front of my Xander face," Willow's desirability swoops beneath his cognitive radar, never made apparent until the possibility of reciprocating it becomes hopelessly complex ("Buffy," 5.10). After their brief physical liaison, Willow forcefully tells Xander that she must choose Oz over him — just as, in the future, she will have to choose Tara over Oz. In her words: "If I want to make things right with Oz, my hands, my — all my stuff— has to be for him only" ("The Wish," 3.09).

Love is verbalized and actualized by these characters in unique, specific ways. Spike names himself "love's bitch"; Anya's love makes Xander "feel like a man"; and for Buffy, love and pain are perversely conflated, twined and warped together in a symbiotic embrace from which neither can be separated. But Willow is the only character who describes love as deficit, as lack. It is disembodying for her — she must become not abject, like Spike, but *object.* She must belong to Tara, to Oz, to Xander, in order to be inscribed by meaning, by the validity that others place in her. But what, then, to make of Tara's enigmatic comment, "I am, you know — yours" ("New Moon Rising," 4.19). Mendlesohn describes Willow's role in the relationship as a dominant one, stating, "Willow takes [her] gained confidence and employs it in the attraction of the painfully shy Tara, in which she repeats, in reverse, the primary dynamic of her relationship with Buffy" (Mendlesohn, 59) — that is, the dynamic of submission/control that several critics have identified between Buffy and Willow, leading to a queer reading of their relationship. That aside, in regards to Tara's sentiment, it does seem as if Willow is doing most of the taking, not Tara. It is she who *already* belongs, and Tara who is looking for belonging.

Yet, it is Tara who confronts Willow about her addiction to magic, and Tara who effectively ends their relationship.[15] Long after Tara has readjusted herself to life without Willow — helping Buffy research the particulars of her resurrection, and offering her emotional support — Willow herself continues to fall deeper into a state of emotional wreckage and sensory oblivion ("Smashed," 6.09). Magic becomes not merely a form of sublimation for Willow, but a radical embodiment, as demonstrated when she mystically imbues one of Tara's old dresses with corporeality (6.09). The dress physically embraces her, a shadow figure — born of cloth, air and intent — and for the first time Willow is "real," while Tara is just a magical construct ... a memory.

Magic is not a power that Willow manipulates here in order to invoke Tara, like a flicked switch or a pushed button. The power itself is what makes *Willow* real. By allowing it to embody her, she positions herself within a core of physical and social interstices — erotic desire, comfort, authority, selfhood — and is thus part of a Foucauldian system of interplay and difference where "power is immanent ... to [all] other types of relationships" (Foucault, 94). And, as further episodes illustrate, she cannot separate herself from the simultaneity of magic/body. Willow herself observes that "I *am* the magic" — a statement then reaffirmed by the image of a hundred magical books pouring their printed knowledge into her body, bringing her role as "information system" to a new level by making her the living intersection of flesh and text (6.22). Willow's body, and Willow's magic, intersect upon a field of power that makes both subjects radically interchangeable. They are caught up in a power that, as defined by Judith Butler (who revises and recasts Foucauldian conceptions of power dispersal), "forms, maintains, sustains, and regulates bodies at once, so that, strictly speaking, power is not a subject who acts on bodies as its distinct objects" (Butler, 34). Willow is thus no longer "distinct" from her power, her magic, because she has allowed it to embody her.

It is Tara's subsequent death, abrupt and shocking, that pushes this Willow/magic relationship into crisis. Hit by a stray bullet meant for Buffy, Tara has time merely to look at Willow in confusion, and ask "your shirt?" — it is covered in a fine spray of her own blood — before collapsing ("Seeing Red," 6.19). This radical and almost perfunctory silencing of Tara, who is denied a glorious swan-dive like Buffy, or a long, protracted moment of pain like Angel, has been the source of much audience outcry and criticism. Tara's death is further complicated by the fact the she and Willow begin the episode in bed together, after a night during which "there was plenty of magic," as Tara herself states wryly (6.19). This violent juxtaposition — from sex to death in one episode — has invited criticism that "whether viewers are aware of [it] or not, murdering a lesbian just minutes after she has sex suggests a causality between lesbian sex and death" (Mangels, 1).

In all fairness, it does not happen *minutes* after the two have sex. But the observation is still valid, and it cannot simply be sidestepped that, by removing the Tara-Willow relationship, Joss Whedon has removed one of the few positive and "graphic" (perhaps a better term is "visualized") lesbian relationships on a television. And, although this "gap" has allegedly been filled by the arrival of Kennedy — Willow's new love interest, who attempts to inject a bit of ease and frivolity into her sex life — the shadow of Tara remains. When Willow temporarily "becomes" Warren — a spell of atonement engineered by Amy to punish Willow for her efficacy, her specialness — she blames the transformation on Kennedy's kiss. For, in that brief moment of physical satisfaction, Willow admits that "I killed her. I let her be dead," speaking of Tara ("The Killer in Me," 7.13). This moment of loss, of foreclosure, results in Willow pointing a gun at Kennedy's head: case in point that Tara's death still haunts her, and will continue to delimit what she allows herself to feel, and who she lets into her life. Also, of course, her death precipitates what at first seems to be a clichéd narrative convention (scorned lover becomes grief-fueled killing machine) which repositions the Tara-Willow relationship (formerly unique and layered) within a realm of televisual kitsch. Perhaps.

But it must also be remembered that the happiness and well being of these characters is constantly being frustrated by powers seemingly beyond their control. Angel and Buffy are held in romantic abeyance due to a magical curse ("I Only Have Eyes for You," 2.19); Xander cannot marry Anya for fear of repeating the scenario of mindless conflict that his parents have presented him with ("Hell's Bells," 6.16); Giles finds romantic satisfaction with Jenny Calender, only to learn that she has been killed (in an equally swift and appalling manner) by "evil" Angel ("Passion," 2.17). These characters gain verisimilitude — and thus audience appeal — through their suffering, reversals, mistakes and attempts to negotiate a thoroughly obscured ideal of humanity. Willow and Tara are no different, and thus should not be treated differently by the show's narrative.

Extra-textual ramifications aside, it is Tara's death that fragments Willow's already-compromised identity beyond repair, causing her to become wholly subsumed and embodied by magic. At first her goal is simple — kill Warren, who is directly responsible for the shooting, and also his friends Jonathan and Andrew, who are guilty by association. But after her first kill — a gruesome act of *dis*embodiment, in which Warren is actually flayed — Willow's plans grow more abstract. While supposedly pursuing Andrew and Jonathan, she spends most of her time challenging and subverting her surrogate family — the Scoobies — by excavating their fears and undermining their accomplishments. Willow does not need magic to do this. Magic gives her the voice, the confidence, but it is through ordinary speech acts that she violates and tears down her friends. This psychic battle culminates in a physical one with Giles — whom she accuses of being "under the delusion that you [are] still relevant here" — wherein she brings him close to death, and extracts the magical power that he has "borrowed" from a Coven; the power allegedly meant to contain her (6.22). This confrontation will ironically be recast as a teacher-student relationship in "Lessons," (7.01), as Giles attempts to teach Willow focus and control over her power. The rhetoric that he employs, however, is merely a positive, slightly Gaian spin on what Willow has already enunciated: "I am the magic." Giles can never truly teach her what this ambivalent relationship means how it must be maintained, or how it will transform her.

Still — returning to "Grave" — it is the Coven's stolen power that taps into Willow's "spark of humanity," allowing Xander's own speech act to penetrate her. What might seem terribly hackneyed (good triumphs over the corrupted soul) is made interesting by the profound ambivalence of the situation. For Willow attempts to destroy the world not out of villainous, moustache-twirling ire — or because she feels betrayed by a world that falsely imagines her and renders her an outcast — but because she wants to annihilate human suffering. Her connection to the source of all magic allows her to experience a terrifying collectivity of earthly pain, anger and despair, the depth of which she cannot withstand. And she could not experience this without Giles's "gift" of the Coven's power. Thus, the emotional event that drives her to extinguish all human life is the same event that allows Xander to reach her, and foster her dying "spark" of individuality. And that notion of the spark is made entirely more ambiguous by Spike's later speech to Buffy ("They put the spark back in me, and now all it does is burn" ["Beneath You," 7.02]), leading the audience to question just how this soul-concept truly influences *Buffy*'s characters (7.02).

This syncretism of interdependent forces — not the binary life/death, but rather life *in* death, monstrosity *in* humanity, informed and embodied by each other — creates a wildly subversive and critically fascinating vision of the "real" social architecture that exists outside of the show, not just that which drives conflict *within* the show. If, as Baudrillard suggests, "it is the TV that renders true," then the exigencies of these characters are shared and simulated by their audience (Baudrillard, 29). The fact that the world must be brought to the brink of apocalypse in order to save one human life — Willow's — is not lost upon the consciousness of the viewer. What is being said here may not be a master-narrative that guides *Buffy*'s moral universe, but it *is* still a suggestion that these characters are not separate from the monsters that they fight — just as the prototypical construction of "evil" within the show lingers on the borders of good, and is given form within that liminal space. Willow *is* the magic, and as Xander observes, there is no real demarcation between "crayon-breaky Willow" and "scary-veiny Willow," because both are reflections of a continually evolving source.

This investigation, then, must begin and end with the same question: Who is Willow? And, perhaps more accurately, why does she matter? As has been discussed, it is Willow's ambiguity that makes her interesting as a character — her lack of positioning that makes her the object of theoretical debate. She is Buffy's twilight sister and confidante, yet has the mystical power to destroy the Slayer. She is dismissive of Xander's friendship and foibles, yet all of her rage, grief and desire for vengeance cannot withstand his brilliant, calm declaration of unconditional love. She is the academic equal — and mystical superior — to Giles, yet it is Giles who "teaches" her to reaccess her lost humanity by reminding her that she is part of a vast, organic system. In short, Willow resents her surrogate family, yet is informed by them, and desperately needs to anchor her free-floating subject to what she assumes are their "solid" identities.

Willow reflects all that her friends imagine her to be. She is Xander's kindergarten playmate, and the awkward, foolishly dressed "nerd" who gives a boring report on C.S. Lewis in the episode "Restless." She is the "rank, arrogant amateur" Giles supposes her to be when she naively brings Buffy back from the dead, and also the computer whiz who can effortlessly control what he terms "that infernal machine." She is Buffy's font of relationship advice, and also the black-eyed witch whose magically-induced strength allows her to match the Slayer blow for blow, and summarily defeat her.

Willow inhabits all of these subjectivities, and none of them make her as legible as the other characters in the show, because she can move so quickly and seamlessly between them. Willow — alone among the Scoobies — has the power to choose between redemptive and destructive behavior. She is not bound by prophecy (like Buffy), or mediocrity (like Xander) or logic and propriety (like Giles). She is free and thus — completely dislocated, bewildered and confused. For no identity satisfies her, no power can ever truly embody her, and after losing herself in "dark" magic, no amount of atonement can erase the memory of what she inflicted on others through word and deed. Her hybridity, her ability to choose, comes with the loss of any meaningful sense of belonging, intimacy or certainty. Like Buffy, she is faced with the knowledge that she doesn't know "how to live in this world if these are the choices. If everything just gets stripped away. I just don't see the point" ("The Gift," 5.22). But, also like Buffy, she knows that the illusion of safety, of a morally governed universe, of a destiny not eclipsed by suffering and most likely death, is her only comfort. And it is, after all, the maintenance and defense of any human certainty, however small, that drives these characters to avert apocalypse season after season: not the assumption that there is any one suitable "way" to live in the world, but rather the continual realization that the world itself is worth saving, that causes them to fight, even against themselves.

Willow's role within the program is as ambiguous as the program itself. She is not a model heroine, nor is Buffy, since neither can ever fully juxtapose themselves against negative powers — whose meaning is forever deterred by signifiers like "darkness," "the First" or Spike's "big bad" — without violating the gossamer-thin line that separates them from those powers. Willow, more than anyone, knows how easily these lines can be transgressed. Again, like the program itself — which the viewer expects to be what Jacques Derrida might call a text with an "edge," but is instead an open-ended system — Willow's negotiation with the monstrous is a journey through dark, open terrain rather than a carefully defined block of cells (Derrida, 256). She is engaged in a process of becoming and is, in her own words, "not all grown yet."

It is most important to remember that Willow has driven *Buffy*'s narrative from the beginning, and that the rich history of her character — all of the awkward moments, turned phrases and bursts of emotional intensity — has in itself composed the material of that narrative. For *Buffy* is read by the audience not as a plot-driven system — an endless recession of soporific story echoes, returns and repetitions — but as an evolving dialogue between its characters. Willow does not, then, have to arrive at a final transformation or defining moment, because — like the other Scoobies — she *is* the story. And, although the show has ended, Willow's story has not.

In other spaces — be they fanfiction, cameos on *Angel* or simply the wealth of unarticulated stories that swirl around a "completed" narrative — she will continue to tell (un)tell, and retell herself, pushing against the very limits of what can be said, of what might be embodied, in her search for existence without foreclosure. She must be crayon-breaky Willow/scary-veiny Willow at the same time, and find both lovable, both inhabitable — because it is not, as Buffy suggests, being "finished" ("Afterlife," 6.03) that is most important, but rather the dark and seductive expanse of the story itself, with its critical gaps, eager to be reimagined. Chapter Two, then, will stretch us further across that gap as we discuss the character who straddles both gender and generic identities, yet who also ties the Scooby Gang together: Xander Lavelle Harris.

CHAPTER TWO

"This Carpenter Can Drywall You into the Next Century": Xander Harris as Hero, Big Brother and Male-In-Progress

> "Although we seem to have a difficult time defining masculinity, as a society we have little trouble in recognizing it."
>
> —Judith Halberstam, "Female Masculinity"

> "It's time for me to act like a man. And hide."
>
> —Xander, "Bewitched, Bothered, and Bewildered" (2.16)

Xander's exact place within the Scooby Gang, *Buffy*'s chosen family,[1] has always been uncertain. The title of this chapter suggests two possible identities for Xander: there is "big brother," which Buffy calls him in the surrealist episode "Restless" (4.22), and there is also "butt monkey," which he calls himself after falling under the clearly feminizing thrall of Dracula (5.01). I have chosen these poles because, it seems, much of Xander's social interaction remains focused on walking a thin line between "big brother" and "butt monkey." He is constantly invested in proving his heroism, and by extension his masculinity, to the crucial women in his life—Buffy, Willow and Anya—but more often than not he fails spectacularly on both counts. This chapter, therefore, will focus primarily on Xander's negotiation of his own masculinity, which remains the key sign for his placement within the family unit. Xander's masculinity has much in common with the sort of dominant white masculinity that masquerades as a cultural norm rather than as a political category[2]; however, Xander also manages to exist on the margins of hegemonic maleness, forever undermining his own sexuality.

What interests me the most about Xander is that, regardless of how much he complains about being disempowered, the last season of *Buffy* suggests that he does in fact have a formidable superpower: that is, the power of *sight*. As I will discuss a bit later, Xander's agency, if it exists at all, exists as a technology of remembering and preservation. He sees his family so clearly because, in his own words, "nobody's watching me" (7.12),[3] and in this sense he is able to hold his family together by reminding them of who they are. Xander becomes, like the television show *itself*, an archive of these characters' dreams, failures and personal triumphs. He is figured as the eye/I of the camera, which Laura Mulvey has defined as a male spectacular position, interested in capturing and inscribing female bodies. But Xander's own insecure maleness, combined with the nurturing support and definition that he gives his family, creates a viewpoint that is profoundly queer.

In so many ways, I have always been, and continue to be, the inarticulate and perennially uncool figure that Xander represents. I, too, have been known to "laugh in the face of danger, then hide until it goes away" (*Buffy*, "The Witch," 1.03). Most *Buffy* fans have a character to whom they've indelibly linked themselves. The average university English department is divided evenly among those faculty who would like to sleep with Spike, and those who feel as if they have always embodied the social awkwardness of characters like Willow and Xander. To study a show like *Buffy* at all is to be, in some ways, the Xander of your respective department. I have come to embrace that role. I am the Zeppo.

Zeppo, refers to Zeppo Marx, the allegedly "invisible" member of the Marx Bros. comedy troupe. I raise this bit of cultural ephemera in order to point out that *Buffy*'s creator, Joss Whedon, and his team of writers have made quite a visible effort to draw our attention to Xander's *invisibility* as a character. Indeed, an entire Season Four episode, "The Zeppo," was devoted to showcasing Xander's own hopeless ineptitude as a fighter of evil. Cordelia Chase, who — as only a character in the Buffyverse could — eventually makes the transition from prom queen bitch extraordinaire to an avatar for the forces of good,[4] tells Xander that "it must be hard being ... a little nothing" (*Buffy*, "Zeppo," 3.13). As I combed through seven seasons worth of Xander-related quotes to compile this chapter, the words *nothing, invisible, hide* and *background* kept coming up. I had originally intended on discussing Xander as an interesting site for alternative and marginalized masculinities. But, as variations on the word *invisibility* continued to emerge, it became apparent that Xander was just as intimately connected with dominant forms of white masculinity — with a masculinity that has historically presented itself as a transparent cultural norm.

In an oft-cited quote from her book *Marked Men*, Sally Robinson states that "what calls itself the normative in American culture has vested interests in *both* invisibility and visibility" (Robinson, 3). I would like to align this statement, which serves as an entrance into Robinson's discussion of the wounded white male, with a statement of Xander's that I find equally compelling: "It's time for me to act like a man. And hide" (*Buffy*, "Bewitched," 2.16). It is significant that Xander says this while being chased by a horde of schoolgirls, all bewitched into thinking that he is the cherished object of their affection. The humor that the show constructs here is a tad sophomoric: something along the lines of "isn't it funny and ironic that Xander has to hide from these cute girls?" But, as is often the case with *Buffy*, there is also a subversive edge just waiting for someone to point at it.

To "be a man" on television is *not* to hide; and indeed, Xander knows that this desire to hide is precisely what pushes his masculinity into crisis. The visible marker of his heterosexuality — that is, his relationship with Anya — is constantly undermined by Xander's many ironic assaults on his own masculinity. He is not only hiding in plain sight as a white man, but pointing snidely at his own hiding place in the hopes that somebody will notice him. Yet, as scholars within masculinity studies are now insisting, the notion of "being" a man, of being "normative" within dominant white cultural production, continues to depend upon a tension between visibility and invisibility.[5] For dominant white masculinity to retain cultural capital, it needs to erase alternative masculinities — most especially queer and female masculinities.[6] But it also needs, in effect, to erase *itself*; to render itself invisible as a political category, and instead to re-present itself, to continually reinvent itself, as the ground from which culture emerges.

As a great deal of recent scholarship, as well as simple observation, have shown, *Buffy the Vampire Slayer* as a cutting-edge, subversive television show is by no means immune to this formula of cultural erasure. The population of mythical Sunnydale, California, is overwhelmingly white, and when Black or Asian characters find their way into *Buffy*'s narrative, they tend to do so as peripheral figures.[7] Kendra the Vampire Slayer, whose appearance and subsequent death shocked audiences in Season Two, was a brutal caricature of the pan–African woman; an Asian vampire slayer, who Spike kills (predictably during the Boxer Rebellion, that staple of the eighth grade Social Studies curriculum), is never even given a name. The Slayage Conference on BtVS and Angel, held May 2004, devoted an entire panel to discussing the fourth-season episode "Pangs"—which, through its rather unexamined message of cultural tolerance and white guilt, looks a great deal like the "very special episode of *Buffy*" that Joss Whedon promised he would never write.

The point is that it's impossible to talk about the show's subversive potential without also talking about its various mechanisms for deferring and containing that subversion. Like Xander, the program itself is implicated in a complex relationship between visibility and invisibility. Xander, as a character, seems to be at the heart of this paradox. He is hiding in plain view. He is very clearly a white male, but just as clearly *not* invested in what he thinks being a white male could mean. His insecurity makes him a sort of Everyman while simultaneously distancing him from everything that dominant white masculinity has a stake in. He has a demon for a girlfriend (one who spent 1100 years torturing unfaithful men), a lesbian witch for a best friend, and he was once (just one time!) Dracula's butt monkey. These wildly absurd variables, among other things, help to push Xander's masculinity into crisis. But he is not exactly a wounded white male, and not exactly a transparent white man. So what is he?

In the episode "Potential," Xander tells Dawn, "I see more than anybody realizes because nobody's watching me" (*Buffy*, 7.12). Dawn suggests that this could be his superpower, but Xander remains unsure. Six episodes later, the evil priest Caleb plucks out one of Xander's eyes, calling him "the one who sees everything" (*Buffy*, "Dirty Girls," 7.18). Obviously, the question of who Xander is watching, and who is watching *Xander*, establishes itself here as a focal point within *Buffy*'s narrative. The title of this paper alludes to Xander's "superpower," but one of the most interesting aspects of this character is that, unlike his surrogate family, Xander consciously disavows the notion that he could possess any sort of power in the first place.

It is only other people who ascribe power to Xander; it is never visible, or rather, it remains invisible until it becomes authorized by someone else's citation of it. Only once does Xander admit that "I saved the world with my mouth" (*Buffy*, "Same Time," 7.03), but again, this intervention occurs within the realm of the symbolic rather than through a display of magic or might.[8] All of Xander's victories, it seems, are queered by the notion that this is all just speech; that he probably doesn't even believe what he's saying; that his mouth may be saving the world, but the rest of him remains in hiding.

Judith Halberstam, among other gender theorists, argues convincingly that masculinity has historically been filtered through and constructed by non-male bodies, including biological-female, queer and transgendered bodies. In her work *Female Masculinity*, Halberstam states that "manliness is built partly on the vigorous disavowal of female masculinity[,] and partly on a simultaneous reconstruction of male masculinity in *imitation* of the female masculinity it claims to have rejected" (Halberstam, 49).

In applying this idea to *Buffy the Vampire Slayer*, the obvious candidate for female masculinity is Buffy herself. Time and time again, Buffy has made what Halberstam calls "convincing and powerful assaults on the coherence of male masculinity" (15). Physically strong, authorized to lead, figuring centrally within more than one prophecy, and wielding a stake called "Mr. Pointy," Buffy signifies across a variety of spaces that dominant white masculinity is invested in. Much discussion has revolved around what alternative masculinities she might embody. But very little discussion has concerned itself with the alternative *femininities* that Xander, and the other male characters in the show, might also embody.

Xander's femininity, as well as Buffy's masculinity, are fractures that the show must deploy and then contain in order to ensure the continued acceptance of its audience. The possibility of Xander's queerness,[9] which arises from his masculinity-in-crisis, must be continually disavowed through his sexual relationship with Anya. Similarly, although Buffy often hovers around the margins of lesbian identification, her heterosexuality is firmly and repeatedly announced through her various relationships with Angel, Spike, Riley and even Principal Wood. The character who opens the queer Pandora's Box, so to speak, is Willow, when she manages to enter into a sexual relationship with Tara after having long-term, physical and narratively significant relationships with Xander and Oz. Willow's sexuality is never made especially coherent, and her own lack of what she calls "lesbo street cred" (*Buffy*, "Tough Love," 5.19), has been criticized by viewers as an attractive and ratings-friendly form of bisexuality constructed by a largely straight team of writers.[10]

Willow's magic eventually reinscribes her as the most powerful member of the Scooby Gang, and her sexuality only complicates this further, placing her within the lesbian body that Buffy herself could never be allowed to inhabit. Let me preface this by saying that, if Willow does produce masculinity, it is by no means butch. She clearly performs the role of the femme with her tight-fitting Ts, glossy lips and long, perfectly conditioned hair. All of the aggressively masculine characteristics that she takes on as "Evil Willow"—physical violence, cold logic and brutal honesty through speech—are summarily expunged when she transitions back to "Good Willow." But it is *Xander* who helps to erase this aggressive form of masculinity; and he erases it precisely through his sensitive language, his masochism and his stubborn insistence that he loves Willow "even though you're about to do something apocalyptically evil" (*Buffy*, "Grave," 6.22).

Whether or not Xander "feminizes" Willow, or reasserts her femininity under the auspices of searching for her "humanity," is a point open for debate. But the fact remains that Xander's primary female influences are: a hypermasculine Vampire slayer, a lesbian witch who, until only recently, wore dark pantsuits and flayed men alive, and a former vengeance demon who grew quite used to hearing her male victims scream, "Oh, God, please stop hitting me with my own rib bones!" (7.03). Xander's only "normative" masculine influence is Riley, who, self-described as a "corn-fed Iowa boy," is actually the poster child for dominant white masculinity.

But, as his relationship with Buffy unravels, it becomes clear that

Riley's own embattled masculinity cannot cope with Buffy's more formidable strength, nor with her desire for fatal men (a desire that inverts, becoming wildly sadistic, when she begins having sex with Spike). Xander, it seems, is continually confronted by alternative female sexualities and incoherent masculinities. This makes him remarkably visible as a male, but simultaneously invisible as a character denied any form of agency, be it martial, sexual or symbolic. He remains the Zeppo, surrounded, in keeping with the era, by Dietrichs and Valentinos.

But if Xander has no agency, then what are we to make of his contested ability to "see" things? Without overanalyzing the heavy symbolic content of Xander's own blinding, it's safe to say that his vision must be a considerable threat to the forces of evil. But what, exactly, is Xander able to see? His own queer masculinity? The sexual and gender dysphoria that other characters seem blissfully unaware of? The paper-thin boundaries between female masculinity, masculine femininity and queer gender that all of these characters seem to transgress at one time or another? The utopian queer theorist in me wants to proclaim that Xander is able to see all of this, as well as the fragile bonds that hold his chosen family together. But I also know that part of Xander's project as what Spike would call a "nancy boy" is to reincorporate alternative masculinities into a more acceptable and attractive dominant masculinity.[11] An unavoidable effect of Xander's masculinity-in-crisis is that he still gets the girl, still emerges as an action hero, and still, in his own words, gets to "feel like a man" (*Buffy*, "Woods," 5.10) primarily because Anya loves him.

At the end of the day, Xander remains very straight, very white and vigorously sexual to the point of resembling a college freshman. Even partially blinded, he manages to survive the final confrontation between the First Evil and (significantly) *her* minions, whereas Anya, who has proven herself to be more physically capable than Xander in dozens of situations, is brutally killed without a moment of narrative pathos. These various (and often funny) queerings of Xander's masculinity serve only make his vindication as a straight white male profoundly ironic.

There is a visible tension in the show between Xander's desire to be a heroic straight male (with heroism being coded as "straight"), and his various performances as a non-heroic, emotional, terrified and physically inept anti-hero. Lorna Jowett discusses Xander's homoerotic subtext in her forthcoming book *Sex and the Slayer* (Wesleyan: 2005), and I am particularly grateful for the editorial input that she gave me on drafts of this chapter. If not for her suggestions, I would have forgotten completely about Xander's "gay me up" comment in the episode *First Date* (7.14), as well as the extended parodic conversation on queerness that follows. I would love to reproduce that conversation in its entirety, given that, as a queer spectator, I find it to be one of the funniest exchanges in the show's history. Given length constraints, however, I will settle on making a few short references to it, because I think that it critically underscores Xander's own masculine insecurities, and his overriding desire to be a heroic older-brother figure who gets to save his sisters-in-distress, rather than, as is usually the case, the other way around.

After returning from a particularly life-threatening date with a demon, Xander seems to relinquish his tenuous hold on heterosexuality, and tells Willow: "Gay me up. Come on, let's gay." Xander's use of the word "gay" as a verb is more than a little disturbing, as it suggests that characters can easily transition from gay to straight, and that Willow, being a lesbian, can give him directions on "get[ting] this gay show on the gay road." There are several criticisms at work here, the first being a clever upbraiding of male homophobia. The repetition of the word "gay" allows it not only to bend common rules of grammatical usage, but to become a site of absurdity, a vocal non-sound, or what linguists might call an empty morpheme. It's the equivalent of having a character shout "gay, gay, gay" at the top of his lungs until it no longer seems threatening — until, indeed, it no longer contains meaning at all.

This allows Xander to, in a playful way, confront his own homophobia. By suggesting that "I'm mentally undressing Scott Bakula right now," Xander can flirt with an exotic sexuality while still safely cohering as a straight male, and simultaneously suggesting — even if the show doesn't intend to — that queerness is a kind of last-ditch effort, a solution to failed heterosexuality, and a fun alternative to the rigors of the hostile dating world. That Xander is bleeding as he says all of this, and being carried by Buffy, only further skews his masculinity, presenting him as a wounded white male whose sexuality, like his body, is in a state of fracture. But, as already discussed in this chapter, the sign of the wounded white male has historically served as a site for the *reassertion*, not the deconstruction, of heroic male heterosexuality. Like Spike, Xander gets to appear vulnerable, taking on the elements of trauma that actual queer bodies have experienced, while still retaining his essential straight masculinity. In this sense, he can playfully gesture to his own anxieties around queerness, while never actually exploring those anxieties in a manner other than parody.

Xander's primary claims to heteromasculinity arise from his brief stint as a soldier — from which he still retains valuable military training — and his later identity as a carpenter and handyman. He is, after all, one of the only gainfully employed members of the Scoobies who works a traditional job, which suggests that part of his masculinity emanates from a working-class identity. While Faith is the failed working-class subject, who refuses to labor and hence becomes marked as a dangerous psychotic, Xander is the appropriate laborer who derives a sense of normalcy and accomplishment from his work. Much of this masculine normalcy gets asserted in scenes with Anya, and we should pay particular attentions to scenes where the two of them are driving. Notice that Anya never drives, and Xander never attempts to teach her how to drive. We also rarely see Anya arriving home from work, or calling in sick, or mentioning "work" at all in a way that isn't entirely conflated with her capitalist money-obsession. For Anya, work remains a kind of rarefied pleasure, whereas, for Xander, it is what he "has to do," and thus gestures to the conflation of essential masculinity with blue-collar labor. But Xander is also constructed as being more clever and sensitive than his work buddies, which means that the show is drawing upon the symbolic vocabulary of the working-class male while simultaneously disavowing him as unenlightened and primitive.

At first glance, it may appear that Giles is the masculine "head" of the Scooby family, but keep in mind that Giles spends much of his time *leaving* the Scoobies. He is also coded, again and again, as an intellectual rather than action-oriented masculine presence, and as a slightly foreign, slightly out-of-touch figure. Xander, however, is a core masculine presence who develops, in later seasons, into the essentially patristic "big brother" character who holds the family together, in no small part because of his normative masculinity. Discourse on the family has traditionally revolved around images of the male provider, and Xander, as he grows into his "carpenter" persona, comes to embody that image. His embattled masculinity remains a palpable threat to the coherence of the Scoobies as a "real" family — that is, as a family unit that, despite its radicality, still remains legible to the majority of audience members — and so Xander must be continually reinscribed as a straight male even as he lingers on the edges of that signification.

Lorna Jowett also pointed out to me that Xander is at his most sexually ambiguous when he interacts with Riley. Upon seeing the Initiative headquarters for the first time, he asks "Can I have sex with Riley too?" ("Goodbye Iowa," 4.14). And his incomplete "soldier training" must always exist in tension with Riley's "official" training as a soldier — his lifelong commitment to the military, which is like a roundtrip ticket to straight masculinity, as compared to Xander's mystical brush with being a soldier. Scenes which attempt to use this "training" to reassert Xander's heterosexuality — such as his admonition to a real soldier that "you hold your gun like a sissy girl" (2.14) — usually end up as parodies, rather than resignifications, of this essentialized masculinity. Xander will never be as "cool" as he thinks Riley is, and will never have that sort of breezy ability to emanate heterosexuality or heroism. Xander, like most straight male viewers, has come to associate heroism and efficacy with a particular brand of straightness that consists of absolute confidence in one's physical abilities, as well as unswerving loyalty to a cause.

Riley is, of course, everything that Xander is not. He is not especially funny, not particularly conflicted about his masculinity, not concerned about his sexual prowess, and not torn between variously unpleasant career choices. Riley knows exactly who he is, and Xander doesn't have the first clue about who *he* is. Masculinity, in this sense, gets strangely conflated with self-possession, with knowledge and identity-formation. To "be" a man is actually not to "be" anything, but rather to *know* something — to know who you are and where you're going. Riley seems to have this roadmap, whereas Xander does not. And Xander's humorous request to "gay me up" seems, thus, to be a kind of surrendering of direction. Xander finally admits what he perceives to be his failed masculinity here, and invites the possibility of becoming a different sort of man. The troubling suggestion implicit in such a "change" is not just that sexuality is malleable, but that a queer man would represent the "bottom" of the sexual-identity ladder, the absolute basement of self-knowledge. To be queer is to *admit* that you are a failed man, and thus to stop worrying about being a man altogether. Given that *Buffy* has no positive or enduring gay male characters to counteract this statement, and that Willow offers no real protest in this scene, we are left with this idea hanging in the air.

I feel like I have criticized Xander's flexible masculinity enough in this chapter, and I don't want to belabor the point. He remains one of my favorite characters, and I do understand that his comic negotiations of what it means to be a straight man are actually meant as positive gestures, suggesting that — as is, I understand, the case — most straight men don't have the first clue about how to "be" a man. Queer men understand this far more intimately, and the answer, for them, is often brutally simple: to be a man is not to be queer. Masculinity is defined in opposition to their sexual knowledge, their self-knowledge, and thus cohering as a "man" forces them to foreclose all of the understanding they have about themselves. When this foreclosure is not an option — when one already belongs to this category of straight masculinity, and is not actually seeking admission — then the process becomes one of negotiation rather than disavowal.

Xander's negotiations are meant to be funny and gentle, but it remains the case that, for queer audiences, every ironic jab at hypothetical queerness is a violent intrusion on someone's living queer reality. Jokes about turning gay, about the prospect of "gaying" or being "gayed up," are funny to straight audiences because *being gay* is funny to them; and they are funny to queer audiences because most queers experience this sort of humor as a kind of laughable irony, a playful self-criticism that is part of their tactics for survival in a predominantly heterosexual world. But for those whose living space is threatened by legislated homophobic violence, for those who are looking for representations of themselves in popular television and finding nothing, and for those who look up to *Buffy* as a show that rhetoricizes tolerance and inclusion, these ironic asides can appear patronizing at best, and insulting at worst.

Perhaps, then, what Xander "sees" (with his alleged superpower) is that his biologically male body allows him to flirt with all kinds of symbolic sexualities, while still cohering as a hetero man simply because that sign's flexibility is what has made it so historically impervious to female and queer assaults. Although he occasionally dons a form of queer masculinity, Xander remains what Halberstam calls "the femme pretender … [who] performs the failure of her own masculinity as a convincing spectacle" (250). Xander "performs the failure of his masculinity," but that performance is a licensed one, and must be continually reconstituted as an essential white maleness that only grows more transparent once he literally (and symbolically) becomes a carpenter.

But, regardless of this failed mimicry (or successful pass, depending upon how one views it), I believe that queer and female audiences may still have the pleasure of the final cut here. And I don't mean to conflate female with queer—only to point to an audience beyond this essentially masculine core. For Xander "sees" many other things besides his own privilege as a straight white male. He sees past the aggressive facade of "Evil Willow," and realizes that what she needs, beyond magic, justice or even redemption, is the bare offering of unconditional love. He sees past Buffy's insecurities, and tells her, quite rightly, that her version of love needs to include "scary, messy, no-emotions-barred need" (5.10). He sees past Anya's peculiar and literal-minded view of the world, and understands her to be, like him, a displaced person surrounded by individuals of power and prophecy.

But most of all Xander sees the genealogy of laughable and painful moments that compose who and what his friends *are*. He sees the gaps they try to fill between monstrosity and humanity, and understands that their comic negotiations of the supernatural are just as profoundly negotiations of adulthood. Over seven seasons these characters have grown up quite a bit, and their identities may no longer be as coherent as they were during the pilot episode, when Willow dressed in plaid skirts and Xander skateboarded ineptly, charmingly, into Buffy's frame of vision. But Xander continually reminds his friends who they once where, and who they have become. He sees them because, in his own words, nobody is watching him. And this outsiderness makes him a kind of queer observer: fiercely in love with these people who define his life, but forever removed from their orbit.

Now that I have sketched out a framework for looking at Xander's contested masculinity, I would like to discuss how that masculinity positions him within the Scooby Gang family. If Willow is defined by a kind of specular identity (as discussed in Chapter One), a lack waiting to be inscribed, then Xander is defined by his comic negotiation of maleness and masculinity. He emerges, at times, as Halberstam's "femme pretender," always aware that his performance is a failure, but also as a male caricature who is inept at conversation and other "intimacies" far better at fixing windows than interpreting prophecies, and traditionally brave because he goes into battle without the aid of slayer-strength or magical power. Like John Wayne's character in *Stagecoach* (1939), he does what a man "has to do," but his reasons for "doing" masculinity remain incoherent. Is he truly the big brother to Buffy and Willow, a kind of patriarchal organizing force among the Scooby Family? Or does his masculinity-in-crisis make such a role impossible? My answer to this is, no: it simply makes the role a lot more interesting.

As previously mentioned, in the episode "Restless" (*Buffy* 4.22), Buffy names Xander "big brother." A great deal of academic criticism has been focused on this surrealist episode, much of it published in *Slayage*, the online journal of *Buffy*-related scholarship edited by Rhonda Wilcox and David Lavery.[12] Interestingly, although most *Buffy* critics tend to mention "Restless" peripherally — commenting on its Dadaist dialogue and provocative imagery — none have discussed it as an episode that links the core members of the Scooby Gang together as an extended family. When I first watched "Restless," I was immediately struck by the tender image of the Scoobies sleeping "safely" on Joyce's couch, which was then juxtaposed against a montage of disturbing and often incoherent images — each one escalating in violence. Xander, as usual, is the bearer of movies and popcorn, offering his extended family the predictable measure of comfort, geniality and distraction from the forces of evil that they have come to expect. Xander's own dream sequence within "Restless" seems, at first glance, to be the most charmingly literary (with its unapologetic allusions to Coppola's *Apocalypse Now* [1979], and by extension Conrad's *Heart of Darkness* [1899]), and the least dramatic.

However, the "evil" that Xander faces at the end of this dream is none other than his own father, who informs him coldly that "the line ends here with us, and you're not gonna change that. You haven't got the heart," before plunging his hand into Xander's chest and removing the offending organ himself. This evisceration makes sense in terms of the episode's own thematic logic, since Giles, Willow and Xander all have symbolic body parts removed by the spirit of Sineya, the First Slayer. But Xander's dream, more than the dreams of the other Scoobies, offers a wide spectrum of family-related imagery that speaks to Xander's own imprecise position within a chosen family.

When Xander warns Buffy — who, in his dream, is playing in a sort of paradimensional sandbox that shifts from a safe space to a forbidding desert — that she should be careful because "you can't protect yourself from ... some stuff," Buffy replies enigmatically, with "I'm way ahead of you, big brother." Xander appears confused by the statement, even re-echoing it as a question, but Buffy's dream incarnation remains sedate. She obviously knows what she's talking about, as evidenced by her calm smile (she is also holding a child's shovel). But why, exactly, does everyone seem to know Xander's place in this family except for Xander himself?

Part of this stems from Whedon's adoption of conventional dream logic, which, without going into early psychoanalytic writing on the subject, we can agree tends to place the dreamer within a continual and often escalating knowledge gap. Obviously, the characters in Xander's dream should know more than he does. But I'm especially interested here by *what* these characters know in relation to Xander's potential "big brother" identity, and what Xander himself seems not to have the foggiest clue about. When we, like Xander, see the image of Giles and Spike on the swings together, dressed in matching tweed suits, the sheer strangeness of the pairing creates a moment of both charming parody and deadly confusion. Why deadly? Because, as we know, Giles and Spike — especially at this point in the show's story arc — hate each other. The sight of them sharing an absurd father-and-son round of playtime, while Buffy plays at the edge of what could very well be Baudrillard's "desert of the real,"[13] is on the surface merely an eruption of comic nonsense. But Giles's cheerful claim that "Spike's like a son to me," followed by a pan to Xander's clear expression of disbelief, suggests an anxiety that is cleverly being shaped by this dream world — namely, Xander's own rocky relationship with Giles, who has always served as the Scooby Gang's surrogate parent.

Giles and Xander have always had something of a disciplinary relationship, with Xander often ending up on the sharp end of Giles's acerbic criticisms. Although Giles shows a marked and surprising tenderness for Buffy, excusing many of her transgressions as an indulgent father-figure would be expected to, he very rarely offers Xander that sort of long-suffering clemency. But Xander and Giles do share certain secrets. He is, for instance, the only person who knows that Xander didn't *actually* lose his memory after being possessed by a hyena spirit ("The Pack," *Buffy* 1.06)—that he remembers, in perfect detail, every cruel thing he said to Willow when she was still at her most bookish and vulnerable during the show's first season. And Giles, despite his obvious misgivings about Anya's work-in-progress humanity, assures Xander that "I'm sure you'll spend ... many years of non-hell-dimensional bliss [together]" ("All the Way," *Buffy* 6.06). Indeed, the conversation that the two have in "All the Way," revolving around house-buying, cohabitation and other matrimonial matters, is very much a dispensation of paternal advice on Giles' part.

Surrounded, as he is, by supernatural "daughters," it comes as no surprise that Giles should engage in the gruff, hard-nosed type of relationship with Xander so often typified by a father's connection to his only son. This affection is, of course, mediated by the ever-present "Britishness" of Giles' demeanor, which we have to remind ourselves is not only a benchmark stereotype of televisual and cinematic discourse, but, in *Buffy*'s case, a trope of intellectual legitimacy that has been dragged out of the stable so that it might be deconstructed rather than merely deployed. Like Xander, Giles is constantly undermining his own position as a stiff authority figure who, as we have seen, has very little power with which to police the slayers, witches and ex-demons in his care. Even if Xander does lack a superpower, he is still well beyond the scope of Giles' imagined authority, and, like any wayward son, has the capacity to make his own mistakes—although those mistakes, unlike Buffy's or Willow's, are rarely on the cosmic scale.

Still, given this father/son dynamic existing permanently in the background, it is possible to read Giles' claim that "Spike's like a son to me" as a kind of betrayal. For, if most of Xander's insecurities stem from his unstable biological family—a family whose visual absence for most of *Buffy*'s seven seasons is a telling disavowal—then the idea that Spike might be usurping Xander's position as "big brother," however ludicrous, becomes starkly legible to him as a very real threat. The confusion on Xander/Nick Brendon's face as he watches Spike swing higher and higher ("a watcher scoffs at gravity," Giles cries), is, I think, mitigated by a much deeper ache of longing.

It is unmistakable: Xander wants that tweed suit, wants desperately to be on that swing, even if he'd rather die than admit it. His "real" family is permanently disappointing, even incoherent, and Giles, although he has proven himself many times to be fallible as a Watcher (and as a pedagogue), is the most influential masculine presence in Xander's life. The incongruity of Xander wanting, if only for a moment, to be a Watcher, and hence, to "be" Spike — who is nothing at all like a Watcher, and represents a long-standing and especially vicious threat to the Watcher's Council — demonstrates the sort of incestuous intertext that *Buffy* in general, and this episode in particular, has become famous for.

During the show's seven-season arc, we experience Xander's biological family as a hovering sort of non-presence. In the episode "Amends" (*Buffy* 3.10), Xander admits to a tradition of sleeping outside during Christmas Eve in order to avoid his family's psychotic arguing. "Amends" concludes with a freak snowfall whose exact source, be it mystical or simply coincidental, is never made apparent. This snowfall is what darkens the sky above Sunnydale long enough for Angel to avoid his suicidal date with sunrise — for, after his initial (but not his last) meeting with the First Evil in this episode, Angel becomes convinced that his murderous history as Angelus has placed him beyond the path of redemption. As is often the case with *Buffy*, it is this bit of meteorological curiosity — not a firm decision on the part of the characters — that gives Angel an escape clause from what might have been a deadly piece of melodrama. The image of Angel and Buffy walking, hand in hand, through the snow-covered streets of Sunnydale is then juxtaposed against the comically haunting image of Xander, asleep beneath a thin veil of snow, wrapped in his childhood sleeping bag.

The notion of Xander deliberately exiling himself from his own family is one of several family-rejection scenarios that occur among *Buffy*'s Scooby Gang. It is never presented as the most crucial rejection — Tara's family, for instance, is violently controlling in the episode "Family" (5.06), and Angel actually kills his family in order to achieve a traditional vampiric rebirth ("Becoming Pt.1," 3.21) — but Xander's disavowal is certainly the longest-running. Beginning with "Amends," it surfaces again in Season 5's episode "The Replacement" (5.03), when Xander, watching TV in his basement with the rest of the gang, acidly describes the sounds of his parents' fighting as "incompetent burglars." In the later episode "Forever" (5.17), after Joyce's death has prompted everyone to pay more attention to their families, Xander defends his choice to visit Willow's family rather than his own by stating, "I'm not going to *my* place. Those people are scary."

This is one of many ironic contrasts in *Buffy* wherein the idea of what might be "scary" is endlessly mutated along the increasingly vague axes of humanity/monstrosity. Although Xander should, by all accounts, find vampires, mummies and demons to be infinitely scarier than his parents, it is a fact that he does not. This is no easy exemplum meant to demonstrate that "real" life can be just as frightening as fantasy, but rather one of many psychological gestures within the show towards an unmooring of generic horror. *Buffy*'s characters have becomes naturalized to the unnatural — they are unafraid of most supernatural phenomena — but the truly insurmountable horrors are the ones that would normally have no place within a horror text — families, relationships, sexuality and the continual negotiation of gray living space between the outrageously fictional margins of good and evil.

Xander's own definition of horror emerges not from any invasive, "outside" forces of evil, but from the unsettling syncretism of the horrible "outside" with the intimate "inside." His family, along with his other insecurities regarding masculinity and performance, arise from the Kristevan idea of *l'abjection* which, in her own words, is "something that disgusts you [...] a revolt against an external menace from which one wants to distance oneself, but of which one has the impression that it might menace us from the inside" (1996: 118).[14] This "menace ... from the inside" has its external culmination in the episode "Hell's Bells" (6.16), when Xander sees his perennial fear of failure — his failure to "be a man," with all of the uncertain spaces that might suggest — in a mystical vision.

The vision has long been a narrative staple within *Buffy*. Whether it takes the form of a prophecy (like the one that Buffy is connected to), a dream or a waking reverie, the vision always conveys vital information that is, by nature of its medium, connotative and gestural, as opposed to the "hardcore" data on vampire lore, demonology and other mystical errata that the Scooby Gang is constantly researching. The show employs a critical tension between qualitative data, as represented by the knowledge media stated above, and mythic or impressionistic understanding — dreams, visions and emotions.

That the ultimate signification of Xander's own worst fears regarding his life with Anya comes to him through a *vision*, rather than through publicly accessible knowledge, is indicative of the premium that *Buffy* places on intuition and emotional understanding. Despite Anya's continued assurances that "it wasn't real ... what he showed you wasn't real," Xander is unable to reconcile the possibility that it might *become* real, even if that possibility is remote. What he sees in the vision — a dystopic representation of himself and Anya, projected far into the future, as a bitter and unsatisfied couple — is more a concretizing of his own formidable anxieties than a projection of any conceivable future. It doesn't matter if it is, or could ever be, "real," for the fact remains that it has always been psychologically real to Xander. Part of what makes these characters so accessible is the narration of their most intimate fears, and chief among Xander's fears has always been the cruel inevitability that he might become exactly like his parents.

"Hell's Bells" showcases the Harris family as a pastiche of televisual stereotypes — the alcoholic father, the enabling-yet-shallow mother, and the requisite crew of annoying aunts and uncles whose most embarrassing characteristic is their own total acceptance of mediocrity. What strikes me as peculiar about Xander's family is, quite frankly, their lack of peculiarity. They are almost boring in their adherence to the generic codes that have come to define the "problem family" within American televisual discourse. It appears, at first, that Xander's own demonization of his family is far more exotic than the family itself. At its worst, "Hell's Bells" gives us an inter-family brawl, with Xander's aunts and uncles hurling food at Anya's astonished paradimensional relatives. Where is the crisis here? What, exactly, is so insurmountable that the Scooby Gang — which has, by this point, weathered six seasons worth of apocalypse — can offer Xander no possible resistance with which to expel his own fears?

The crisis, as I have already outlined, is psychological rather than mystical, and although one often emerges from the other in *Buffy*, we have come to understand that no amount of martial or magical force can repair psychic rifts among these characters. It is the ordinariness of Xander's dysfunctional family that makes this episode's outcome so strange, but it is also this ordinariness that makes his psychological upheaval that much more critical. For Xander is not rebelling against a cruelly abusive family, or even a family that doesn't care about him at all — for we are never given any certain indication that Xander's family has ever rejected *him*. Indeed, their presence at his wedding to a former vengeance-demon, even if that presence happens to be disruptive, is still a gesture of acceptance and inclusion towards their son.

No — if Xander is rebelling against anything, it is the postmodern horror of being forced to take his place among an endless procession of middle-class American families. The idea that his constant brushes with the supernatural have not somehow radically changed him — that he might still retain the fundamental laziness, mediocrity and petty dissension that he sees daily in his own family — is one that Xander cannot face. It is actually the horror of suburban normalcy that he is fleeing from; and, as Sunnydale itself demonstrates, there must be an evil rotting out the foundations of post–Fordist American suburbia. There must be, and there is — a visible evil, given supernatural form in *Buffy*, but also subtly implicated within the various poses of white, middle-class urban life.

Xander's flight from commitment, then, is informed by his own internal critique of the stubborn ordinariness that he can never escape from. He will always be the Zeppo. He will always remain in the background, never given a prophecy or power to make him somehow greater than the awkward, tongue-tied Xander Lavelle Harris whose courtship of Buffy was, from the very first episode, always constructed as laughable. But what about his "big brother" identity suggested earlier? How do we reconcile Xander the failure with Xander the hero, who, in his own words, "saved the world with my mouth"? And how does he eventually become the "one who sees everything," whose powers of perception make him a kind of living archive of the Scooby Gang's organic evolution as a chosen family?

Let us return to Xander's own boast which forms the title of this chapter — his challenge to Willow that, despite her dark magic, "this carpenter can drywall you into the next century" ("Grave," 6.22). The dialogue between Xander and Willow at the close of this episode is some of the best found anywhere in *Buffy*, and to fully comprehend the intertextuality being brought to bear within this confrontation — the violent collision of much younger, much more innocent versions of Willow and Xander with the weathered and experienced humans that they have become — the audience needs to have plotted their relationship from the show's inception. It is a testament to the strength of this relationship that Willow warns Xander to "get out of my way" rather than simply liquefying him with the power she obviously possesses. Xander's address to her of "black-eyed girl" makes it clear that he is speaking not to "Evil" Willow, but to the girl he recognizes underneath; similarly, it is that fragment of the old Willow that warns Xander, and that is unwilling to destroy him.

The dynamics of this final scene illustrate, probably better than anywhere else, the flexibility and crucial significance of Xander's role as "big brother." Willow's mockery of him is coolly arrogant, but also contains a bit of ineluctable logic: "Is this the master plan? You're going to stop me by telling me you love me?" For, indeed — how can this speech act be a resistance at all? The only thing standing between Willow and her wish to destroy the world — literally standing *within* the stream of negative energy that links her to a mystical temple, thereby disrupting the flow bodily — is Xander's form, his words, his intent. This is no longer the boy who asked, on the verge of tears, "Who's gonna help me pass trig, you know?" ("Becoming Pt.1," 2.21) when Willow was in a coma, but rather an adult fully prepared to sacrifice himself in order to save Willow from self-annihilation. An adult who, it seems, is also supremely confident that his verbal effort to "humanize" her must succeed; either supremely confident, or so exhausted by his own perceived inadequacy that he no longer cares what the consequences of failure are, so long as the effort is made.

Given the propensity of dreams within *Buffy* to suggest, even to outline, story arcs that won't come to fruition until several seasons later, I have to believe that Buffy's assurance to Xander in "Restless" — "I'm way ahead of you, big brother" — is a gesture towards this very moment, when Xander's only weapon against Willow's apocalyptic magic is nothing more than his emotional connection to her. This connection, we must remember, is one that predates the arrival of Buffy, Oz, Tara or any of the other people who have made a significant impact on Willow's life. Even in the pilot episode, Xander is certain that Willow can help him pass math — along with a host of other subjects that he is clearly inept at — and, only two episodes later ("The Witch," 1.03), he cheerfully proclaims her to be "my guy friend who knows about girl stuff!" Later, in Season 3, when Willow "chooses" Oz over Xander, those who have followed their friendship from the beginning know that this "choice," like something out of the *Symposium*, is an impossible one. She enters the Buffyverse with Xander, and in the final episode she is standing at his side. The two have never been separable, or even separate, for they, like the oldest and most intimate of friends, are linked at an almost cellular level.

Xander, therefore, is the only possible candidate to bring Willow back from the edge of her soul's oblivion. When she threatens once again to destroy the world, even if it means destroying him, Xander's smile is wry — but triumphant — as he states that "it doesn't matter. I'll still love you." This complexly simple idea of unconditional love is a text lying underneath much of *Buffy*'s fantastic narrative, and it is a love that signifies across different human spaces — romance, family and friendship. It is, after all, a sort of loving *heteroglossia* that depends upon the intersection of different modes, different histories, in order for it to be legible. Willow and Xander's relationship begins as a long-suffering acquaintance, but the audience quickly comes to recognize that Willow loves her awkward, silly friend, and loves him in the visceral way that only a fiercely shy adolescent *could* love. That love becomes reciprocal only at the moment of its impossibility, and any erotic attachment that they might have enjoyed is sacrificed for the integrity of the friendship. It is only with the passage of time — with the arrival of Anya into Xander's life, and Tara into Willow's — that this fumbled erotic connection deepens into an abiding familial one.

This "big brother" identity is thus a tender matrix of varying human loves — the original love of a friend, which becomes, if only briefly, an erotic love, and then the older, calmer love of a big brother for the sister he knows as "crayon-breaky Willow." Each intimacy is informed by the one that comes before, and only at their intersection does the Willow-Xander relationship become a complete circuit that spans across all of the gaps in signification, a presence not to fill, but to ease, the ruin that Tara's murder has left behind.

Despite her commitment to Buffy, and her deferral to Giles, it is neither of the two that makes Dark Willow hesitate — it is only Xander, who has always known Willow, who recognizes her even after she has become illegible to herself as a dark text whose characters burn too painfully to be read; it is only Xander, who is able to confer through his clumsy declaration of love that he is *not* the skateboarding boy who needed her math notes, that she is no longer the hesitant girl who shocked herself by breaking the yellow crayon in kindergarten, that neither of them are wholly these children any more, but that, regardless, the shadow of that childhood connection is eternally preserved by a love ten-thousand-fold more powerful than Willow's grief-fueled magic. A love that signifies, that shines, because it is not delimited by friendship, by family, by erotic attachment, but is rather a coherence of all three human realities.

Two threads have informed this chapter — Xander's own masculinity in crisis, and his shifting role as the "seer" among his chosen family. These identities constantly overlap, and in so many ways it is Xander's masculine insecurity that makes him a peripheral watcher, just as it is his fraternal devotion and nurturing qualities that split his subject as a heterosexual male. If Xander sees anything, it is the frailty of his family members, and the love needed to quietly buttress those frailties against the "great dark" always attacking them, the dark that is always on the outside and always on the inside. His connection to Buffy and Willow is, by nature of its complicated origins, an incestuous one — for he desired both of them at one time or another, and arguably desires them still. But that desire is continually mediated by a familial connection, by an evolving and exquisitely complex friendship, which suggests that the durability of his connection to the Scoobies is a direct result of its erotic indivisibility.

To choose a family beyond our biological one leaves open a space for legitimate desire, for sexuality, but that desire will always be overlaid by familial strengths — by traces of *home*— that make erotic lack inseparable from comfort, mothering, safety. The chosen family offers erotic possibility even as it forecloses any kind of simple relationship, any merely sexual connection. This aporia is a curious one that I mean to explore further, but it begins, I think, with Xander — for he begins by desiring both Willow and Buffy, and "ends" by supporting them, by brothering them, by seeing the interstices that bind them together as inevitably as true north, and telling what he sees. He doesn't always tell it prosaically, or at the right time — like any storyteller, he can't always get things right — but he tries. He is stubbornly mortal, physically unremarkable, and finally even blind in one eye; but his effort is supernatural.

He knows that if he says "I love you" to Dark Willow, if he keeps saying it, then eventually he will reach the core of her, beneath all of that toxic pain, where only the voice of a hopelessly awkward boy, unable to pass trig without her, might sound clearly. He knows that if he acted more aggressively, if he postured, if he adopted a clearer and more dominant form of masculinity, then his voice would be an incursion rather than a persistent murmuring from the margins. For Xander complains quite a bit about his marginality, but does very little to shift the stakes either way — in the end, he seems comfortable occupying a middle ground between straight white male and queer mother figure among the Scooby Family. It is an interesting vantage point, and a point from which he alone can see the brutal collisions of love, power and immortality among his family members; these checks and balances which are fallible human attempts to reconcile cosmic instability with everything that is boring, everything that is beautiful and everything that falls between.

This is not to say that Xander cannot still be a butt monkey. His comic mediations, his witticisms, will always go before him, blurring any serious thoughts about his immanent heroism. But it is these missteps that make his braver acts so much more fascinating, because Xander can be an unforgivable idiot, but he is an idiot who continually risks his life for other people. And he is never wholly invisible. Dawn, Buffy, Giles, Willow — they all see him standing at the edge of things, and they know that he isn't going anywhere. He will continue to fix their windows, to trim, adjust and square away, quietly acting as both the heart and the eyes of his family. But the question remains — what drew Xander to this chosen family in the first place? What made him think that it was possible to step away from his failed biological family, from his intense fear of mediocrity and sameness, and enter into strange new dynamic — forever complicated by magic, death, apocalypse and, just once ... syphilis?

There is no easy answer. But *part* of the answer — a crucial part — is the subject of Chapter Three. The alleged organizing principle behind this chosen family, but also the figure almost entirely dependent upon it.

Buffy.

CHAPTER THREE

What It Feels Like for a Slayer: Buffy Summers and the Paradox of Mothering

> "The in-between zones are the shifting grounds on which the (doubly) exiled walk. Not you/like you."
>
> —Trinh T. Minh-ha, *When the Moon Waxes Red* (70)

> "Being the slayer made me different, but it's my fault I stayed that way. People are always trying to connect to me, but I just ... slip away."
>
> —Buffy, "Touched" (7.20)

Just before I began writing this chapter, I had a sort of personal collision with family structures and their ambivalence. My grandmother died, and, as a result, I had to stay with my parents for nearly a week while we made arrangements for the funeral and cleaned out her house—a house that had been quietly accumulating material history since the late 1960s. My parents and I had to negotiate the attendant sadness and emotional labor of planning a funeral with the back-breaking physical labor of removing a lifetime's worth of possessions from a house practically drenched in memories. What to throw away, and what to keep? Funerals always involve interpersonal, as well as material, accumulations and divestitures. The behavior of family members during funerals often becomes a gauge of their historic personalities, and becomes also a primary factor in the decision to keep, or sever, ties with that individual once the event is over.

How does this relate to Buffy Summers? Well, it relates in a variety of ways, but primarily it is a kind of litmus test: that is, do Buffy's own familial relationships, before and after her mother's death, in any way mirror familial relationships in the outside world? Are the crazy, irrational and often extra-dimensional family ties in *Buffy* the television show at all concomitant with the lived reality of a contemporary family — my family, for example? The comparison may be a daring one, or it may be an autobiographical ploy. I will leave you to decide. Either way, I intend to use my own experience as a member of a non-nuclear family to frame and contrast Buffy's experience. I have waited until the third chapter to treat Buffy herself because, I think, some critical background and lead-up has been required. To even begin to understand this show's eponymous character, we need first to analyze her core friends/siblings in order to develop the relational context and episode-specific vocabulary necessary to look at Buffy, who is both a matriarch and a dependent of her extended family.

If my own family experience is a frame for this discussion, then my entry point within the show itself is Buffy's characterization as a mother-figure. Up until Season Five, Buffy's biological mother, Joyce, is the primary mother-figure for all of the Scoobies, with Giles standing in for Buffy's absent (and clearly negligent) father. But after Joyce's death, Buffy is suddenly invested "officially" with the caretaking responsibilities that she had always exercised unofficially. Suddenly, Dawn, her little sister (if, by "little sister," we mean a former ball of universe-destroying energy given human form by conveniently pan–European monks), is *her* responsibility — Buffy must not only ensure her physical safety, but also feed, clothe and nurture her. It would be impossible to say that Buffy does not at least attempt this, to the best of her ability, for the remainder of the show's duration. It would also be impossible to say that this lifelong endeavor — the safeguarding of a loved one from physical and psychic harm — is a viable or sustainable project, given that it fails as often as it succeeds. Still, mothers try. Buffy tries. But do her many attempts somehow align her with a contemporary North American ideal of what a mother should be? Or does she subvert this ideal entirely, not simply by virtue of being a vampire-slayer in a fantasy program, but through extremely (extra)ordinary actions that we might recognize across a range of non-nuclear families?

In many ways, the simple presence of non-nuclear families had historically been regarded as extraordinary, even impossible, within the North American television climate. Given that a great deal of televisual families today are extended, single-parent, or multiple-parent models, I will have to explain that last statement. By "nuclear family," I am referring not simply to the statistical two-parents-under-one-roof definition, but to the connotative criteria of all nuclear families on television which remain always beneath the surface but never quite overt: race, sexuality and economic access. Although by 1995 only 25.6% of families on television were "nuclear" in an organizational sense (Robinson and Skill, 151), they still remained "nuclear" in their adherence to middle-class economic and moral values, and were predominantly both white and heterosexual.

Buffy's family, both biological and extended, is no deviation from this norm. By virtue of televisual fantasy, her mother is able to pay for a massive three-story house in suburban California, as well as support two children, on the salary she makes working at an unspecified art gallery. The Summers kids don't go to school hungry — indeed, Joyce, like most 1950s televisual moms, is constantly thrusting a brown-bag lunch into their hands as they run for the bus. Both siblings are able to wear fashionable clothes, and Buffy herself has a revolving closet full of colorful, stylish outfits; this may have begun innocently enough (with the series opener) as a trend towards subverting the "final girl" of B-grade horror movies, but it becomes, with repetition, an undeniable symbol of class-based capital to the majority of viewers who cannot afford to shop at "Bloomies," as Buffy affectionately calls the uber-*riche* department store (*Family*, 5.06). No — money doesn't become a problem for the Summers family until Joyce dies and her hospital bills consume the funds put aside for Buffy, leaving her with a house that's losing money daily and a pile of unpaid debts.

Just as the Summers house comes to represent a safe and historically significant locus for the Scoobies, it also comes to preeminently signify the capital that Buffy and her family possess as middle-class white Californians living in a predominantly color-blind suburb. The sheer fiscal impossibility of that house, which would be prohibitively expensive for a single-mother to maintain — especially in what is obviously a gentrified and middle-class neighborhood — points to the televisual maintenance of fantasy that makes shows like *Friends* and *Party of Five*, with their equally impossible homes, believable.[1] One respondent to a participant media study launched by Kelly Albada (2000) summarizes the point when she says about *Party of Five*:

> The parents are dead, and all the older kids are working hard to keep the eight-bedroom house. Yeah, you know, a four-bedroom house is like $1100 per month. Shit. And where are they living like in New York or somewhere, Seattle or somewhere ... [Albada, 93].

In the case of *Party of Five* it is actually San Francisco, although the spacious apartments that appear in *Friends* (Manhattan) or *Frasier* (Seattle) also apply to this critique. To engage with televisual families, we generally must enter a middle-class utopia, wherein the realistic pressures of urban poverty have been neatly thrust aside.

But these repetitive images of nuclear and extended families living in "de-classed" urban spaces don't merely point to television as an efficient purveyor of capitalist fantasy. They also suggest a sort of transparent agency possessed by middle-class white families, who always seem able to maintain their fiscal stability despite visually obvious paradoxes or tragic narrative obstacles. Even on a critically acclaimed show like *Six Feet Under*, the only non-white family — Federico (Rico) and Vanessa Diaz, who appear to be the sole Hispanic couple living in the show's Los Angeles suburb — are constantly at odds with their finances, trying to balance the care of two children with Vanessa's salary as a nurse and Rico's (fluctuating) salary as a sometimes-partner of Fisher and Sons Funeral Services. The Fishers, despite the death of Nathaniel Fisher, Sr., and the subsequent efforts of a rival company[2] to buy out their family business, never seem as financially strapped, or even as money-conscious, as the Diaz family.

I need to situate this discussion of Buffy as a mother figure within critical debates around economic access — as they pertain to families both nuclear and non — because so much of Buffy's characterization as a mothering agent on the show emerges from her fixed location within a space of white, middle-class solidarity. She becomes, I will argue, not merely a "super-mom" to Dawn — battling all kinds of supernatural forces in order to safeguard her younger sister — but a "super middle-class mom" who upholds dominant ethical and economic frameworks through her conspicuous access to exclusive cultural spaces, even as she allegedly "subverts" the nuclear family on television. The Summers home may welcome and nurture people who would normally be a threat to nuclear-family values, such as a lesbian witch, an ex-vengeance demon (do family-values experts even *know* about ex-vengeance demons?) and two sisters with an erotic attachment to the undead — but that doesn't make the house any less of a saturation site for racial exclusions, class-based assumptions (everyone is middle-class) and the complete disappearance of anything resembling urban poverty.

I should point out, before going any further, that "middle-class" as a homogeneous category is itself a fiction, given that it suggests a broad spectrum of diffuse and complex economic realities that it cannot possibly contain. My understanding of, and relation to, the "middle-class" experience — growing up as a white teenager in an exclusively white suburb — is both a privileged and an introspective understanding, with my ability to critique middle-class values stemming crucially from my immersion in them. Like the writing staff of *Buffy* and *Angel* (all white), I am a product of those values. I have been, and continue to be, rewarded by them, and to take an adversarial position against those values is to, in effect, stand in opposition to my own history, my own adolescence. It is not a position that I can take up uncritically — for I know that, just as *Buffy*'s various subversions of middle–America necessarily emerge from, and in various ways serve only to reconstitute, the middle–American ethos, so are my "outsider" critiques of middle-class exclusions being relayed across the privileged spaces in which I grew up, and the privileged spaces that I currently inhabit as a white male academic.

This point was driven home to me recently when I was talking to a good friend and colleague. We had somehow gotten on the topic of high school graduation, and she said something along the lines of: "So, you obviously worked somewhere during your summers in high school." I blinked, a little taken aback by this assumption — as only someone who grew up in relative financial security could be — and replied that, no, I hadn't worked "officially" until after I graduated high school. I had done the requisite "volunteer" work for my parents, both of whom managed retail stores at one time or another, but my duties as stock boy rarely resulted in anything close to a formal paycheck. My friend simply raised one eyebrow at the idea of having summers off as a high school student, and said, kindly but critically: "Must have been nice."

I realized then more firmly than I ever had before that, like many kids hovering somewhere around the discursive edges of "middle-class," I had romanticized a particular ideal of relative poverty. Given that we had always been a single-car family, that my mother had, at times, relied upon roommates to help pay our rent, and that my parents are still struggling today with their townhouse mortgage, I had somehow managed to conceptualize myself as occupying a "lower-middle-class" space. Not being able to afford name-brand clothes, not being able to eat out very often, not having a swimming pool or a big backyard — these inequalities had come to represent my closest brush with poverty. I had functionally rewritten myself as "poor" because it was a space I could conveniently enter, a space that I had the power to imaginatively access, even as people actually *living* within that space were proscribed to it, unable to match the mobility that I was trying so desperately to jettison even as I actively exploited it.

In much the same way, *Buffy* flirts with popular and safe constructions of poverty, even as it firmly entrenches its heroine within images of middle-class empowerment. Buffy, after all, only works at the Doublemeat Palace for a few months before she is offered an implausible administrative position at the newly rebuilt (and allegedly de-vamped) Sunnydale High-School. But this is just long enough to exploit the popular ideal of the laboring single-mother, even as it hurriedly reconstitutes that selfless ethic into yet another middle-class professional space (this time a school counselor) while avoiding any prolonged engagement with the material realities of single-motherhood and the quest for a living wage.

It may seem like I'm being too hard on *Buffy*, especially given the praise that academics have heaped on the show, not to mention this book's central argument that *Buffy* represents an array of postmodern families. But I would caution against uncritically valorizing any television program, no matter how avant garde it presents itself to be. And *Buffy*, despite its subvocal commitment to various forms of feminism and gender empowerment, is still very much a product of white, middle-class narratives which remain palatable to large audience. Much of its critical success arises from a highly flexible model of "subversion" that teases middle America while quietly reconstituting much of its core value system, including the whitening of its citizens and the erasure of its impoverished and barriered communities.

If we intend to look at Buffy as some kind of gender crusader, then we also need to acknowledge her ultimately conservative portrayal as a femmed-up, parada-wearing consumer, who necessarily incorporates her economic background into her parenting style. One crucially overlooked indicator of this is Dawn's major transgression against Buffy and the Scoobies, designed as a ploy for attention — her shoplifting. Monitored closely by Buffy, rarely able to leave the house, and prohibited from helping the Scoobies in any tangible way, Dawn is exiled and alone. Buffy, however, doesn't make this connection until it becomes clear that Dawn has been stealing ("Older and Far Away," 6.13). It takes a glimmering pile of consumer goods to make Buffy realize: *something might be wrong here.*

The Dawn-Buffy relationship is a unique one in that it goes through so many significant narrative changes, never truly arriving at anything normative in terms of a nuclear-family model. Dawn begins as a televisual trope: the bratty younger sister, whose job it will be to taunt, irritate and undermine her older sibling in any way possible. This job is, of course, made easier by the fact that Dawn is too young to have a job (nor does she need one, given the financial stability of the Summers family), and that her school commitments are lax enough to allow her to spend vast amounts of time at home without having to do very much studying at all. This gives her the leisure to be a critical force in Buffy's life, becoming a kind of "mini–Buffy," complete with the same colorful outfits, lip gloss and acerbic sense of humor. This is, however, only a starting point for Dawn. Over the course of several seasons, we discover that she is not so simple a character at all, and, in fact, that she is not even entirely human. Still, it is crucial to note that Buffy never consciously rejects Dawn, even when she discovers that her "sister" is actually something called "the Key" — a mysterious energy force with the metaphysically unpleasant power of melting dimensional walls.

Given that Dawn has now been established as non-human, and a potentially destructive energy force, it doesn't seem as if her relationship to Buffy could get any more complex. But, as with most relationships on the show, the most exotic edges of complexity emerge not from clear narrative signposts, or even from visualizations of the supernatural — no, the "real" complexity lies at the level of language, at the strangely braided and intermeshed language acts whose power to shape these characters suggests, season after season, that it's all about, to paraphrase J.L. Austin, "doing things with words." Language controls magic; it controls relationships; it controls research and exposition, which remain central loci of power within the show. When, in "The Gift" (6.22), Buffy says of Dawn — "she's me. The monks made her out of me" — their sibling relationship is effectively rewritten as a kind of symbiosis. Dawn is Buffy, and Buffy is Dawn. They both have "Summers blood," and in the end, that shared blood is the only thing powerful enough to stop all of the dimensions in the universe from crumbling.

There are all sorts of pat phrases that Buffy might have used to describe her connection to Dawn — "She's my only sister"; "I can't lose her"; "She's all I have left." The idea of siblings clinging to each other after the loss of one parent (or both) is yet another televisual staple, exploited to the fullest by past shows like *Party of Five*. But Buffy's protectiveness of Dawn, which borders at times on ruthless surveillance, now has to be understood in terms of Buffy's relation to Dawn as "me" — that is, as a version of Buffy herself. From the monks' point of view — which must be limited, given that they are a plot device granted theological "authenticity" rather than a group of characters — it makes perfect sense. Buffy must protect Dawn, because she is, in effect, protecting herself. It's all very Darwinian. But this detour into the Age of Reason leaves us with a substantial problem. *Buffy*, as a show, is predicated on its heroine's sacrifice of her own "normalcy" in order to protect people from the forces of darkness. Although she begins the series as a self-centered teenager fleeing from her responsibilities as the Slayer, Buffy evolves into a leader who is perfectly willing to give up her own life to save the world.

But is she really? If Dawn is Buffy, and Buffy is Dawn (I promise this is the last time I'll repeat this syllogism), then symbolic logic dictates that Buffy is really saving herself. Of course, symbolic logic has no place in the Whedonverse, where emotion always outweighs logic — or, more diplomatically, where emotion is mediated by logic, but never eclipsed by it, for emotion has produced the conditions within which logic itself has been allowed to operate. It seems patently ridiculous to apply this sort of Newtonian framework to Buffy's actions in order to suggest that, because X = Y, Buffy is really just serving her own self-preservation instinct. It is a lot more complicated than that.

But self-preservation does have a hand in her decision-making process. We should note that Buffy, up until the last possible moment of "The Gift" makes every effort to find a way to save Dawn. She even threatens the lives of the other Scoobies if they come near Dawn, claiming fiercely that "the last thing she'll see is me protecting her" (5.22). Dawn, however, is willing to give up her life — not for Buffy, but for everyone else, every*where* else, every world in existence. "You have to let me go," she says. Dawn tries to act in order to save the world. Buffy blocks her because she *can't* let Dawn go. She is willing to jeopardize the fate of countless dimensions because she doesn't want her sister to die. A fair reaction. It would be my reaction. But Dawn's logic is altruistic here, while Buffy's is visibly selfish. She is not acting in line with the Slayer's philosophy — indeed, she is acting precisely against it.

Of course, breaking rules — gender rules, sex rules, power rules and most other hegemonic discourses — is what *Buffy* as a program has always been about. It stands to reason that Buffy herself should be able to deviate from her own mission statement as Slayer, given that she has been uniquely building that mission statement since the show's inception. It is also possible that Buffy is not breaking the rules so much as bending them, if we accept that her position as Slayer is a morally flexible one, and that it depends upon the tricky mediation of local ethics with global ones. By "local," I mean Buffy's own uniquely human desires which still revolve around a constellation of moral imperatives, and by "global" I mean the sort of post–Kantian[3] ethical frameworks that she must apply to the world in general.

The world needs to be saved, and is worth saving — the Scoobies have proved this several times over. But their efforts to save each other often initially get in the way of saving the world, only to end up ultimately facilitating the whole world-saving business. The world is worth saving, then, precisely *because* of the Scoobies' emotional attachments to people within it — or, in Buffy's own words, because "my emotions give me power" ("What's My Line II," 2.10). It is possible to be more driven to help globally because local people — loved people — are at risk. The two protective desires inform each other, and this interconnection is nowhere more evident than in "The Gift," when Buffy saves the world (and countless others) almost incidentally, as a consequence of her need to save Dawn alone.

Who, or what, is Buffy saving after all? Is Dawn simply a version of herself— a smaller, more annoying version of Buffy with a penchant for stealing shiny things? I would contend that Dawn is, as her "Key/Human" status dictates, a kind of paradox. She is both a past reflection of Buffy herself before she became the Slayer (and shouldered allegedly "adult" responsibility), and also a local representation of everything about the *world* that Buffy finds worth saving. Dawn is a past emanation of Buffy's innocence, her capriciousness, her inherent strength before it was necessarily mediated by the logic of leadership. Dawn is, in so many ways, the person who Buffy used to be, and the person who Buffy — in her darkest moments — wishes she might be again. As in the episode "Normal Again" (6.17), when Buffy almost gives in to the idea that she could really just be "a girl in a mental hospital," instead of "some kind of superhero," Dawn must always represent the pre–Slayer version of Buffy who gets to love uncritically, make selfish decisions, say whatever happens to be on her mind and perhaps most importantly, the version of Buffy who *gets* saved rather than the Slayer doing the saving. To be saved, *Buffy* tells us continually, is a luxury that should never be taken for granted. And there is in Buffy, as there is in most people, a strongly "pre–Oedipal"[4] desire to be saved that emerges exactly at those times when it shouldn't.

Buffy is, then, not simply saving a fragment of herself, or even a complete version of herself, but rather a complex site of emotional and psychological convergence. In a familial sense, Dawn represents her duties as older sister, made more urgent by the loss of their mother and the conspicuous absence of their negligent father.[5] But from a much deeper psychic standpoint, Dawn also represents everything that Buffy has lost — her freedom, her innocence, her childish wonder, her fear of the supernatural, her chance for a normal life and most acutely, her connection with Joyce. By saving Dawn, Buffy is trying to recuperate this growing inventory of losses. By saving Dawn, she is saving her past, present and future. It is not solely an act of self-preservation, because there are multiple selves at stake here. Buffy is acting as Slayer, sister, mother and individual, all at the same time, and each category would be impossible if not for the symbolic constitution of the other categories,[6] just as it is impossible to explain what Dawn means to Buffy without looking first at the multiple and overlapping symbolic terrains that she inhabits. If Dawn is indeed "the Key," then there can be no more complex lock for her to open up than Buffy's own subjectivity.

As I have mentioned in previous chapters, family life on *Buffy* tends to be either an invisible force in the background (Willow's unseen father, for instance), or a site of chaos and disruption (Xander's querulous family and Anya's extra-dimensional relatives). The Summers family seems to occupy a middle ground between these poles. Although Buffy's father has absconded to tropical locales with his secretary ("Family," 5.06), Joyce seems outwardly to be able to deal with raising two kids on her own. Of course, up until Season Five she was only raising one kid — Dawn was, we must remember, somewhat unceremoniously inserted into her life, along with a complex network of false memories to legitimate her presence (thanks to the monks). On the surface, Joyce seems perfectly capable of raising both a vampire slayer and a dimension-destroying Key, while still retaining a respectable social circle and keeping pace with her job at the gallery. It takes a biological intervention — a brain tumor — to convince Joyce and everyone else that her role as the Scoobies' mother figure is both indispensable and incredibly complex to maintain. This role goes largely unacknowledged for the first four seasons of *Buffy* primarily, I would contend, because of particular middle-class assumptions about Joyce and her role as a single mother that the audience is encouraged to make.

To understand Buffy's mothering role, we need to look at the layered relationships between Buffy, Joyce and Dawn. Those relationships really operate in the background until the arrival of Joyce's brain tumor, which shows up as "a shadow" in Season Five ("Shadow," 5.08). There is a plentitude of ways to read Joyce's illness — perhaps it is the physiological manifestation of her own inability to take care of Buffy, or a representation of the human mortality that Buffy herself has never quite been able to understand. Perhaps it is a plot twist, which Joss Whedon wryly claims to have invented in more than one interview. Perhaps it is just the bare and agonizing fact of cancer, which still seems fantastical, even to those who live with it. To suddenly wake up and have cancer, to be told "you have cancer," remains as wildly implausible as being told "you are a vampire slayer" or "your blood melts dimensional walls." Yet there it is. Joyce's illness is many things, but it is not "metaphor cancer," like Xander's "metaphor intestines" that Anya would like to see writhing ("Entropy," 6.18). Given that Joyce's death is in many ways patterned after Joss Whedon's experience of his own mother's death, (Season 6 DVD commentary), it would be insulting to suggest that *Buffy*'s creator was utilizing a "cancer narrative" in order to wring emotion from the show's audience.

No — as Whedon himself claims in his commentary for "The Body" (5.16), the goal with this episode, and with Joyce's illness throughout, was to capture thc "boring" quality of grief. A brain tumor is, in fact, "boring" when compared with the exotic array of supernatural forces that Buffy and her friends deal with on a daily basis.[7] But in many ways, the exact reverse is true. It is the supernatural that, through its very saturation within the show, has become boring. What happens to these characters *outside* of the graveyard is what fascinates the audience, and Joyce's death, one of the most disruptive events ever to occur in Buffy's life, is also the most natural. It would be easy, from a theoretical standpoint, to claim that this sort of thing merely re-emphasizes the tension between "normal" and "monstrous" that the show itself depends upon. But I think there is more at work here. Joyce's death is not simply a reverse-eruption of the normal into the monstrous, as opposed to the usual routine of the monstrous invading the normal in Sunnydale. It is a turning point for Buffy, forcing her to realize that, despite living in a suburb with an unusually high mortality rate, the *fact* of death, of natural death, of a body simply *breaking down*, had never really occurred to her until now.

That realization brings with it a whole host of others — that her mother was indispensable, that she worked every day, that she performed a vast spectrum of emotional labor — for Buffy, Dawn and the Scoobies — and that she was, in some way, always *there*, until quite suddenly she wasn't. There is no music in "The Body" because people do not die with a soundtrack. There are no misty camera filters, or cathartic hospital bed scenes, or tearful recollections of past events, because those are techniques of comfort — and Joyce's death is not comfortable.[8] It is swift, and it is brutal, and it is almost inconceivable in its finality; a kind of mathematics, even; a kind of formula that has led to this, to death, quite unexpectedly, while our backs were turned, while we were writing something on the chalkboard, while we were getting up for a soda. This is how many people experience the death of a loved one — not as a pastiche of comforting images, as a slow and almost poetic descent into illness, but as a sudden and inscrutable theft. Joyce dies so quickly that she is still sitting on the couch, wearing nice clothes, perhaps poised to go shopping, or buy groceries, or pick up Dawn from school.

For Buffy, this is a powerful reversal of physics, for she has grown used to vampires desiccating into a cloud of powder, vanishing before her eyes. But this whole episode is built around the heaviness, the vorticism, the black hole of Joyce's body, which does not vanish or crumble or become any easier to deal with. Its materiality sucks in everything that we have come to understand about the show — its music, its laughter, its relationships, its "kill the big bad" mission objective, and finally, any sense of comfort that its characters might offer us. All that remains for Buffy is what Virginia Woolf might call "the hours"; that is, the process of being, of breathing, of assembling her days, of continuing on and walking carefully around the rift that Joyce's absence has left in her life — her own personal Hellmouth. To grieve her mother's loss, Buffy must, in effect, *become* Joyce. She must take up her mother's duties as she took up the Slayer's duties, and what she finds, not surprisingly, is that it is a million times harder to be a single mom than it is to be a vampire slayer.[9]

For the first three episodes of season six ("Bargaining I and II" and "Afterlife"), Buffy inhabits a kind of post-resurrection fugue, unconcerned with the daily trials of maintaining the Summers household now that Joyce is gone. It isn't until "Flooded" (6.04) that Buffy has her "hemorrhaging" finances explained to her, and asks in astonishment: "I'm broke?" Anya, Willow and Xander all pitch in to soften the blow, but the reality is that Joyce's "hospital bills ... pretty much sucked up all of the money." This leaves Buffy with a house that, as Anya puts it, is "just sitting here, doing nothing ... [costing] money." The pained look on Buffy's face is evident here as she tries not only to understand her fiscal situation, but also to connect, however unwillingly, her mother's death with her present state of near-destitution. Of course, in Sunnydale, "near-destitution" is still a relatively flexible space, where Buffy get to apply for a bank loan rather than for social assistance, and where the Summers house is never repossessed.

There have been a lot of strange variables in the financial history of the Scoobies up until this point. Buffy, for instance, has no income, but is able to afford very nice clothes. She even affords a year at UC Sunnydale (whose tuition costs, we imagine, must be prohibitive), despite the fact that she never applies for a student loan, wins a scholarship or asks Joyce for money. More recently, Willow and Tara appear to be staying in the Summers house rent-free (they don't have jobs, either). Anya and Xander, the only gainfully employed Scoobies, are able to afford what looks suspiciously like a luxury apartment in Sunnydale, yet have no money left over to give Buffy and Dawn. It is Giles, whose precise salary as a Watcher has always been kept under wraps, who comes through in the end with a mystery check to cover Buffy's immediate expenses. Giles, who just flew to England, and then flew back to California. Giles, who no longer runs the Magic Box (that's Anya's job, now). Giles, who, despite all of these money-sucking activities, still seems to have quite a nest egg put away somewhere, which he pulls out just in time for Buffy's fiscal crisis.[10]

I am being a tad patronizing here, but one of *Buffy*'s great weaknesses as a show with supposedly unlimited subversive potential is its absolute unwillingness to treat the economic realities of its characters. It is true that "Flooded," as an episode, is constructed around the very problem of Buffy's finances, and that this problem leads her to take up a menial and unfulfilling (and, predictably, near-fatal) job at the Doublemeat Palace. My problem with this apparent "look" at Buffy's economic reality is that, 1) it is just that—*one* look, a single episode wherein Buffy's financial problems end up seeming more humorous than anything else, and 2) her job as a fast-food employee never has any kind of verity or immediacy, given the ways in which the Doublemeat Palace is constantly spoofed as a factory full of mindless zombies, producing burgers made with a special "meat process" that actually involves nothing but vegetables (6.11). And, yes, I am aware of the absurd gravity with which I just pronounced that "the Doublemeat Palace has no verity." It does sound a bit silly.

But that silliness is exactly what transforms this normally implausible idea—Buffy slinging burgers—into something that the audience can handle. That silliness is what firmly reinscribes Buffy as middle-class even as she flirts with the experience of a fast-food employee, allowing her, quite usefully, to occupy spheres of middle American respectability *and* poverty pathos at the same time. This gives her an all-access-pass into the world of a struggling single mom, while simultaneously allowing her to retain her "normalcy" as the Slayer, and as a Valley Girl, with a wink and a nudge towards those fast-food employees who are "lifers." Various images serve to bolster this idea that the Doublemeat Palace is in fact a fantasy, including Buffy fighting vampires in a graveyard while holding on to her "meat-medley" burger ("As You Were," 6.15) and, later in that episode, Buffy putting the now-squashed "medley" into her modern fridge, in her enormous kitchen, in her enormous house, before promising to take Dawn out for supper because neither of them can stand to eat another burger. For the Summers kids, eating burgers remains a change from routine, rather than the routine itself, as it is for many American families who can't afford to eat much besides fast food, or who can't afford to eat much at all.

Allow me a brief aside. By and large, most people with whom I spoke regarding the topic of this chapter — Buffy as a middle-class mom — objected to my critique in some way. These were *Buffy* fans, of course (as well as academics), and a certain measure of loyalty to the show is always expected. But I was a bit surprised to find that even the staunchest of feminist critics defended Buffy, citing her various concessions to poverty that I have already discussed — the talk among the Scoobies about money trouble, Giles being forced to write Buffy a cheque, and, finally, Buffy taking a job at the *Doublemeat Palace* in order to keep from losing her house. Most *Buffy*-loving colleagues that I talked to felt that, within the framework of a network television show, this was at least a glimpse of poverty, as opposed to the wholesale eradication of it that usually goes on within major-network vehicles (including every Aaron Spelling show). So, perhaps I have been too hard on the Summers kids. Perhaps any visualization of an economically-struggling family on a popular show is better than nothing. And, as many people gently reminded me, *Buffy* has never reported itself as a show about reality.[11] Why should I expect, then, a hyper-realistic portrayal of poverty in a show about vampires, vengeance demons, and characters who get "the funny syphilis?" ("Buffy vs. Dracula," 5.01).

The problem, I think, lies not in my perhaps over-enthusiastic critique of the show but the way that televisual media are still received by academic critics. Despite the growing field of television studies, as well as the pervasive influence of television — both historically and presently — on our lives, television shows remain the atmospheric limit of scholarly study. Many critics love to moonlight in television studies, giving conference papers on *Buffy* and *Angel*, crafting courses around television shows, or writing articles on *Survivor* and other staples of the "reality TV" phenomenon. But few would define themselves as media critics — as opposed to literary critics — and just as few would admit that studying a television show is as crucial, as meaningful, or as financially attractive (in terms of the applicability of government grants) as studying a literary text, or a body of theory, or sociological trend. When I began telling people about this book, I hear very few comments along the lines of "What a great idea," or "That show must really be fascinating." No — mostly, what I heard were questions, and sometimes overt challenges. "Why would you want to study *that* show?" "Isn't there something more pressing you'd rather write about?" "Isn't it hard to find materials written on a television show?" "Is it really that great? I never understood all the hype." "Aren't you afraid how that will look on your CV?"

These are all real questions that I was asked, and I include them here to illustrate a point. Most academics see popular culture in general, and television in particular, as an antidote to scholarship rather than a complement to it.[12] After devoting so much energy to analyzing other media, they gladly welcome television as an escape from obsessive deconstruction, and if they do critique a show, it is always framed as a playful and low-stakes sort of endeavor. I am reminded of a former student, who told me about his friend, an undergraduate film major. The act of deconstructing movies in terms of cinematic vocabulary — *montage, mise-en-scene,* continuity, point of view and other concepts crucial to film — had become so instinctual to him that, in order to "enjoy" a movie without critically analyzing it, he needed to be drunk or stoned. Books, however, he could enjoy. Books posed no deconstructionist quandary, given that his primary discourse was film. But my poor student — both an English *and* a Film Studies major — wasn't so lucky. He was, in essence, doomed to deconstruction, no matter what medivm he was studying. So it is possible for an academic to regard visual and print media equally as objects of cultural analysis. But that equanimity of focus seems to bring with it an attendant sense of fracture. If there is no longer a division between our productive "scholarly" time spend reading, and our leisure time spent watching television (all of which falls somewhere along the continuum of organized capitalist time), then that would mean we don't ever get to relax!

My answer to this is — no, we don't. We *don't* get to relax, nor should we think of writing off most of popular culture as "relaxation"; not when we are fully aware that "popular" culture is both highly embedded in networks of economy and access, and that it is simultaneously the most widely consumed, yet academically ignored, form of visual culture being produced in the first world and relentlessly marketed to the third world.[13] We don't get to ignore popular culture when it has become, in the words of Nestor Garcia Canclini, "a process of multi-national assemblage, a flexible articulation of parts, a montage of features that any citizen in any country, of whatever religion or ideology, can use" (1996: 18). We don't have the luxury of relegating television shows to an uncritical realm of leisure, when so many current debates around globalization (including Canclini's work) suggest that competing claims to audiovisual space within North America and beyond are radically altering the ways in which regions conceptualize their own locally produced culture, as well the ways in which states conceptualize their own citizenship practices. The only television show that makes me relax in any way is *The Teletubbies*, and that's only because I've convinced myself that it's Dadaist.

If I am being hard, then, on *Buffy* and its economic unreality, it is because I am certain that practices of subversion — as they are allowed to operate within the climate of internationally marketed television — depend upon certain conservatisms, certain compromises, certain backdrops of popular tradition, in order to exist. This formula works well with serial shows: All we need to do is begin adding non-traditional variables to the generic structure in order to see what happens. *Buffy* is a show based on a white, middle-class, attractive Californian twentysomething who wears pretty outfits and slays vampires. Simple enough. Let us imagine, for an instant, that Buffy herself was not white. It would be appropriate to make her Hispanic, given that the Hispanic population represents the largest ethnic group in the state of California. Now let us imagine that Buffy was living below the poverty line — and by this I am not drawing a fallacious connection between California's Hispanic population and legislated poverty, nor am I suggesting that if this character were Hispanic, she would have to be poor. Except that, she *would* have to be poor on *television*, given that the majority of Hispanic representations on television (I have already mentioned the *Six Feet Under* case) draw upon popular imagery related to poverty, including inner-city communities, gang membership and drug-dealing.[14]

The fact is that Buffy herself could never be anything but white and middle-class, because "white" and "middle-class" are assumed characteristics in a popular show about teenagers (or twentysomethings) living in California. If, as Ella Taylor suggests, "television comments upon and orders, rather than reflects, experience, highlighting public concerns and cultural shifts" (Taylor, 3), then shows like *Buffy* must faithfully encode systemic racisms (or ethnic exclusions) to meet the basic expectations of a white-majority audience. For the show to cover subversive ground in terms of gender, sexuality and institutionalized power structures — especially governmental and military structures — it must simultaneously uphold certain inventories of corporate symbolism. We cannot ignore the visually obvious fact that all of the Scoobies are unusually attractive, and very well dressed, and pretty much independently wealthy — given that they either don't require full-time employment, or have the flexibility to take and leave jobs as they choose. This financial stability is actually a precondition for most fantasy and sci-fi dramas, since the characters need to be able to devote most of their attention to fighting paranormal forces, and can't exactly call in a raincheck for dealing with the Apocalypse because they have to work a split-shift somewhere.[15]

In spite of its attempts to create a "poor" character who is actually not that poor at all (and a selfless single mom who actually has the capacity to be quite selfish), *Buffy* does cover a lot of important and evocative ground. The Summers remain a complex hybrid family, bound both physically and metaphysically to each other, and Buffy's often improvisational tactics for filling the space that Joyce left behind are, by turns, painful, funny and brilliant. It is true that, in the moment that Riley appears at the Doublemeat Palace, and Buffy responds to his military debriefing by insisting that "my hat has a cow" ("As You Were," 6.15), we as the audience understand that fast-food preparation will never be a significant aspect of Buffy's career future. Indeed, it is less than a month later that she begins working at the newly rebuilt Sunnydale High, in a counselor position that, miraculously, required no references or training. The cynic in me wants to say that it is not miraculous, since the symbolic capital of middle-class whiteness remains durable enough to allow any character to get any job, regardless of her background, because she is helping to maintain the Fordist imaginary of progress through hard work. I know that if it were merely a plot issue, in that Buffy needed to be working at Sunnydale High for the story arc to make sense, then she could have more realistically gotten a job as a janitor.

But, regardless of how the show's story arcs are bound up with economic meta-narratives, *Buffy* still tries harder than any other fantasy–sci-fi program to situate its characters within a realm where economic choices affect their lives. Anya's suggestion that Buffy could start charging for saving people's lives, although it is rejected out of hand, points meaningfully to the divide between fantastic spectacle and lived economic, as well as political, reality that characterizes most television dramas of this sort. Characters in fantasy–sci-fi programs tend to occupy various spaces where economic particularities don't apply, such as enclosed para-governmental agencies (*Nikita*), magic shops that serve more as community-building locations than as actual workplaces (*Buffy*), investigative agencies that deal in demonic, as well as intergalactic, currency (*Angel*), smuggling rings operating outside of legal constraint (*Firefly*) or proto-feudal economies that seem to only trade gold and gems (*Xena*) in return for itinerant labor, usually of the "save the distressed person / get the gold" variety. In fairness to the show, *Buffy* does treat various economic challenges, including buying an apartment, paying hospital bills, running an (albeit magical) business and, most importantly, performing Anya's "dance of capitalist superiority" ("All The Way," 6.06).

My concession here is that *Buffy* tries, and although trying is not enough, it is always a start. I am simply suggesting that we look at the show's fantastic and unconventional family-building strategies in light of the middle-class backdrop that allows those strategies to take place — the economic assumptions around which these peculiar and wonderful families cohere. The vast, warm, welcoming house that provides a safe locus for the Scoobies, as I have intimated before, must remain a rather ominous inscription of capital; in many ways, it is the ultimate manifestation of the supernatural for the majority of single-parent families, who could never hope to afford such a lucrative piece of real estate in suburban California.

There is a crucial exchange in "The Gift" in which Buffy admits to Giles, "I don't know how to live in the world if these are the choices" (5.22). It is not simply the reality that Dawn might die, but the still-present reality of her mother's death, and the overarching knowledge that being the Slayer means being consigned to impossible choices. "I just wish Mom were here," Buffy concludes softly, before leaving — and in many ways this encapsulates the paradox of motherhood that exists among the Scoobies.[16] For Buffy is, essentially, a mothering force within her extended family — she protects Willow, Xander, Anya, Giles and Dawn, and tries to ensure both their physical and emotional wellbeing. She provides the house in which they stay, organizes all of their social events, gives them advice — and criticism — when it is needed, and ultimately tells them what to do and how to do it. In "Restless," when Xander warns Buffy that "you can't protect yourself from ... some stuff," her smile is wide because she knows that, although he may be right, she will still channel every ounce of her energy into just that — protecting her family from "stuff" of all varieties.

Yet Buffy just as desperately wants to be mothered; she, like Dawn, wants to be made to feel safe, protected and "finished." Her biological father is gone, and Giles represents an erratic substitute; he fears that Buffy might be growing too dependent on him even as he fiercely depends on *her*, more and more, with each passing apocalypse. Unlike its traditional positioning within nuclear-family discourses, mothering in *Buffy* is bi-directional, and protean enough to produce mother-figures who need to be mothered themselves, as well as big brothers who need an awful lot of supervision from their keenly observant sisters. Buffy and Faith's relationship, although it seems on the surface to be more of a sibling-dynamic, is also based on mothering, with Buffy trying to instill a loose ethical framework in Faith while she, as a force of anarchy, resists. But in the moment when Faith, having taken over Buffy's body, declares to the sadistic vampire Boone that "you're not gonna kill those people ... because it's wrong" ("Who Are You," 4.16), it is not just a moral epiphany — it is a mirroring, a *true* mirroring, of the maternal lessons that Buffy was trying to impart. Buffy, at times, mothers even when she doesn't realize it, with varying degrees of success.

As the only child of a single parent, I am drawn to the image of Buffy as a kind of crusader for single moms — an emblem of the capacity for economically disadvantaged parents to be strong, to claim power, to oppose the forces that encroach upon their families. In *Buffy*, those forces, which in the "real world" would be clearly economic and governmental, are often rewritten as supernatural, mystical. There is not just "copper rebar" that needs to be replaced in the Summers' basement, but a demon assassin that Buffy must fight as the basement floods rapidly. With strange juxtapositions such as this, *Buffy* tries to show not only that the ordinary can seem supernaturally difficult, but that, just as often, the only way to address complex philosophical questions is through the practice of everyday life. "The hardest thing in this world," Buffy herself says, "is to live in it" (6.22), and constructing a family, even a supernatural family, remains tangibly difficult within the show. It is a difficulty, though, that offers incredible rewards, just as the maintenance of "difficult" families in the real world offers a realm of empowerment, community and love that, although no less complex, remain worth the physical (and sometimes metaphysical) effort.

As a member of a non-nuclear family, with two biological parents, two step-parents, three step-siblings and a host of clashing political and economic backgrounds, explaining how my family "works" can seem as complicated at times as having to explain *Buffy*, with its family of vampires, witches, werewolves, energy-forces and vengeance demons. But it does work, somehow. With all of its strange satellites, its differences of opinion, its ambiguities of authority and its gulfs of geographic separation — I think it does work. Like the extended families of *Buffy*, it is the various implausibilities, paradoxes, gaps, gray areas and gleams of fantasy that make my family, along with countless others, "work" in its own peculiar fashion. The Summers may not be a wholly accurate representation of a single-parent family, and Buffy may not be the ultimate vampire-slaying mom. But their family, for whatever reason, makes sense to me. I admire it. I even love it a little. And that connection, even if it comes by way of an avenue of fantasy, is worth exploring.

The next chapter will explore the fathering role of Giles and Wesley as Watchers in particular, and the overarching paternalistic function of the Watcher's Council in general, in order to address some of the fathering tactics in both *Buffy* and *Angel*. It will also explore the relationship between Angel and Connor, whose various cycles (father kills mother, son tries to kill father, son saves father's life) point to a highly dramatic (and engagingly perverse) representation of the father/son dynamic. Fathering, like mothering, in these shows often seems to be about constant surveillance, as well as visual inscription. But just who are these fathers watching, and who is watching them? These are a few of the questions that this next chapter will attempt to address.

CHAPTER FOUR

"Daddy's Home — I'm in Real Trouble Now": Fathers Who Watch in *Buffy and Angel*

> "It is in the name of the father that we must recognize the support of the symbolic function which, from the dawn of history, has identified his person with the figure of the law."
> — Jacques Lacan, "Écrits" (67)

> "She said I was an absent male role model. Absent my ass. I'm twice the man she is."
> — Rupert Giles, "A New Man" (4.12)

Fatherhood in *Buffy* has always entailed a great deal of watching from the sidelines, and an attendant sense of frustration at the inability to make anyone — least of all the Scoobies — listen to self-fashioned paternal wisdom. This type of passive fathering finds its clearest representation in the Watcher/Slayer relationship, as personified by Buffy and Giles,[1] wherein the pedagogy of the Watcher's Council is more often than not deflected, subverted or overtly criticized by Buffy herself. *Angel*, however, presents a more dynamic version of fathering with the relationship between Angel and Connor, which allows Angel a great deal more flexibility as a father figure to physically, as well as mystically, intervene in the life of his son. Both parental relationships are nontraditional, given that Buffy is the Slayer and Connor is the prophesied offspring of two vampires — Angel and Darla. Both also incorporate relatively "ordinary" elements of fatherhood, while allowing those elements to mingle with the more exotic and supernatural fare that has come to characterize *Buffy* and *Angel* as fantasy texts. The purpose of this chapter is to explore what I have called the "passive" fathering tactics of the Watchers — Giles and Wesley — in comparison to the "dynamic" fathering tactics of Angel as a kind of vampire super-dad, who, like Buffy, risks his life (or un-life?) and soul to protect Connor, even when that intervention manifests itself as a violent and unwarranted psychic intrusion.[2]

In the early episode "Never Kill a Boy on the First Date" (1.05), Giles tells Buffy, "I was ten years old when my father told me that I was destined to be a Watcher." When Buffy asks if he was excited, he replies irritably that he "was going to be a fighter pilot. Or possibly a grocer." Giles' parents are rarely mentioned; Wesley's relationship with his father, however, is made explicit in the episode "Lineage" (5.07), when the audience begins to understand what formative style of parenting might have created the originally docile, and now emotionally distant, Wesley Wyndam-Price. In the character of Wesley's father, Roger Wyndam-Price, the paternalistic structure of the Watcher's Council finds its ultimate expression. Formerly personified by the pedantic Quentin Travers, who ruthlessly tests Buffy's abilities more than once in order to ascertain her suitability as the Slayer, the Council has always been presented as a shadowy and injunctive apparatus, concerned just as much with policing a specifically imperialist brand of western morals as it is with monitoring the Slayer herself.[3] But Travers has no emotional attachments that make him interesting, whereas Roger's relationship with Wesley provides a kind of ideological blueprint for the organizational philosophies, and guerilla tactics, of the Council proper.

Standing on the rooftop of Wolfram and Hart with a gun pointed at his father, Wesley says, "I've done everything you ever asked, and I've done it well … [but] I suppose I don't know what you really wanted. You never had any use for me as a child, and you can't bear the thought of me as an adult" (5.07). As it turns out, in true Whedonesque fashion, Roger turns out to be a cyborg rather than the real Mr. Wyndam-Price. But Wesley doesn't know this as he addresses his father, and, really, this episode isn't about robots. Wesley's words resemble a general refrain — a declamation that any son could be making to any father, and just the sort of challenge that operates within all of the paternal relationships on *Buffy* and *Angel.*

Family within these shows remains a site of both satisfaction and disappointment, and any familial relationship encodes pain and loss just as much as happiness and fulfillment. But fathering in particular is a problematic institution here. We have absent fathers, murdering fathers, vampire fathers, cyborg fathers, demon fathers and, quite simply, human fathers who are negligent and abusive.[4] The question of how Wesley and Giles, as Watchers, might fit into this troubling arena, and how Angel attempts to disrupt many of these images while, at times, unconsciously fulfilling what has become a doomed prophecy of fatherhood on both shows, is one that this chapter will discuss in depth.

I have given myself a lot of ground to cover here, so it might be best to begin with some demographic context. As I have discussed in previous chapters, this book is not simply about plotting interesting theoretical discussions around family systems within *Buffy* and *Angel*, but about comparing those alternative models with current critical discussions around family studies and social welfare. As the child of divorced parents, I remember my mother working two jobs and living with roommates so that we could afford to eat, just as I remember my father searching for work and occupying a string of unremarkable apartments, before literally stumbling into a career that turned out to be financially viable. My stakes in the idea of what "family" means, and how it is presented on television, are personal rather than simply theoretical. I am the product of a non-nuclear family, and have thus always been intrigued by the persistent symbolic of the nuclear family—how it has survived all kinds of postmodern assault over the past several decades, only to re-emerge, in many ways, as a more flexible version of its former self in popular media.[5] *Buffy* and *Angel*, I think, by virtue of their generic as well as emotional concerns as media vehicles, offer some of the most unconventional yet endearing "families" to be found anywhere on television. But it is important to remain critical, and thus to maintain a sociological and demographic backdrop by which to measure the efficacy of these alternative families.

The least visible father figure in *Buffy* is Buffy's biological father, who, as Buffy has already stated in "The Gift" (5.22), is "living the cliché" with his secretary in Spain while neglecting to pay any kind of child support. He doesn't even show up at Joyce's funeral. Mr. Summers is part of the "terrible father" category in both shows, and is joined by Roger Wyndam-Price, Mr. Harris (Xander's psychologically abusive and alcoholic father), and Angel's father, who is generally disgusted and disappointed by anything that his son does — although we get the impression in "Becoming I and II" (2.21 and 2.22) that this may be the result of an entire adolescence spent drinking and "wenching" on Liam's part. In the "good father" camp is Fred's father, who, like her mother, is sensitive and overprotective of his only daughter; and of course Angel, who, despite accidentally allowing Connor to be sent to the worst hell-dimension in existence, still makes a supernatural effort to protect his son at any cost. The rest of the biological father figures remain ambivalent. There is Cordelia's father, who is defined only in terms of his current economic status[6]; Willow's father, who is never seen; and Giles' father, only mentioned in passing.

Fatherhood, with its various cultural and legal responsibilities, continues to be a problematic site within current debates around family studies. Much of the information pertaining to family structure that the general public is allowed to access (or, rather, that they are given glimpses of) comes from government-administered census data. That information, however, is skewed in terms of the groups that it commonly excludes from economic analysis, such as common-law parents, and the "benefits" that it inscribes as universal, such as child support.[7] Suzanne Peters admits that "adequate information about the impacts of court-awarded support levels and their after-tax consequences on sole-parent families has been very difficult to generate," citing the limits of census data and the virtual inaccessibility of concrete figures pertaining to the division of wage labor in most Canadian families (Peters, 50).

The organization of American census data is no more progressive than its Canadian counterpart, with common-law families, and families with same-sex parents, being forced to occupy a categorical "other" that keeps them from somehow statistically invading the data around nuclear families.[8] In both the United States and Canada, it remains the case, in Peters' view, that "compelling evidence of the positive developmental benefits of high-quality child care, particularly for children growing up in otherwise disadvantaged families, has been widely available for years.

Child care policy, however, has see-sawed on the political agenda" (Ibid). It is difficult, if not impossible, to conclusively tell just how many fathers are paying appropriate child-support benefits, and how those benefits factor into the elusive living wage that the majority of single mothers must view as a kind of utopian economic fantasy, rather than as a humane and viable reality.

Connecting this back to the show, it seems that much of the appeal of Rupert Giles as a character emerges from his many attempts, both bumbling and poignant, to fill the absence that Buffy's biological father has left in his daughter's life. He is, however, not just "raising" Buffy, but the rest of the Scoobies as well — for they all defer to him, in one way or another, as an indefinable sort of parental figure. This role is further complicated by Giles' background, which is a fictive "Britishness" made popular within a countless array of popular film and television shows, but, I think, most clearly personified in the James Bond franchise, and in the more recent Harry Potter films. This is a transplanted ideal of British masculinity, buffed and packaged by Hollywood, which depends upon the delicate tension between its own performative binaries: sexy vs. stern, intelligent vs. irascible, clean-cut vs. rakish, and cosmopolitan vs. confrontational. Giles is a dapper combination of Roger Moore's 007 (Jonathan's favorite, incidentally) and *Harry Potter*'s Prof. Dumbledore, with his suave clumsiness and wry sense of humor.

But Giles is also, we must remember, a product of Britain's colonial history — or, more accurately, America's popular perceptions of Britain's colonial history.[9] In this sense he is quite a good sport, for he puts up with a tremendous amount of ribbing about his nationality from the Scoobies, including Buffy's various descriptions of him as "boring, old and English" ("Lies My Parents Told Me," 7.17), and the entire gang's constant citation of "British" as coldness, lack of emotion, repression, inability to communicate, and general uptightness. In the infamous episode "Pangs" (4.08), however, Giles is officially inscribed as the stereotypical British colonizer: He calls the Scoobies "bloody colonials," and seems callously unconcerned about the various atrocities and depredations visited upon Native American peoples in general, and Sunnydale's ancestral Chumash population in particular. This lack of concern is echoed, with emphasis, by Spike, who protests that he "can't take all this namby-pamby boo-hooing about the bloody Indians," and goes on to explain that "you came in and you killed them and you took their land. That's what conquering nations do." His description of Buffy and Willow's "empathy" (if it is indeed that strong) with the murdered Chumash as "namby-pamby" even goes so far as to de-masculinize the very idea of compassion, suggesting that masculine rationality allows no room for colonial guilt.

This episode has received a lot of criticism from academic, as well as popular, channels, and, in spite of that, I am going to criticize it just a little bit more. I think that it was a highly misguided and patronizing attempt to discuss cultural relativism within *Buffy*, and that the didactic, as well as subversive, value of laughing at what is clearly a tokenized aboriginal history within the all-white-all-the-time universe of Sunnydale is virtually nil. There arc numerous funny-racist moments wherein any interrogatory or critical message that the episode might have had is completely dissolved, as when Buffy protests to the Chumash warrior Hus, after he has described the genocide waged against his people, that "Uh, you can have casinos now"; and Willow's naively shocked descriptions of missionary violence being cut against comic dialogue revolving around Thanksgiving dinner, specifically the debate between regular peas and "mushy peas," which Giles prefers. At no point does this episode succeed in being even relatively thoughtful or non-racist — instead, it falls into virtually every Hollywood stereotype imaginable. Even the shooting script describes Hus, before he is named, as "Indian," knowing full well that the symbolic baggage of the word will be more than enough to convey a detailed visual.

But, coming back to Giles, it is the American deflection of imperialist sentiment onto this "British" character that remains the least subtle, yet most effective, discursive feint in terms of making the episode digestible to a white, middle-class audience. Giles, by virtue of being an overt colonizer, gets to bear the full weight of institutionalized American guilt around the historic treatment of Native American peoples, as well as the ongoing systemic racism directed towards American citizens who are also members of an indigenous community. Giles here becomes sole representative of what Edward Said calls the "act of geographical violence through which virtually every space in the world is explored, charted and finally brought under control" (Said 271), and in the process, the free-floating guilt and distress that Buffy and Willow feel as American citizens, and thus co-colonizers, is projected entirely onto the willing symbolic pastiche of Giles's "British" colonizer's body. Here, it is subsumed by the love that these characters bear for Giles, and by his crucial role as Watcher, pedagogue and father figure. The racist and self-questioning distress is thus defused, dismantled and rendered sanitary, as it becomes simply another aspect of Giles' quirky Britishness. The episode closes with Giles sitting at the head of the dinner table, dishing out mashed potatoes, happy and wise and ecumenical once again, while Hus and his warriors, much like vampires, conveniently dissolve into mist.

Giles, then, serves a dual role as father figure. He represents the stereotypically colonial and patristic elements of Britain's past, but he is also a site of reconstitution for these elements, as well as other negative ideologies among the Scooby family. In short, because he is a moral barometer for the group—and a barometer calibrated firmly to white, middle-class values—Giles has the luxury of saying all kinds of questionably racist, sexist, classist and homophobic things while still cohering as a loving, supportive and highly intelligent father figure. And, in the event that the audience is upset by something that Giles says, they are offered the Hollywood simulacra of "Britishness," that televisual copy without an original, as a rationale for any kind of peculiar or potentially harmful sensibility. They can think, "Oh, that's just Giles being British," instead of, "Oh, that's clearly Giles being a classist wanker." In this sense, his character fulfills a time-honored role within serial television, as well as within a more historically diverse collection of North American literary mythologies—that is, the wise patrician who is gentle but firm, reasoning but intuitive, and who gets to express popular white, middle-class sentiments while conveniently veiling them beneath his character's aura of harmlessness.

Wesley, however, is a bit of a different story. He is allowed a great deal more character flexibility than Giles, and the writing staff of *Angel* have granted him access to much darker places than Giles would ever be allowed to go. In part, this is because Wesley was coded from his introduction on *Buffy* as a younger, less wise version of Giles, and thus the audience expected him to make colossal mistakes. More generally, Wesley is different because *Angel*, as a show, is different from *Buffy*. As Joss Whedon has stated in numerous interviews, *Angel* is a show about adulthood, whereas *Buffy* is a show about adolescence. Wesley is given the opportunity to make cataclysmic "adult" mistakes because he isn't fixed within a parental image like Giles, just as the Angel Investigations crew, although close-knit in its own way, never coheres as visibly as the Scooby Gang because *Buffy*'s characters have the kind of friendships that exist only in high school and college — people who see each other every day, who never doubt each other's loyalty and devotion, and who practically live each other's lives. The Gang is able to spend its evenings in Xander's basement, or in Buffy's vast, echoing house, or in Giles' apartment with its strange pea-green walls, because their lives are still very much in transit. The characters on *Angel* actually run a business — sometimes quite badly — and most of them, despite their obvious love and commitment to each other, spend a lot of time alone ... Angel most of all.

As a result of these generic shifts, Wesley's role as a parental figure is more ambiguous than that of Giles — but it still remains visible. Although he begins his career as Faith's (unsuccessful) Watcher, he experiences a sort of renaissance by becoming Angel's Watcher instead. Of course, Watchers are designed to watch Slayers, not vampires, and so the thought of Wesley being "assigned" to Angel doesn't make much sense at first glance. But, given that we know very little about the Watcher's Council and its precise organizational and legislative errata, I think it's safe to say that 1) Watchers don't just watch Slayers, and 2) as proven many times by Giles, a good Watcher almost never follows the rules set out by the Council. The person that Wesley watches most closely — aside from Fred, which is an observation of a different kind — is Angel. This surveillance reaches its height during the end of Season 3, when Wesley translates the Troclon Prophecy and believes that Angel will kill his newborn son Connor ("Couplet," 3,14). Angel walks into Wesley's office as he is writing something, and, when Wesley says, "You startled me ... I thought I was alone," Angel looks down at Connor, asleep in his crib, smiles, and says, "So did I." His paternal pride is shadowed by the scrawled translation on Wesley's notepad, which reads *the father — will kill — the son.*

The story arc that follows from this moment will change Wesley irrevocably, making him unrecognizable to his chosen family, and bringing him closer to his own ironic description of himself as a "rogue demon hunter" than he might have ever thought possible.[10] His conflict with Angel over Connor's safety, which eventually culminates in Connor being thrown into a hell-dimension and Wesley having his throat cut, seems at first like a masculine battle of wills: Angel's paternal instincts vs. Wesley's analytical logic. I believe, however, that the real conflict arises when both Wesley and Angel try to occupy dual parental roles. Both attempt to steer the Angel Investigations family in a particular direction, and both are convinced that they know what's best for Connor, as well as what's best for their loved ones in general. In the process, they enact very different parenting styles, and represent opposing models of fatherhood that I would like to compare with the model offered by Giles. If the Watcher's Council is a dictatorial and inflexible version of fatherhood, then the versions offered by Wesley, Giles and Angel are both reactions against, and recapitulations of, that master-model.

In their book *Media, Home, and Family* (Routledge, 2004), Hoover et al. discuss the findings of their participant analysis on television audiences and their reactions to televisual families. One father who was part of the study, Rob Carson, offers what is both an honest and critically interesting depiction of his role as a father. He describes the idea of "family" as "a power trip. It's a way of getting a place in society, in which I have more prestige and authority than I would if I didn't have a family [he laughs]" (55). While Carson is certainly trying to be funny and humble at the same time, his observation points to the varied and bidirectional flows of power that exist within all family structures, and which culturally cohere around the role of the father. Both Hobbes and Hegel saw the family as a transmitting unit for cultural mores, with Hegel focusing on its moral underpinnings—which echoed national constructions of morality—and Hobbes focusing on its role as a civilizing contract (Shapiro, 4). But whether the family was transmitting civic efficacy or Enlightenment morality, the message itself necessarily originated with the father. Michael Shapiro suggests that "fictitious universality continues to haunt the contemporary discourses on the family" (55), and numerous debates focusing on whether the father still constitutes a core within this universality—itself a product of Enlightenment narratives around imperialist "fathering" and civilizing—continue to be relevant within family studies.

Angel represents a version of fatherhood that, strange as it may seem, connects with both the paternalistic rationales for imperialism and the televisual stereotype of the "super dad"—the ideal parent who manages to take care of his son while remaining indefinably cool. He accomplishes this primarily through the help of his extended family, the crew of Angel Investigations, who always seem able to offer free babysitting in between fighting demons and decrypting ancient prophecies. The character seen most frequently with Connor, in fact, besides Angel himself, is Lorne, whose coded identity as a mother figure in *Angel* is both highly complex and sexually ambiguous.[11] Cordelia and Fred are also happy to watch Connor, and even Wesley volunteers a few times—although his final babysitting job turns out to be an abortive kidnapping. As in *Buffy*, there is a specific episode wherein Angel obsesses over financially providing for Connor ("Provider," 3.12); and, as in *Buffy*, the episode becomes a comedy, and the crew's money problems get smoothly solved.[12] As a result of this, Angel gets to worry more about physically protecting his son from harm than about emotionally preparing him for adulthood, which is a task that he shares quite liberally with his friends.

Now, we can say that this division of parental duty among the crew is, in fact, a radical revision of patriarchal family systems, and thus a step forward. Of course, this sort of sharing can also produce what Boss and Greenberg call "boundary ambiguity" (Boss and Greenberg, 23)—that is, the decay of family roles, which brings with it a concomitant decay of certainty around social interaction and identity formation. As David Cheale suggests, echoing the work of Pauline Boss on family crises, "extremely closed and extremely open family systems are both identified with unhealthy forms of family life" (Cheale, 69). With all of this parenting duty being spread amongst a singing demon (Lorne), a clairvoyant demon-hybrid (Cordelia), an eccentric physicist (Fred) and a ruggedly heterosexual vampire hunter (Gunn), the crew most definitely represents an "extremely open family system." But what, exactly, is Angel's role within that family? How is he watching them, and how is Wesley watching him? And what, specifically, is the significance of the gaze within models of fatherhood?

We should remember, first off, that Giles has no paternal competition among the Scooby Gang—he is the sole father figure present. In "Grave" (6.22), when Willow, upon seeing Giles, proclaims that "Daddy's home. I'm in real trouble now," she is not just acknowledging his symbolic parenting authority, but rather citing him as an effective father figure. She makes no mention, after all, of her own biological father. But

Wesley is never granted this sort of *carte blanche* parenting role—he must share it with Angel, who appears most visibly as the crew's father figure, but who in fact defers a great deal of that authority behind the scenes to Wesley himself. The crew, then, has two fathers, while the Scoobies have one, which in itself suggests that *Angel* is willing to disrupt the family coherence of its characters in order to explore new spaces of interpersonal connection and intimacy.

Wesley's introduction within the show, and his *reintroduction* to Angel—given that they met previously, and quarreled at length, in Season 3 of *Buffy*—doesn't exactly suggest fatherhood potential. Aiming a crossbow at Angel in the episode "Parting Gifts" (1.10), he says coolly, "I'm the one asking questions here," before Angel knocks the crossbow out of his hands and smoothly interrogates him. Wesley's self-fashioned "rogue demon hunter" aesthetic, which Angel refers to here as an interesting "motorcycle" look, is a premonition of the dark, unsavory, and caustic persona that he will come to adopt in Season 4, after his brush with death. But for now, in Season 1, Wesley still very much resembles the awkward schoolboy with an encyclopedic Watcher's vocabulary that we got to know in *Buffy*. By the middle of this episode, he is already happily commenting on flora, as well as ancient prophecies, and seems quite comfortable in his new role as rent-a-Watcher for Angel's crew.

But it is precisely that vocabulary, that licensed realm of knowledge based on occult histories and magical texts—combined with an equally impressive knowledge of all manner of sciences—that immediately places Wesley in an oppositional role to Angel's status as father figure. Angel has first-hand, physical, visceral knowledge of the demon world, but Wesley is in possession of something far more culturally powerful—call it a sort of demonic cosmopolitanism. He has all of the *techne* of western academia, including research skills, analytical reasoning and competency in several different languages. While Angel can act only upon particular, physical manifestations of "evil," Wesley has the abstract power to *define* evil, that is, to decide what prophecies to look at, what books to study, what facts to collect and, ultimately, what action the crew should take in each demon-hunting situation. In this sense, Wesley is the one directing Angel, and Angel himself becomes the blunt instrument of the operation, while Wesley remains its cerebral core. Who, then, is the crew actually deferring to? Who are they following, and whose judgment are they trusting?

These models — research and reasoning vs. action and instinct — represent not just crucial strategies for operating within the world but, more specifically, different styles of parenting that reflect different ethical commitments. Angel's conceptualization of the crew as his "family" is one based on emotional attachment, protectiveness and loyalty. In the finale of Season 1 ("To Shanshu in L.A.," 1.22), when Angel bursts into Cordelia's hospital room and the nurse asks "Are you family?," he shouts "Yes!" without even thinking. Later, when Angel seems ashamed at the prospect of having to drink blood in front of her, Cordelia chides him ("Don't be embarrassed. We're family!"), suggesting that her intimation of what "family" might mean is as instinctual and flexible as his own. Wesley, however, is much slower to regard the crew as anything close to a family unit, and his commitment to them, more often than not, manifests itself in a form of vigilant surveillance. While Angel simply wants to protect his loved ones, Wesley wants to educate them and, in so doing, to provide them with the very particular ethical framework necessary for telling good demons from bad.

I am not positioning Wesley as some type of colonizing force here, as that would be far too simplistic. But he does, by virtue of his academic background and boarding-school demeanor, resemble in many ways the stereotype of the western intellectual operating within the savage frontier — with the frontier, in this case, being L.A., and the chief "savage" being Angel. In the episode "Loyalty" (3.15), just before Wesley kidnaps Connor, he has a peculiar conversation with Angel about unconditional love. Angel tells him that "if anything ... ever happened to Connor, I don't know what I'd do. I love my son." Wesley's reply is cryptic: "Love can be a terrible thing." To his way of thinking, it is Angel's love for Connor that blinds him to the fact that the child is in danger; love convinces Angel that he, a vampire, can actually be a good parent to this child, when the very idea seems somewhat ludicrous — as ludicrous as the idea of a barren vampire, Darla, carrying the child to term in the first place. Angel protests that unconditional love is indeed possible, but his declamation is shadowed by an earthquake, which turns out to be one of the signs that the dreaded Troclon Prophecy is actually coming true. In the end, Angel's emotional and surprisingly vulnerable words must exist in relief to the ineluctable force of Wesley's logic, which dictates that, however much Angel seems to love Connor, he is still going to murder him.

It is during this moment that Wesley makes up his mind to kidnap Connor, which forever changes his relationship with Angel, and sets into motion a series of events which culminate in Angel plunging to the bottom of the ocean. In this instance, love is indeed "a terrible thing," for it is Connor—returned much older, and much angrier, from his hell-dimension—who locks Angel in a box and lets him sink. Wesley's logic, meanwhile, sees him bleeding to death in a park, alone, eyes staring fixedly at the ground as he wearily contemplates his own betrayal. Later, in his hospital room, knowing that Angel wants him dead, Wesley experiences a loneliness even more consuming than what he felt when he was on the verge of death—for now he has to face life, "the hours," knowing that his family no longer supports him. "You should have trusted us," Fred tells him, in as angry a voice as she can manage. "You were supposed to be our friend" ("Double or Nothing," 3.22). In this case, Wesley's analytical reasoning seems to have come up against unconditional love, and failed. But does this one mistake somehow cancel out all of the research, all of the advice, all of the exposition on Wesley's part that has, in the past, been crucial to Angel Investigations? Is this a failure of language, a bad translation—or is it possible that Wesley and Angel are *both* right, and that both follow valid ethical frameworks to their necessary conclusions?

This is not simply a debate of logic vs. passion but, more specifically, of public vs. private. In their study of families on television, Hoover et al. suggest that "Public/private [is] a false distinction, in that both meanings are contained in the term 'family' and both work together to construct what the term has come to mean in public scripts" (Hoover, 53). Wesley's model for "parenting" the Angel Investigations crew is very much based on public performance and the maintenance of civility. He does not address Fred, Gunn, Angel and Lorne as family members, so much as instrumentalize his familial connection to them in order to structure their view of the world. Like Giles, he is intensely concerned with translation, with linguistic consistency, and thus with the possibility of a "correct" interpretation of ancient texts. But, unlike Giles, who tries to quietly steer Buffy's adolescence into an appropriate moral field, Wesley must fight to have his reasoning heard amongst a group that, by general consensus, acts more often on instinct than on careful analysis. With Cordelia, who says exactly what she feels; Gunn, who shoots first and asks questions later; Angel, who always acts to protect his loved ones; and Lorne, who is literally a register for emotion — Wesley represents the sole arbiter for introspection and research. His aforementioned cosmopolitanism, which Timothy Brennan describes loosely as the perceived "expertise and political responsibility of academic professionals" (Brennan 23), marks him as something of an intellectual missionary, with all of the unsettling connotations that such a colonial identity suggests.

If Wesley is attempting to transmit public virtues and civilizing discourses, then Angel is doing the exact opposite. He acts within the private sphere, ensuring the physical and emotional wellbeing of his family members, as well as encouraging them to love and support each other. When Wesley tells him that "love can be a terrible thing," his reply "I used to think that" echoes a maternalist sentiment that seeks to supplant Wesley's logic with a more powerful ethic of care.[13] Furthermore, Angel's physiological limitations as a vampire — his aversion to sunlight, most of all — literally confine him to the private sphere, given that he can't even leave the house during the day. Wesley, then, becomes the public representative of Angel Investigations, while attempting to complicate and problematize much of the "private" discourses that Angel himself seeks to advocate. Angel's own politics are, in fact, closely in line with a sort of maternalist feminism, which Mary Dietz describes as "informed by the virtues of the private realm, and a personhood committed to relational capacities, love, and caring for others" (Dietz, 72). Wesley's politics are more in line with the universalist traditions of the Enlightenment, which privilege the humanist scholar.

Shapiro suggests that "family space ... serves as a critical locus of enunciation, as a space from which diverse family personae challenge the relationships and historical narratives that support dominant structures of power and authority" (Shapiro, 3). The family, although it has historically served as a mirror for state politics and critical civilizing practices, also represents a site where public and private intersect — a site where both of those realms, themselves a creation of eighteenth-century paternalist thought, can be radically challenged and revised. In the case of Angel's extended family, it is clear that both Wesley's pragmatics and Angel's ethics of care are necessary to provide stability and support, as well as something that closely resembles a communitarian space. It is only when one of these parenting styles attempts to subsume the other —

as with the case of Wesley trusting his own logic over Angel's intuition—that chaos ensues, and the family system is disrupted. By providing a site where public and private overlap in a positive way, Angel's family challenges traditional and paternalist conceptions of the nuclear family—especially the "isolated nuclear family" proposed by Talcott Parsons, among other adherents of sociological systems-theory, as "the only type of family that does not conflict with the requirements of an industrial economy" (Parsons, 5). It should not take a vampire with a soul to issue such a challenge, but in this case, having one around certainly helps.

Where, then, does this leave Giles? If Wesley and Angel both represent aggressive vehicles for maternalist vs. universalist politics, then Giles must fall somewhere between these competing discourses. Unlike Wesley or Angel, who continually intervene in the lives of their family members, Giles actually realizes that, in the case of Buffy, he's "just standing in the way" ("Once More with Feeling," 6.07). He leaves Sunnydale more than once, returning when he's most needed, but then quietly fading into the background afterward. Both Giles and Wesley represent exotic versions of "Britishness" that act as holding sites for American anxieties around imperialism and cultural values. However, they move past these stereotypical identities by becoming something in-between the Hollywood antipodes of "American" and "British," and thereby reinvent themselves as surprisingly durable and ideologically flexible characters. Wesley's Americanization is far from subtle, transforming him into an Indiana Jones simulation—complete with leather jacket and Bond-esque knife gadget that resembles a slicker version of Angel's high-powered stakes in Season 1. Giles, however, experiences more of a dialogic transformation, in that his language and demeanor becomes less sardonic (i.e., "British") and more licit and honest, conveying the sort of rugged individualism that characterizes the American capitalist spirit within cinema.

This transformation first becomes evident when Giles and Wesley meet in Season 3 of *Buffy*, and the audience is given a chance to compare the "old" Giles—that is, Wesley—with the "new" Giles, who has been re-educated by the Scoobies and thus become a British-American hybrid. Although Wesley has been assigned to take over Giles' Watcher's role, telling him that "the way you've handled this assignment is something of an embarrassment to the Council" ("Bad Girls," 3.14), nobody actually listens to Wesley—least of all Buffy. Later, when they are being threatened by the grotesque demon Balthazar[14] (who lives in a sort of modified demonic hot tub), the Watchers' individual conflict styles become quite visible. "Stay calm, Mr. Giles," Wesley insists, while Giles simply admits "They're going to torture us to death anyways." After Wesley, unable to bear the thought of losing his kneecaps, offers to tell Balthazar everything, Giles irritably refers to his younger counterpart as "captain courageous" in a "snappy comeback" manner that Buffy would be proud of. These undermining tactics come to a head in the later episode "Checkpoint" (5.12), when Buffy, with Giles' help, rejects the Watcher's Council completely, thereby expelling the foreign agents of patrimony and vindicating the brand of American neoliberalism that the show's white, middle-class audience has come to accept.

The Council itself, like all bureaucratic superstructures on *Buffy* and *Angel*, represents a cold and power-hungry juridical force that, not unironically, quite closely resembles the production and assimilation codes of organized capitalism. They deal in abstract labor, making decisions with what Giles calls "the stroke of the pen," while ignoring the fact that, as David Harvey describes it, "there could be no abstract labor at all without a million and one concrete labors occurring throughout the world … [but] the qualities of concrete labor respond [to] and internalize the force of abstract labor as achieved through global trade and interaction" (Harvey, 16). The Scoobies, up until this point, have internalized the Watcher's Council's standards for dissemination and production, while the Council has largely ignored their unique living situations and interpersonal relationships. Now, the regimented and quasi-legal declamations of Quentin Travers, the head of the Council, must compete with the emotional and familial language of Buffy and her friends. We know, of course, who wins, because the show has already established a universe wherein emotion always surpasses logic, and the particular always triumphs over the universal. But I am interested in what, exactly, is being defeated here — because it looks a lot like a rejection of both "foreign" imperialism and late capitalism. Yet both of these indexical forces, along with their material realities, are what make *Buffy* coherent as a television show in the first place. How can Buffy reject the powers of organized bureaucracy, the capitalist production of time and space, the ethos of cultural relativism, when all of these powers are what make her existence possible?

Buffy claims that the Watchers need her, the Slayer, to "give your lives some semblance of meaning," and that "without a Slayer, you're pretty much just watchin' *Masterpiece Theater*" (5.12). This disruption of the watcher/watched binary echoes Homi Bhabha's idea of visuality as a colonizing device—what he calls the *scopic drive*—and proves to be a material representation of his challenge that " in the objectification of the scopic drive there is always the threatened *return* of the look" (Bhabha, 81). Buffy here is looking back at the Watchers, and not just as a Slayer returning the colonizer's look, but as a young woman quite evenly returning the looks of a Council padded with white, middle-aged men. Laura Mulvey's conceptions of the feminine body as a passive register for the male gaze, of woman's "to-be-looked-at-ness," (Mulvey, 1975), also come to the forefront here, with Buffy deflecting a sort of masculine inscription even as she deflects the inhumane analytics of production that characterize the Watcher's Council as an imperial vehicle. It seems, however, that there is just a bit *too* much deflecting going on here, and that some of it is a highly self-abnegating gesture of rejection that refuses to acknowledge how what is being rejected actually makes Buffy herself, and her world, coherent.

The Watcher's Council cannot wholeheartedly be rejected, because it represents a universalizing discourse upon which all of these characters' interactions have been built. Travers and his men may appear to be a sort of ethereal legitimacy whose dictates influence the lives of particular people—that is, part of what Stuart Aitken calls "a series of myths that does not account for the diversity of day-to-day lived experience [and which] constrains our understanding of the spatial relations within families and between families and communities" (Aitken, 11). But they are also the defining edge of law and authority, the organizing principle behind the Slayer's mission, and the administers of a sort of Foucauldian notion of "governmentality"[15] which, as Nikolas Rose describes it, "[acts through] the instrumentalization of the micro-fascisms of everyday life—of the band, the gang, the sect, the family" (Rose, 26). They are not precisely "governing" Buffy and her friends, because, within the conditions of governmentality as a controlling apparatus, "there is no such thing as 'the governed,' only multiple objectifications of those over whom government is to be exercised, and whose characteristics government must harness and instrumentalize" (Ibid, 40). Buffy is then, in a sense, trying to reject the power relations that make her legible — both as the Slayer and as an individual.

Giles is trying to reject these relations as well, which seems to be an even less possible feat, given that he is wholly a product of the Council's ideologies, and has effectively "been" a Watcher since he was ten years old. The notion that he can simply step out of this hegemonic system is a highly optimistic one, and much of that optimism emerges from a nineteenth-century construction of American individualism — typified by public figures like Roosevelt — which argues that being "one's own man," when combined with Fordist models of production and entrepreneurialism, can grant access to the best and most ethical life possible.[16] Giles' rejection of the Council is very much a rejection of the faceless, bureaucratic "master" in favor of an emotional ethic of individualism, instinct and relational humanity. But it remains to be seen whether, to paraphrase Audre Lorde's famous statement, "the master's tools will [ever] dismantle the master's house" (Lorde, 110), and thus whether it is at all possible for Giles to "reject" the Council when his very rejection is structured in the vernacular, the cultural mode and the properties of addressivity that the Council itself has given him.

The psychoanalytic ramifications of this rejection scenario — which could be described as son rejecting father, vassal rejecting master, and laborer rejecting the capitalist world-system — are varied and important. Due to the constraints of this discussion, however, I cannot address them all, and hope that other work on *Buffy* and *Angel* will take up this unique challenge. The Council does not precisely represent "governmentality," or western imperialism, or even, more appropriately, the networks that give shows like *Buffy* and *Angel* life — and thus also have the power to take them away. It is instead a curious mixture of all these forces and also, generally, a tyrannical manifestation of the multiple and radical fatherhoods seen on both shows. Despite many of the caring and protective qualities that motherhood and fatherhood share on *Buffy* and *Angel*, it remains the case that we don't see a lot of governmental "mothering" agencies on either show.

A notable exception to this lack of "evil" mothering forces is the character of Maggie Walsh, who heads the Initiative. Maggie appears at first, to be a hard-nosed matriarch who is, protective of her all-male soldier family. She seems especially concerned with the progress of Riley, who she often gives special attention to, addressing him as a surrogate son whose job it is to "make her proud." But, as Maggie's story unfolds, she transitions into a controlling and dictatorial mother who has been secretly drugging her "boys" with chemicals designed to augment their strength and ensure their unswerving loyalty to the Initiative. Interestingly, it is Buffy, not Riley or any of the other soldiers, who immediately suspects Maggie's intentions, and who begins ruthlessly questioning the organization and ethical practices of the Initiative.

Maggie's crowning creation is "project 314," which turns out to be the homicidal cyborg Adam. When Adam addresses Riley for the first time, he calls him "brother," and says, "After you met Maggie, she was the one who shaped your basic operating system. She taught you how to think. How to feel" ("Goodbye Iowa," 4.14). Once again we have a character being shaped not by his biological family, but by an extended replacement. Riley's distance from his "real" family is made all the more significant by their geographic separation (they live in Iowa), along with his immersion in military culture. Riley's immediate family is not in Iowa, but in the Initiative, where he finds a protective older brother (Forrest), a sibling who looks up to him (Graham) and an extended group of soldier-siblings with whom he can be comfortable and feel sustained. When Buffy tries to tend to Riley after Adam has stabbed him, Forrest growls that the military will take care of him, and he is whisked off to a secret hospital. The "band of brothers" family model is clearly operating here, and Buffy's Scooby Gang are suddenly civilians, on the outside.

That Maggie is killed by her own Frankenstein-like creation is, I think, more a subversion of classic horror narratives than it is a gesture towards horrible mothering practices. Even at her worst—when she attempts unsuccessfully to kill Buffy—Prof. Walsh still seems to depend upon her "boys," calling desperately after Riley as he storms out of Initiative headquarters. She has a genuine love for Adam, even if that love is coded as perverse, and her death by Adam is rather a destruction-from-the-inside event, rather than a subversion by the Scooby Gang. Plus, her body, shown later, becomes a site of grief for Riley and the other soldiers—she is never given the entirely inhuman cast of the evil fathers on *Buffy* or *Angel*.

Still, in both shows, we tend to primarily see ruthless "paternal" agencies bent on propagating a universalist worldview that more or less forwards the production values of late capitalism. This connection between fatherhood and capital requires more exploration; that will yield a wide array of fruitful and important discussion around televisual families in general, and the families of *Buffy* and *Angel* in particular.

That said, I would like to conclude this chapter with a less analytical and more "instinctual" look at fatherhood within both shows, focusing on the different ethics of care that Giles and Angel convey, and how those ethics simultaneously define and complicate their masculinity. As I have discussed in earlier chapters, specifically in the case of Xander, it is possible for straight men in these shows to adopt a kind of queer aesthetics of motherhood, while still cohering visibly as heterosexual men and even, in the case of Angel, as action heroes. *Angel* as a show is predicated very much on the unassailable heterosexuality of its star, which, because of its durability as a symbolic category, gets to experience all sorts of humorous assaults while still remaining legible. It is in this way that straight white masculinity continually reinvents itself, and, in Sally Robinson's words, it "comes clothed in the language of crisis, and ... that crisis use a vocabulary of pain and urgency to dwell on, manage, and/or heal the threats to a normativity continuously under siege" (Robinson, 5). Both Angel and Giles get to appear as loving, sensitive and sometimes highly emotional men, without their heterosexuality ever being questioned by the audience because it is constantly being deconstructed and then reassembled by controlling discourses of sarcasm, as well as by Shakespearean fool–type agents like Spike.

Despite the potential for straight masculinity to hold up under pressure, however, Giles and Angel still represent interesting alternatives to the universalist fatherhood model produced by the Watcher's Council. Giles is willing to admit his own inefficacy as a father, singing in "Once More with Feeling": "Wish I could play the father / ... But now I understand / I'm standing in the way" (6.07). Angel continually understands why Connor is so angry at him, but just as doggishly tries to be a loving father in spite of this. "When you live as long as I do, eventually you lose everyone" ("Double or Nothing," 3.18), he tells Cordelia, after the infant Connor has been taken from him by Holtz. "[But] then one day you wake up, and you have something else." Angel realizes that, although his connection to Connor will never expurgate all of the guilt that he's accrued over the centuries, it will, in the end, make him more human than vampire. *Buffy* and *Angel* both complicate this literary ideal of the "monster" struggling to be human by suggesting that vampires and humans can actually learn from one another, that vampires can, at times, appear more "human" than humans, and that the existence of a hybrid vampire-human subject—in the form of Angel and Spike—although it can never be properly defined, is possible.[17]

It is clear that Angel loves his son, just as he loves the rest of his extended family. He takes visible delight in watching, and caring for, the infant Connor, joined by Lorne, who quietly schools him in proper mothering tactics. Lorne says of Angel that "I'm sensing a serious 'mama bear' vibe" ("Dad," 3.10), which is an appropriately ambivalent construction of Angel's parenting model. When Angel finally chooses to give up Connor—to give him a chance at a "normal" life by erasing his memories and placing him with a loving foster family—it is clearly the hardest choice that he's ever had to make. Connor, of course, realizes what happened; as numerous sci-fi television shows have taught us, the course of memory erasure "never did run smooth." But when Connor tells Angel that "I don't want to make a thing. I get what you did ... I'm grateful" (5.22), we know that he is truly Angel's son, because only someone genetically related to Angel could accept something like that with such casual stoicism. Still, Connor shows up one last time to help Angel defeat the "hopped-up-uber" liaison to the Senior Partners, Hamilton, stating with Angel's partented sarcasm that: "Come on. You drop by for a cup of coffee, and the world's not ending? Please." Their last exchange, suitably, is one of familial banter, shadowed by a much deeper and durable ground of love.

Giles has many representative moments of paternal love, but one of the most powerful occurs not between him and Buffy—as might be expected—but between him and Willow. In "Grave," Giles returns from England to stop Dark Willow, although his plan appears at first glance to be something of a suicide mission. The exchange that he and Willow have—with Buffy, for once, standing in the background—resembles that of an angry and petulant daughter upbraiding her controlling father. "Remember ... when you were under the delusion that you were still relevant here?" she asks him, only to react in astonishment when Giles manifests enough magical power to actually contain her. But this is not the moment. In both *Buffy* and *Angel*, the crucial moments never occur with fanfare, or martial skill, or triumphant music. They occur, always, between the margins, in the diverse relational spaces between characters, and within ironic dialogue that often contains a brilliant and heartbreaking poignancy.

This moment is a simple one. Willow is now hanging in the air, contained by a blue energy field, and looking peaceful, almost asleep. After this startling display of power, Giles seems to deflate slightly. He pauses by Willow, looking at her, and says, quietly, "I'm very sorry about Tara." Giles acknowledges, here, that Willow's magic-fueled rampage is not about world domination, or even about subsuming her own feelings of inadequacy beneath layers of power — it is, instead, a flight from grief, a running away down endless dark corridors, in the hopes that she might escape the unbearable sadness of losing her lover and partner. Willow says to Buffy, "There were moments — just moments — when Tara would look at me and I was wonderful" ("Two to Go," 6.21). Giles understands this, and his own grief is the grief of a father who doesn't know how to make his daughter stop hurting, but needs to try, regardless. Like a father, too, Giles maintains confidence in the power of his family to stay together. Even when Willow seems to have won, he senses that Xander is about to engage her in his crucial dialogue about unconditional love, and, lying in a pile of debris with Anya trying to support him, he manages to smile and say, "There ... it isn't over." It isn't over, because his family, he knows, has the innate ability to support itself, even if he isn't at the helm. In this case, Xander takes on the role of both brother *and* father, making Giles, although he never actively voices it, conspicuously proud.

These various and nuanced models of fatherhood prove that, in *Buffy* and *Angel*, no one parenting style can make a family cohere, and that balance only occurs when the ethics of care join with the pragmatics of logic and research. Fatherhood is more troubled than motherhood in both shows, and more often than not takes on the guise of a controlling and patronizing apparatus that resembles all manner of governmental and bureaucratic structures. But it still maintains its necessity, and is still continually valorized by characters like Angel, Giles and Wesley, who may not always make correct decisions as father figures, but who almost always act in what they believe to be the best interests of their extended family. What remains important is that two of these characters aren't biological fathers (Giles and Wesley), and the third, Angel himself, is a biological father through highly untraditional means—given that vampires aren't supposed to be able to have children. As a result, both shows suggest that non-biological fathers can "head" non-traditional families far better than their biological counterparts, primarily because they are able to share their parenting duties with the rest of the family, and that they understand that their coherence as "father" depends just as much on the symbolic input, as well as the love and support, of their family members.

The next chapter will treat Cordelia and Fred as ambivalent mothering presences within *Angel*, exploring specifically how Cordelia is a much different "mother" than Buffy, and how Fred's transformation into the chilling Illyria is reminiscent of a sort of abject motherhood—not just the fear that the "pre-oedipal" maternal connection will somehow swallow up the masculine symbolic register, but the more universal fear that a stable and nurturing character—Fred herself—can, like Angel, transform into a monster. Fred's gender complicates this transformation, and merits discussion of how she becomes both the feminine Angelus and also, in the end, a curious hybrid character who is capable of maternal care and calculated violence. One thing is for certain: The mother figures in *Angel* are very different from those in *Buffy*, and in exploring these differences, we can also explore how these dual family models both oppose and inform each other.

CHAPTER FIVE

Demonic Maternities, Complex Motherhoods: Cordelia, Fred and the Puzzle of Illyria

"In fact it is not a question of a human incapacity for a state of absolute happiness, but of an ever insufficient knowledge of the complex nature of the state of unhappiness."

— Primo Levi, "If This Is a Man; and, The Truce" (23)

"I am only bothered because I am bothered."

— Illyria, "Timebomb" (5.19)

Cordelia Chase has what is perhaps the most exotic story arc of any character within *Buffy* or *Angel.* She begins as a self-centered, acerbic and popularity-obsessed teenager in the first season of *Buffy*, and finishes her tenure on *Angel* as a "higher being," whose last favor to Angel is to remind him that he is capable of leading his extended family without the nefarious resources of Wolfram and Hart. In many ways, Cordelia defines herself in opposition to Buffy, and in just as many ways she resembles the Slayer and shares her role as mystical protector. Her relationship with Angel, which begins as a slightly predictable romance, deepens over the course of five seasons into a complex familial attachment based on mentorship and unconditional love. And we, as the audience, get to watch Cordelia evolve from the catty teenager who ruthlessly teased Willow, Xander and even Buffy, to the functional "heart" of Angel Investigations, as well as a co-parent to Angel's son, Connor—a relationship whose incestuous elements are indicative of the erotic flexibility that "family" continues to possess within both shows.[1] More than any other character, Cordelia reminds the crew that they are, indeed, family; she criticizes, upbraids and pushes her family members beyond their alleged limitations.

This chapter will examine Cordelia's role as a mother-figure on *Angel* by juxtaposing her radical ethics of care against the ambivalent familial position of the character who most seems to be her opposite: Fred. Beginning the series as a socially awkward and painfully shy exile from another dimension Fred's transition into the character known as Illyria, a former "pure" demon with a coldly analytical mind and a strange curiosity for human affairs, is not just a masterwork of acting on Amy Acker's part, but a moment of profound fracture within the show. It is one thing for the crew to lose Cordelia, who clearly has duties on a higher plane to fulfill; it is quite another thing to lose shy, retiring Winifred Burkle, and to lose her so completely, to a consumptive demonic force who still physically resembles the family member whom she has effectively murdered.

Both Cordelia and Fred are given storylines that involve aspects of biological motherhood. Cordelia is impregnated by a demon near the beginning of the series ("Expecting," 1.12), which serves as a narrative gesture to her more substantial pregnancy in Season 4. This pregnancy is the opposite of Darla's: Rather than the case of an "inhuman" creature (Darla) producing a healthy human infant, Cordelia is a healthy human who produces a destructive and supernatural offspring. Similarly, Fred's body becomes a site of gestation for Illyria, who uses her as a sort of human cocoon. Both births are monstrous, in that they harm (and, in Fred's case, kill) the mother, while producing something radically different from her in a strange *ex nihilo* fashion, something that wants to destroy her even as it is physiologically nurtured and carried to term by her.

The potential for discussing these monstrous births within a psychoanalytic framework is almost overwhelming, but I don't want to fall into the trap of sketching out fascinating psychological models for these characters which completely divest them of narrative context or emotional significance. I would propose, therefore, a kind of orbital psychoanalytic reading of Cordelia and Fred as mothers — a reading that incorporates some relevant psychoanalytic criticism while staying focused on the *shows* rather than on their instrumental value to Freudian traditions, which really have received enough legitimation through Western academic criticism and don't need *Angel* to help them out.

What I want to explore with this discussion is not how these characters might contribute to the towering canon of clinical writing on motherhood, but on how the alternative motherhoods that they represent offer both challenges to, and hybrids of, various critical writings on maternity and mothering within psychoanalytic and literary traditions. I am more interested in exploring the social rather than the psychoanalytic underpinnings of these radical mothering spaces, given that *Angel*, as a television show, draws more self-consciously on previous televisual narratives than it does on the dense and exclusionary writings of Lacan, Jung or Freud. I would like to propose using the works of Julia Kristeva as a sort of theoretical bridge, given that she attempts to link textual criticism with clinical psychiatric practices.[2]

Lest this chapter appear as merely a recapitulation of Chapter 3 on Buffy and motherhood, I should stress once again that mothering on *Angel* relies on very different models than on *Buffy*, and that it generally goes to darker and riskier places — with Fred's own fatal labor a case in point. I do not want to suggest that motherhood on *Angel* is somehow more "adult," given that *Angel* itself is supposed to represent a show about adult relationships. Destructive and ambivalent versions of motherhood should not cohere as adult simply because they are grittier and more interesting, just as it would be insulting to suggest that teen motherhood does not have radical and life-altering consequences. This chapter's goal, then, is to query why biological motherhood is presented primarily as a negative and harmful principle within *Angel*, whereas symbolic and extended-family motherhood — as personified, for example, by Cordelia's role as the crew's unofficial "mother" — is presented as positive and life-affirming.

I do not think the answer is as simple as the fact that *Angel* and *Buffy* both value non-biological family connections over biological ones. It has to be the intersection of generic elements, narrative structures, individual character histories and audience reception that produces these negative and, at times, frightening simulations of motherhood. And it remains to be seen whether they are, in fact, wholly negative. Although her "birth" effectively results in the death of Fred, the character of Illyria becomes an ambivalent, and at times positive, force within the Angel Investigations crew. And, in a nostalgic sense, Fred's sudden and violent death, like Tara's on *Buffy*, forces the crew to re-cohere as a family.

Her absence is filled in a most interesting way by Illyria, who, despite her homicidal legacy as a kind of fascist demon-princess, is now completely alone, bereft of subjects, stranded on an alien world with her powers severely limited; in many ways, she is as lonely and frightened as Fred must have been when she first landed in the hostile dimension of Pylea.[3] What begins as a derision towards human cultural customs on Illyria's part develops into a knowledge gap that frustrates her, just as Fred's social awkwardness was a site of both frustration and desire in that it forced her to watch from the outside, to linger, a bit like Angel himself, looking in on the warm human dynamics of an extended family she didn't quite know how to penetrate. Illyria's outsiderness, although it manifests itself as icy posturing and imperialism-writ-large, is no less predicated on loneliness than was Fred's.

Cordelia is known in both shows for her particular brand of incisive honesty, and Janet Halyfard suggests that her very name is "an ironic equivalent, to the Shakespearean Cordelia's unrelenting honesty" ("Greatest Love of All'" 2). It is often a self-serving honesty, though, as she tells people what *she* needs them to hear, not necessarily what *they* need to hear. In the early *Buffy* episode "Killed by Death" (2.18), Cordelia tells Giles that "tact is just not saying true stuff. I'll pass." In this, she is the opposite of Giles, whose careful speech conveys the brand of civilized liberalism that was discussed in the previous chapter. Later, in the first season of *Angel*, she elaborates on this personal philosophy by stating, that "I think it, I say it. That's my way" ("The Bachelor Party," 1.07).

Cordelia's truth-telling abilities are interesting, particularly because they have more to do, I think, with cultural entitlement than with a pressing need for honesty. Unlike the character of Drogyn, who is mystically required to tell the truth — a fact that annoys Spike to no end — Cordelia simply chooses to tell the truth (most of the time) because she feels it is her "way." She uses this entitlement to openly criticize Angel,

Wesley, Gunn and, to a lesser extent, Fred and Lorne, using creative epithets ranging from "lunkhead" to "proto-loser." I have to wonder where this entitlement comes from, and how it aligns with Cordelia's later role as a mother. Does her ability to craft honest and unsparing speech in any way presage her ability to produce a child? Are the two related? And how does this compare to Fred's halting, unclear and hesitant relationship with "true" speech-acts?

I suppose the question I'm really asking here is whether *veracity*, traditionally held up as a "masculine" model of speech, has some influence on these characters as mother figures — that is, whether their varied uses of speech somehow make them vulnerable to the destructive forces that invade their bodies, and whether this invasion is not, after all, a silencing of their speech.

In the first few seasons of *Buffy*, Cordelia's above-mentioned entitlement is more of a license to ridicule, and its origins seem somewhat obvious. Her first comment to Buffy in "Welcome to the Hellmouth" (1.01) is that "you'll be okay here ... if you hang with me and mine," and later, upon seeing Willow's plain outfit, she "compliments" her on having "seen the softer side of Sears."[4] That Cordelia so casually harnesses the language of advertising here to ridicule Willow is, I think, testament to her secure knowledge that the advertising itself is on *her* side. Cordelia's entitlement, then, is implicated with her status as an upper-middle-class teenager who can afford to shop at Bloomingdale's rather than Sears, and who conceptualizes L.A. as a mecca of shoes rather than a haven for vampires. She has, like most teenagers who have never experienced poverty, conflated her economic status with her license to deliver the truth.

In this instance, it is more the truth about people's outfits than any sort of sweeping moral observations, but it remains disturbing that Cordelia's knowledge of what it means to be "true" is inextricably bound to her knowledge of what it means to be rich, so that her searing critiques of other people's lives and lifestyles emerge squarely from her visible privilege. She is therefore at her most classist when she upbraids Xander and Faith, who are constructed as opposing working-class models,[5] and who visually as well as culturally clash not just with her concept of "cool," but with her idea of what a legitimate "person" could be.

When Cordelia discovers that her new L.A. apartment is infested with cockroaches — as well as, we learn later, a nasty poltergeist — she laments to Angel that "my apartment ... is like the barrio — or the projects or whatever, and I live there! I'm the girl from the *projects*" ("Room with a View," 1.05). Two things are clear from this statement. The first is that Cordelia has probably never been to a poor Latin-American or African-American neighborhood, and that her knowledge of the terms "barrio" and "projects" are limited to what she has seen on television. The second is that her white, middle-class sensibilities have allowed her to conveniently conflate one racialized space for another, primarily because she, as a privileged white woman, sees no reason to differentiate between the two. The "projects" are as exotic to her as any of the strange dimensions that Angel or Wesley have told her about, and her chances of entering that neighborhood are about as slim as her chances of leaping into the Hellmouth.

Angel, who spent his days as a human pretending to be an Irish working-class man — when he was actually an aristocrat wasting his father's money on drinking — seems to have no problem with Cordelia's appropriation of these loaded terms. In actual fact, the two come from quite similar economic backgrounds. The only difference between them is that Cordelia moved from the financial stability of her parents' home to the (relative) financial stability of Angel Investigations, whereas Angel himself has experienced material poverty to the point that he had to forage through Dumpsters and feed on rats.

I am raising the issue of poverty here because I think that *Angel*, unlike *Buffy*, is more thoughtful in its presentation of financial instability, and that Cordelia remains a sort of middle-class core standing in opposition to these sub-stories of economic inequality and differential access. It is clear that Angel, like most people who have directly experienced poverty or who regularly live below the poverty line, has internal as well as external poor-bashing[6] to deal with. His drive to remain financially viable through Angel Investigations, as well as his desire to financially provide for Connor, is in part a result of internalized critiques around poverty, and his inexpressible shame at having been, however many years ago, hungry and homeless. Unlike Gunn, who seems to have been poor for most of his life, but has responded to this poverty by mobilizing communities of access and aid throughout his neighborhood, Angel has taken the "disavowal" tact and chosen to concentrate on reacquiring financial stability rather than building bridges with other poor communities.

I am aware that this statement might sound a bit heavy-handed. Who, after all, is Angel supposed to reach out to? Other poor vampires? Working-class demon communities? It may seem like I'm criticizing him for not being some sort of outreach worker when, in fact, nothing within the show's narrative points to the idea that he *should* adopt such a role. This is, after all, a fantasy show — not a documentary about poverty in L.A. But the fact remains that L.A., unlike the mythical Sunnydale, is a real locus of economic inequality, and a space within which multiple poor neighborhoods compete with each other, while spectacularly rich neighborhoods define themselves in visual opposition to what they conceptualize as the "barrio" and the "projects."

Gunn and Angel are the only characters on the show who have any idea of what outrageous material inequalities actually exist within such a metropolitan space, yet Gunn's poorness is a "matter-of-fact" signifier that becomes troublingly conflated with his blackness,[7] while Angel's poor history is something that he only talks about or revisits against his will — as in the dream sequence between Angel, Faith and Angelus, when Angel's dark counterpart ridicules "poor Angel" by saying that "his fingers never smelled of anything but rat! I'm so sorry. I give up. I'm gonna live in a sewer!" ("Orpheus," 4.15). He is referring here to the image of Angel wandering, homeless, through the streets of L.A., but he also connects Angel's poverty with "hiding," which is yet another erasure of real poverty in favor of what Anya might call "metaphor poverty." The only characters in *Angel* who have experienced poverty, then, almost never complain about being (or having been) poor, while Cordelia, who has never actually been poor, complains about her lack of financial stability all the time. This comes back to her cultural entitlement as a middle-class white woman to manipulate "truth," which, in this case, is an appropriation of actual lived poverty for the purpose of feeling "barrio," of feeling like the "helpless" that Angel Investigations is supposed to be helping, despite the fact that all of those "helpless" who walk through the door seem to have the financial means to pay for the crew's services.

Why this digression into Cordelia's co-option of poor narratives, or poor experience? And why just Cordelia? Fred, after all, comes from a firmly middle-class background, a white nuclear family that both emotionally and financially supports her, and that background should link her to Cordelia's experience of privilege. Yet both characters "perform" their privilege in very different ways, and Cordelia is much more vocal about her cultural entitlements than Fred is. I want this discussion of poverty, background and home-life to provide a framework for treating both Cordelia and Fred as mother figures who experience quite different "births." I think that their arcs as characters, and their exits from the show, are critically informed by the spaces of privilege that they have been allowed to occupy, as well as their means for articulating that privilege — relentless verbosity, in the case of Cordelia, and embarrassment or guilt in the case of Fred.[8]

These characters' middle-class backgrounds, their whiteness and their unique discursive strategies all combine to make them appropriate mother-subjects for a correlatively white, middle-class audience. They are coded as "acceptable" mothers, even if their progeny are supernatural and destructive, and to replace them with a working-class, African-American mother or — even more unlikely on network television — a working-class Latina mother, would be an unacceptable and indeed unwatchable prospect to that same audience.[9] Their backgrounds, then, are cultural scripts that allow them access to televisual motherhood, but that motherhood has very different manifestations for them which align with their different experiences, and articulatory strategies, of privilege.

Cordelia, a vocal advocate of her own privilege, creates a fully formed supernatural being, Jasmine, who attempts (shockingly) to control the world. Fred, on the other hand, who internalizes her own privilege and cannot express it except in terms of insecurity and social awkwardness, has her body devoured from the inside by the demon Illyria, and ends up metamorphosing into the character who, I think, represents the staunchest and most objective critic of humanity and human affairs on *Angel.* But why in this symbolic framework does *acceptance* of privilege produce a destructive side effect, namely Jasmine, while allowing Cordelia to live, but *ambivalence* around privilege results in the death and subsequent "evil" transformation of Fred?

I should state here that I have not presented these poles — acceptance vs. ambivalence of privilege — as master guidelines for discussing Cordelia and Fred as characters, or even for discussing them as mother-figures. Both have complex narratives, as well as inconsistent and therefore human practices of social interaction, and neither are reducible to their race or economic background. But I do think that *Angel* sets up a serious paradox in the background with these arcs, suggesting, however unconsciously, that the character who embraces her privilege (Cordelia) gets to become a higher being and exit *Angel* as an overwhelmingly positive force, whereas the character who is conflicted about her privilege — and who finds herself in an interracial relationship (with Gunn)[10] — ends up getting possessed by a millennia-old demon who wants only to enjoy the imperial and luxurious existence that she had thousands of years ago. Cordelia's essence, her soul, remains coherent, while Fred's soul is "consumed by the fires of resurrection" ("Shells," 5.16). Only Illyria is left — Illyria, who is morally, as well as visually, the opposite of Fred's essential "Fredness." And yet, the two maintain a connection with each other, and can even appear, at times, as the same person. The message here is more than a little baffling, to say the least.

As stated earlier, these "births" are both negative, in that they produce destructive forces rather than healthy offspring. Therefore, it is not as if Cordelia's birth, as a result of her experience of privilege, is somehow rewarding — it does, after all, land her in a coma. In some ways, we can even see the "birth" of Illyria as a kind of reward, given that Fred, although she is radically different, gets to "live on" through Illyria, whereas Cordelia is taken outright from the show, and receives no interesting blue-haired reincarnation with a penchant for wearing tight leather armor. But it is still the case that Cordelia's offspring, Jasmine, is never meaningfully connected with the "real" Cordelia. The pregnant Cordelia who schemes against Angel Investigations, who drives a wedge between Angel and Connor, and who even kills Lilah,[11] effectively vanishes the moment that Jasmine is killed and "true" Cordy wakes up from her coma. Illyria, on the other hand, is a living reminder that "true" Fred is gone, and that only this false and malevolent copy remains. Fred/Illyria become a joined mother/daughter subjectivity, a dual being whose constituent essences are inseparable; Cordelia is never so intimately connected with her evil child, and is remembered as the healthy, vibrant Cordy that everyone knew best. She has no protracted and wrenching death scene like Fred, and her exit is classically cinematic — she simply vanishes — in stark opposition to Fred's physically violent struggles with a cancer-like illness that liquefies her internal organs.[12]

In fact, it is Jasmine's body that becomes the symbolic register for these images of corruption, contagion and illness. It is Jasmine whose physical beauty masks a putrid and decomposing reality, and whose physical fight with Angel allows her to be visually destroyed, and thus contained, in a way that Fred's illness can never be. Jasmine becomes a metonymic substitute for Cordelia's negative qualities, her selfishness, her cruelty, and thus allows Cordelia to effectively be reborn as a true "higher being," while all of the literal, as well as symbolic, darkness within her is expunged through the birthing process and then eradicated through Jasmine's death. The prospect of a black woman, Jasmine, being not just the supernaturally evil "child" of an enlightened white woman, but also being a site of abjection and scapegoating for white negativity, is as disturbingly racist as it is infuriatingly common within white literature and cultural production. The black body has historically been a locus of traumatic transfer, a site for the breakdown and dispersal of white anxiety around erotic, as well as ideological, scripts, and this symbolic exchange is evident within all sorts of media.

Hazel Carby, describing this process at length in her book *Race Men* (2002), locates it as a complex psycho-historical project of the "western" world that has been operating practically from the first moment of European contact. We can see it visualized clearly in white cultural production — for example, the miscegenation fears in a "classic" text like Harper Lee's *To Kill a Mockingbird*; the disturbing sex/death imagery that surrounds the black serial killer in the 1990s horror film *Candyman*; and the more recent cinematic offering *O*, an adaptation of Shakespeare's *Othello*, whose eponymous black character begins the film as a successful and highly eroticized athlete only to become a destitute murderer before the last reel. All of these media encode the "negrophilia/negrophobia" binary discussed by Kobena Mercer, which is an "aesthetic idealization and erotic investment in the racial other that inverts and reverses the binary axis of the fears and anxieties invested in or projected onto the other in 'negrophobia'" (Mercer, 191). Thus, the necessary white containment of black bodies in visual media, as well as text, must always carry with it an equalizing "scopophila" of the black body, a hyper-eroticizing or hyper-finessing of it, which serves as a surface fixation and visual incarceration of the bodies that are deemed most threatening to white corporeality.

This "idealization/anxiety" clearly operates around the character of Jasmine, who is fetish zed for her supernatural beauty, and whose enthralling of scores of white people — including the Angel Investigations crew — constructs her as the stereotypically seductive black woman who uses her beauty as a discursive weapon. That she even manages to "seduce" Gunn, a black man, is a kind of ironic testimony to her powers of thrall, as well as a suggestion that Gunn's blackness is, as it has been historically constructed by white audiences, a kind of moral weakness rather than a form of racial solidarity. Jasmine states that her followers are "my eyes, my skin, my limbs and, if need be, my fists" ("Sacrifice," 4.20), summoning up the image of a monstrous mother who has organically absorbed her "children," and who, even more threateningly, is able to strike out at "normal" people — being constructed here as "not Jasmine," and hence, by extension, as "not black" — by co-opting their very bodies and inciting revolt. This idea of an organic, as well as an ideological, invasion by an "othered" character is made all the more troubling by the fact that a white woman produces this other, and a white man (Angel) ultimately destroys her. Both characters act like normalizing white bookends to Jasmine's chaotic and vitiating black presence, her monstrous maternity that is threatening to destroy the world through enforced love and servitude.[13]

Both Jasmine and Cordelia are "essentially" mothers, which complicates things, since we have a mythical scenario of a mother being impregnated by another supernatural person (Connor), and then producing a full-grown and seemingly maternal "child." If we try to mobilize Julia Kristeva's theories of motherhood and abjection (*l'abjection*) here, it seems that Jasmine represents a frightening collision of idealized speaking-subjectivity with maternal and consuming "pre-speech," and thus needs to contained and destroyed in order for the characters around her to continue on with their rational existence — otherwise, they might be swept into the ominous space of Jasmine's "love," which serves, in Kristevan terms, as a site for the dissolution of "speaking" subjectivity and the reassertion of a more poetic, flexible and prenatal space, a consciousness before official consciousness.

This is not the space that a character like Angel, clearly in possession of his rational faculties, would ever endorse, although the show's privileging of emotional connections and interpersonal relationships actually gestures towards a valorization of this poetic mothering space. Perhaps this is why Jasmine needs to be destroyed — so that *Angel* can continue to celebrate mothering connections while firmly distancing itself from the possibility that it might ever become "just" a show about mothering, or "just" a series of emotional and affective narratives.[14]

I have previously quoted Kristeva as describing the process of abjection, of distancing oneself from a seemingly horrifying presence, as "above all a revolt against an external menace from which one wants to distance oneself, but of which one has the impression that it might menace us from the inside. The relation to abjection is finally rooted in the combat that every human being carries on with the mother" (Kristeva, *Interviews,* 118). In a western world that privileges literary communication, coded historically as masculine and described by Derrida as "grammatology" (the valorization of written narratives over other forms of extralinguistic communication, including oral traditions and body language) the mother continues to psychologically represent an erasure of language, a return to prelinguistic consciousness, which brings with it an unbalancing of this narrative privilege. We distance ourselves from "nonrational" modes of communication, from a sort of maternal dialogism, not simply because we believe in the efficacy of the narrative sign, but because we cohere as humans in part *because of* the narrative sign. If we lose our narrative, we lose our humanity, and that humanity needs to be preserved textually in order for it to be culturally legible, and valuable, within the confines of western historical and literary production.

When Jasmine says scathingly to Angel, "Look what free will has gotten you" ("Peace Out," 4.21), it is clear that the unconditional love and support that she offered needs now to be recontextualized as coercion and confinement. The only legible sort of love and support that remains within the show's universe is the imperfect and sometimes faltering love of the crew itself, who buttress and hold each other in their own flawed and unique ways. Jasmine's rationalization "I murdered thousands to save billions" is, in a crucial way that the show never examines, an analytical re-presentation of Angel's own mission statement.

The crew, after all, kill "bad" demons to save "good" humans, and often have to rationalize who gets to live and who has to die on a utilitarian basis of what outcome will produce the most "good." Much of what Jasmine wanted to do is actually in line with Angel's own moral code, and she is right to suggest that he has "eaten" his fair share of people, just as she has. But Jasmine's vision of paradise on Earth remains highly flawed, while Angel's musings on the possibilities of a world protected by heroes, a world where the helpless can actually be helped, remains somehow coherent and positive. It is, I think, the disavowal not merely of Jasmine's principles, but of her foreign and dangerous body, that allows Angel's moral compass to reassert itself, and which effectively resignifies the efficacy of his "helping the helpless" project by defining it in opposition to Jasmine's project — which we might as well call "eating the helpless." In the process, Angel gets to expel the black woman who doesn't belong, Cordelia regains consciousness — never giving a lot of thought to such questions as "How did I produce an evil cannibalizing black woman?" — and normalcy reasserts itself. Normalcy, of course, whose final expression is Cordelia's canonization and death, thus erasing all trace of the foreign other by reasserting the privilege and efficacy of the white mother.[15]

While Cordelia's stint with motherhood results in an ultimate absence, Fred's is the exact opposite, producing an overabundant and exotic surplus of presence in the form of Illyria. This "Old One" is one of the original demons, a pure-blooded monster who walked the Earth millennia ago and amused herself by murdering and torturing just about anyone she met. "I walked worlds of smoke," she tells Wesley, "and half-truths, intangible. Worlds of torment and of unnamable beauty. Opaline towers as high as small moons. Glaciers that rippled with insensate lust" ("Underneath," 5.17). Her formal and coldly aristocratic language is an inversion of Fred's stammering speech, her fixed glare an inversion of Fred's wandering eyes and crinkled smile, and nothing that she says, with its echoing and authorial tones, can come close to the warm sincerity of Fred's breathless first address to Angel: "handsome man saved me from the monsters" ("Through the Looking Glass," 2.21). Later, when the "true" Fred is gone, and Angel finds himself up against the impossibly old and far-reaching evil of the Order of the Black Thorn, he wistfully repeats her words to Spike. Their grammatical inconsistency, their strangeness, nonetheless contain a crucial truth that Illyria's speech can only emulate without ever reproducing.

I should admit that I have a bit of an infatuation with Illyria as a character. Fred took a long time to grow on me, and I didn't especially appreciate her role among the crew until she was abruptly stripped of it, taken away, leaving being something that nobody — not even the most dedicated of spoiler-loving fans — could expect. I was fascinated by Illyria, however, the moment that I first saw her, emerging from the ground where Fred had just died, looking slowly, curiously, at her hands, and saying with an air of cruel dispassion: "This will do" ("A Hole in the World," 5.15). That Fred, lovely Fred, was, to Illyria, simply something that would "do," something to fit her essence temporarily, is a horrifying idea. Yet, who can argue with this strange blue-haired person standing where Fred used to be, speaking in a cold register that Fred herself could never have managed while alive, and looking more resigned at her new body than surprised, or even disoriented?

Of course, *Buffy* and *Angel* have a long history of introducing characters whose rehabilitation, or rather, re-humanization, seems impossible (Spike, Anya, even, at times, Angel), only to grant them human status after a long, uphill battle. But I could tell, and I'm sure that most of the audience could tell with me, that this was a rather different situation. Illyria was not, was never, going to be anything close to Fred. She was not going to renege on her evil ways and join the crew in their good fight, at least not in a way that was morally simplistic. This was something that neither show had ever done before — killing a character and replacing her with a completely different character who was her absolute opposite, but who could look and behave just like her as a sort of vindictive simulation of the "shell" that had given birth to her.

There is a moment, before Fred dies, when Spike, gazing at the Deeper Well which leads all the way to Earth's center, observes, "There's a hole in the world. Feels like we ought to have known." In truth, both have known that hole, and known it intimately — both have felt Buffy's death, grieved for her, and then come to accept her return in unique ways. But this is a different sort of hole. This is the staggering possibility that someone, a loved someone, could disappear and not come back — or come back wrong. It is a terrible inverse of Buffy's resurrection — but instead of bringing back some phantasmal after-effect ("Afterlife," 6.03), what comes back is a seemingly corrupted version of Fred herself. Both vampires know, in this moment, that they've lost. That Fred is gone. But what remains?

When Wesley first speaks to Illyria, she is astonished at his boldness. "I thought the humans would have long died out by now" (*Shells*, 5.16), she says, duplicating the demonic hubris — and critical underestimation of human resilience—that many creatures before her on *Buffy* and *Angel* have been guilty of. Wesley tries to use this arrogance against her, telling her that "humans rule the earth ... crying and sweating and puking their feelings all over you. Go back. Sleep." But, as with future conversations that she will have with Wesley, Illyria sees through his attempts at deception. It does not take long for Illyria to become a version of Cordelia, giving everyone the cold and honest truth whether they want it or not. Unlike Cordelia, however, who knows who she is and what she has to do, Illyria is directionless. She is actually in much the same position that Buffy was in when she first returned from the grave, not knowing what is expected of her, not understanding what she's supposed to say or do, and experiencing the world as a kind of assault. Buffy describes her waking life as "hard and bright and violent" ("Afterlife," 6.03), and Illyria describes it as "too small ... it's too small. I can't breathe" ("Underneath," 5.17).

My connection with Illyria here is more than scholarly. I have dealt with depression for most of my life, and I understand very well what it feels like to be rootless, directionless, unable to cope with the world because it all seems like a violent intrusion, as if even other people's kindness is unbearable. Buffy says that, although she doesn't "know about theology, or dimensions," she does know that "I was happy. At peace ... I was warm ... and I was loved ... and I was finished" (6.03). That is, until her friends brought her back to earth, where nothing makes sense any more. Buffy's strange and disorienting apathy after being brought back from this place, her detachment from the people who matter most to her, is a process that most people with depression, clinical or otherwise, can relate to. But Illyria's detachment, her almost existential anxiety, is also a stage of depression. It is one of the deepest and most difficult stages to escape from, where feeling has literally run out, and there is only an absence, only a "hole in the world," left. Illyria's modulated voice, her rolling eyes, her cold posture and visible disengagement from everyone and everything around her, all reflect a critical kind of depression that is difficult to explain to people who haven't experienced it, and which serves as a terrible reminder to people who have.

I am not suggesting here that Illyria's demonic angst at having been torn from her millennia-long slumber is somehow equal to the experience of clinical depression. But I am suggesting that her disconnection, her apathy, like Buffy's when she is initially brought back to life, remains something that people who have experienced depression can relate to. I connected first with Illyria not because she was impressive or beautiful, or even because she was somehow still Fred, but because she was sad. And the more I thought about that sadness, the more I wondered if it had not, after all, existed in Fred to begin with — if it had not seeped slowly into her physiology, her genetic makeup, and thus been somehow transmitted "in utero" to Illyria.

I suggest this because I know that Illyria isn't sad for having killed Fred, and I suspect that the depth of her dispassion cannot be explained away as a hatred for the human world, or a longing for her previous life as an omnipotent demon. I think that Illyria, after a fashion, becomes a mirror for Fred's own living sadness, her outsiderness, her social awkwardness that could never be suitably smoothed away by Wesley, Gunn or even Angel.[16] And she also reflects the grief of Fred's family, who come to fixate on Illyria, to hate her even as they desire her, because she looks and seems so much like what they have lost.

Once she asks Wesley for help, saying, "I must learn to walk in this world" (5.17), Illyria begins her transformation into what I think of as a surrogate Cordelia. By virtue of her outsiderness, she is given license to ask questions, difficult questions, that even Cordelia wouldn't have approached. She has the experience, the unnaturally long life, that Cordelia was never given, along with the detachment and curiosity to ask even morbidly inappropriate questions often at, the worst possible time. This is somewhat like Anya's questioning as well, only Anya's tends to be innocent and bemused, while Illyria's questioning is direct and interrogative, unconcerned by human attachments or proprieties. When Joyce dies, Anya confesses that she can't comprehend human grief, saying, "I don't understand how all this happens ... Joyce will never have any more fruit punch ever, and she'll never have eggs, or yawn or brush her hair, not ever, and no one will explain to me why" (*The Body*, 5.16). Yet Anya's question becomes a plea. She has stakes in the answer — she cares. Illyria's interest is entirely clinical when she asks Wesley if there is "anything in this life but grief?" (5.17). Wesley answers to the best of his ability, but Illyria remains skeptical. She has the luxury of skepticism because she doesn't need, or want, to believe in anything more powerful than herself.

I am tracing Illyria's evolution as a critical force on *Angel* because I think that it relates to both Cordelia and Fred's positions and tenure within their extended family. If Illyria is indeed a replacement for Cordelia, who can actually push Cordelia's line of questioning farther, who can interrogate humanity because she has never known what it is to be human, then her "birth" seems to represent a kind of closing of the family circle. Illyria is the strange fused knot that replaces Fred and Cordelia, the presence left behind who is flexible and ambivalent enough to fill both of their absences, however incongruous that might seem. She unlocks all of the doubt, the sadness, the incomprehension and the fundamental sense of exile that existed in Fred's character all along, giving it the sort of voice and entitlement that only Cordelia could manage. She is, thus, a hybrid of both dead characters, a version of Fred who speaks like Fred never could, and a version of Cordelia who continues to describe her own privilege, her own sense of specialness, while remaining divorced from human concerns and interactions in a way that Cordelia never could.

This leaves us, then, with two ways of classifying Illyria as a hybrid character. Given that Fred didn't say enough about her entitlement as a white, middle-class woman, and that Cordelia said *too much* about her privilege, we can see Illyria as the logical balancing act to these competing models of privilege. Fred, in this sense, is the only likely candidate to produce someone like Illyria, because her shyness, her ambivalence around her own social position, serves as an unspoken threat to middle-class values. Illyria is the containment of this threat — the living embodiment of the privilege that Fred could never quite articulate, and the "finished" model of imperialist entitlement, given a demonic register to operate within so that it avoids any complicit connection with actual human avarice. Illyria, like Jasmine, gets to act as the absorption site for western anxiety around racist colonial scripts, made clear by her demeaning classification of humans and her self-aggrandizement as demonic royalty. Fred *has* to produce Illyria, because Illyria represents her privileged shadow, the parts of her that she has disowned, whereas Cordelia has already accepted, even embraced, those parts. Thus Cordelia creates a monster that can be contained, whereas Fred produces a monster that still *is* Fred, that cannot be destroyed because it is intimately a part of her.[17]

If we accept this hypothesis, then Illyria is, in a sense, Fred's punishment for being an ambivalent middle-class citizen. The corporate elements of Cordelia's personality are rewarded, since she gets to leave in a blaze of glory — still uncorrupted — while Fred must remain trapped in the monster that she has somehow created, the demon that her body has nourished, and the psychic manifestation of all her most negative and harmful qualities. As if this were not enough, she, Fred/Illyria, must exist between worlds, not a "true" demon but nowhere close to human, suffering from mortal vulnerabilities but possessed of a demonic consciousness, an Old One's context, which encompasses worlds and dimensions that poor Winifred Burkle could never understand. Illyria is a specter, a shade, a vestige of everything that Angel and family try to disavow on a daily basis, but can't. And now she is one of them. Her reintegration into the crew represents a reincorporation of divested hostility, an acceptance of anger, shame and doubt, that must ultimately make the crew stronger. So it really is a closing of the family circle after all.

But I also believe that Illyria has another, less abstract purpose as a character, another equally important role to fill. She embodies loss. She is a living absence, a representation of the confusion and debris that death leaves behind. Just as we often see aspects of someone who has recently died in the people who remain, so do Cordelia and Fred's family see constant reminders of their loved ones whenever they look at Illyria, whenever they hear her voice, or watch her walking away. "You are a summation of recollections" ("Origin," 5.18) she tells Wesley, and her comment is more accurate than she knows, for Illyria has become a memorial archive to both Cordelia and Fred. She is the material absence of what their deaths left behind, the excess that can't be rationalized or dealt with simply.

But she is also a space of hope, because she does, after all, learn. She does approach an understanding of humanity, and a curious appreciation that only someone not sure if they even want to *be* human could possibly experience. There is something of Fred still inside of Illyria, and that teaches her, more than Wesley can, about the wonder of feeling, of engaging with the world, of asking questions and *caring* about the answers. It is not a birth, but more of a growing up, a growing into being human, that allows Illyria to experience the inverse of Cordelia's transformation — she transitions from an omnipotent force into a vulnerable human, rather than the other way around. The miraculous thing is that, although it confuses and terrifies her, part of Illyria is pleased by what she is becoming.

When Wesley tries to bring Fred back — in effect destroying Illyria — his plan backfires. Still, he asks her, almost conversationally, "does it sting you ... my betrayal?" ("Timebomb," 5.19). Illyria's reply is fascinating: "I am only bothered because I am bothered." Emotional engagement comes slow to her, and she has never before experienced the sensation of being bothered by something, of being connected to something rather than existing in a state of cold dispassion. She is, in a sense, going backward even as she goes forward, "growing up" by reaccessing the confusing turmoil of emotions that only really exist in adolescence. She calls Wesley her "guide," but he is really a father figure, seemingly educating her about cultural customs and earthly ephemera when, in reality, he is actually trying to teach her how to be human. At first, it is a uniquely *human* failing of Wesley's that motivates him to do this, because he hopes that the process will somehow bring Fred back. But in the end, he continues to teach Illyria for reasons that he cannot entirely fathom, just as she continues to listen, to learn, for reasons that she can't quite put into words.

"You are what I don't understand," she tells Wesley (*Not Fade Away*, 5.22). And that is an apt summation of their relationship. When he discovers that Illyria can change her form to appear exactly like Fred, he angrily tells her: "Don't be *her*. Don't ever be her" (*The Girl in Question*, 5.21), yet he still sees Fred in Illyria, still acknowledges that she is what's left. He insists that "the first thing a Watcher learns is to separate truth from illusion" (5.22), but is the audience so adept at this? Is it really possible to separate Illyria from Fred, to avoid the tempting thought that Fred could somehow still return, or that Illyria could be suitably rehabilitated into something more human, something tender and compassionate and wholly new? This uncertainty, this hesitation, is what makes Fred's death even more difficult to deal with than Joyce's, because Joyce was gone — even when it seemed like Dawn might resurrect her, the result never cohered; even when a likeness of her appeared later in the episode "Conversations with Dead People" (7.07), it was still clear that she was gone. But Fred is never really gone, never *gone* gone, as Buffy might say, because Illyria remains as her ambiguous substitute. She is the materialization of grief that forces the Angel Investigations family to process their sadness, but she is also an illusion, a temptation. And the audience must let go of this illusion, just as Wesley must. Her presence exhorts us to labor, and we cannot fully appreciate her as a character until we accept that Fred is, indeed, *gone* gone.

Still, it is an illusion that Wesley requests as he is dying, and Illyria delivers it. "Would you like me to lie to you now?" (5.22) she asks quietly, and Wesley replies, "Yes. Thank you. Yes," with a smile. This is no simple lie, though. As Illyria transitions smoothly into Fred's old form, smiling that Burkle smile, Wesley knows that it is not *just* Fred that he is seeing. He knows that it is both Illyria and Fred, and that he must say goodbye to both of them, because he has grown close to Illyria, intimate even, in much the same way that he grew close to Fred. Their attachment is more complex, but it is an attachment all the same. Wesley does not say "I love you Fred," but simply "I love you," speaking to Illyria and Fred at the same time. And Illyria responds to Wesley's death in a way that is both human and demonic — when Vail, the demon-mage who killed Wesley, tells her to "take your best shot," she calmly, but with a look of unmistakable satisfaction, drives her fist through his skull.

Does Illyria become human? Or "sort of" human? Her last words are "I wish to do more violence," which doesn't suggest that she has embraced an ethic of compassion. But this violence, unlike passionless demonic violence, has an emotional source: her grief over Wesley's death. Her reaction, then, is a seamless hybrid of demon/human, a rationalization that violence must follow grief, and that killing will somehow expunge the leveling power of sadness that she feels. It is the feeling itself that she wants to kill, not the monsters, or the Order of the Black Thorn, or any other corporeal adversaries. It is grief that she wants to do violence to, and even Illyria, confused as she is about her own evolving humanity, knows that this is impossible. But her urge to try, to flout impossibility, to revolt, is also uniquely human. So perhaps Wesley did teach her something after all — something that stuck.

I admit that this chapter has meandered more than a little. I wanted to discuss the mothering roles of Cordelia and Fred, as well as what I conceptualized as the specific spaces of privilege, and their relation to those spaces, that influenced what sort of "births" they would experience. My original idea was that Cordelia, by virtue of her acknowledged and comfortable privilege, was able to create a monster that could be easily subdued, whereas Fred, whose relationship to her own privilege was more ambivalent, needed to create something that ultimately consumed her. Illyria was thus, within this framework, a punishment for Fred's inability to articulate her position, her shyness, her instability as a middle-class subject. Both characters were coded as suitable candidates for motherhood, given their backgrounds, but both needed to produce very different progeny as a result, with Fred's conception being also a containment of her threatening ambivalence, and thus a spectacular corporealization of imperialist values which could then be deferred onto Illyria's phantasmal and negative body.

But the more we look at these births, the more complex they seem. That Cordelia produces a black woman, Jasmine, who must then be contained and destroyed, is to me a troublingly racist ideation that needs to be explored more fully within a framework of critical race studies. It remains peculiar that both characters are unconventional mother figures, with Cordelia often being more vindictive than maternal, and Fred often being too reserved and inarticulate to express her true loyalty to the crew. Yet both manage to produce powerful and confusing "children" who end up ultimately destroying the vessels that gave them life. If there is a message here, it seems to be that motherhood is a prospect that destroys the maternal body, and that physiological birth — as in the case of both Cordelia and Darla — can only lead to death.[18] On the flip side, "death" itself, or a destructive force like Illyria, is able to gestate within Fred's body, using her up, and emerging stronger because of her.

I don't think that these are the only options, or that *Buffy* and *Angel* conceptualize birth as an immediate presage of death. I do think that both shows like to create anxiety that is as complex as possible, and that the only thing that could make dealing with a character's death more difficult is to introduce the idea of birth, to suggest that they might not really be dead. As Joss Whedon says when discussing the episode "The Body," "grief is boring." It is about getting through each hour, each day, and on the outside it appears simple, but on the inside it remains a constant negotiation of wonderful illusions with cruel and edged realities. These "births" are not just wrenches thrown into the works in order to complicate what is already a complex situation in itself — the removal of a beloved character — but the necessary realization that birth and death are intertwined, that life continues, stubbornly, after someone has died, and that the very process of living through grief is often a strange one, creating new fractured subjectivities, new ways of looking at the world and even, in a sense, new lives.

My corporate analysis of Cordelia and Fred, then, is accompanied here by a more esoteric analysis, a more instinctual reading. Call it a hybrid analysis if you will. I do think that, for every purely analytical and academically informed reading of *Buffy* and *Angel*, there is an equally visceral, gut-informed, soulful reading that has nothing to do with the specters of Marx or gender analysis or psychotherapy. The trick is not letting one subsume the other, and placing them side by side in order to produce a responsible and fully informed treatment of the shows. I am endeavoring to do this, and I apologize if the result skips at times, or becomes less than coherent. I blame it on Illyria.

The next chapter will discuss *Buffy* and *Angel*'s relationship to academic, comparing the family models present in both shows to the "families" within academic communities. *Buffy* has some of the most obsessed and loyal fans of any television show — really, any cultural artifact — in history, and many of those fans are also dedicated academics, working at universities and writing on popular culture. What I want to explore, in this final chapter, is what, precisely, makes *Buffy* and *Angel* so attractive to fans (academic and non), and why the families presented in both shows tend to subsume the biological families of the fans themselves. At the heart of this question is the more complex question of why we love *Buffy* at all, and what we take the show's various and radical families, as well as what they take from us in return.

CHAPTER SIX

Buffy, *Angel* and the Ivory Tower: Open and Closed Family Systems

> "To be scholarly means to be 'complex' ... [to be] one who deciphers a social symbolism inaccessible to laypersons."
> —Timothy Brennan (*At Home in the World*, 72)

> "Yes, Xander, once more you've managed to boil a complex thought down to its simplest possible form."
> —Rupert Giles (*Buffy*, "Passion," 2.17)

This chapter deals with *Buffy*/*Angel* and the "academy"—that is, the institution of academia, of scholarly study—as differing family systems that need each other even as they oppose each other outright. I have the dubious privilege of viewing this opposition from the "inside," given that I am a scholar who studies popular culture in general, and shows like *Buffy* and *Angel* in particular. I am, in that sense, a spy. Maybe even a rogue demon-hunter, like Wesley. Or not. One of the numerous problems with scholarship is that it depends upon binaries, on insides and outsides, for its existence, even as it coyly suggests that such binaries may not exist after all. From my point of view, it has always been difficult to tell the inside from the outside, and just when I'm convinced that I've been given an insider's pass, something always happens to push me outside again. Most scholars of popular culture know what it's like to feel pushed out by their peers, even as they are simultaneously invited back "in" by the conferences, granting organizations and academic publishers who have now discovered that popular culture is an excellent business proposition, as well as a subject that links different consumer-audiences together.[1]

Academics are drawn to *Buffy* for a variety of reasons. It comes as no surprise, says *Buffy* uber-critic David Lavery, that "cultural studies investigators and gender critics and postcolonials would find *Buffy*'s problematic depictions of race, male and female relations, and the body controversial and provocative" (Lavery, "I Wrote My Thesis on You," 11). Viv Burr, a lecturer in social psychology and *Buffy* critic, is engaged by the show because it challenges her, along with other pop culture academics, to participate in the "struggle towards an identity that is something other than academic *or* fan" (Burr, "Fan Identities," 7), thereby assaulting the demarcation between "interested academic" and "obsessed fan" that scholarly analysis in general would like to maintain. *Buffy* has something for everyone — linguists, semioticians, psychologists, historians, queer theorists, postmodernists, classicists, sociologists ... the list could go on, since Buffy Studies incorporates numerous and overlapping disciplines, and is growing all the time.

But it also remains the case that, while shows like *Buffy* and *Angel* are studied peripherally, on the edges of departments, by possibly eccentric scholars like myself, popular culture in general is still something of a cloaked discipline. There is a wide chasm between legitimate film studies and sketchy television studies, and only the brave (or the tenured) often attempt to bridge it. And the truth is that even the discipline of television studies is split between those who study television as a medium — with participatory analysis and charts and cumulative data — and those who actually locate and derive cultural significance from prime-time shows. Media scholars, I would think, can unanimously agree that television programming has wide-ranging and unpredictable effects on people around the world — but whether that influence to "go out and do something" actually translates into *cultural significance*, and whether *The Simpsons* could have the intellectual complexity of a novel by Herman Melville, are questions that the cultural jury is still out on.

Like the radical families that we've already discussed within *Buffy* and *Angel*, the family systems that emerge within the academy are equally unstable, and equally important as objects of critical analysis. The title of this chapter might suggest that the academy is "closed," whereas *Buffy's* families are "open," but it's impossible to make such a reductive conclusion. I would contend, however, that academic communities operate on outrageous principles of exclusion, even as they gesture towards creating spaces of inclusion and equanimity. Cultural studies, in attempting to offer scholarly, and hence "real," interest in shows like *Buffy* and *Angel*, more often than not only widens this divide between what is legitimate and what it superfluous, reinscribing classist narratives around critical complexity and responsible scholarship while simultaneously trying to valorize the cultural objects of its gaze. I am as guilty of this reduction strategy as anyone, given that much of my work traces various complexities within the narratives of both shows, yet, in public spaces, I get to withdraw into my protective classification as a "media scholar" rather than admitting that I'm a "*Buffy* scholar."

Over the course of this chapter, I will discuss my experiences of the academy as an extended family, very much like those seen on *Buffy* and *Angel*, which operates paradoxically by desiring popular culture as an object of inquiry, yet excluding it from traditional curricula because its inclusion is actually a threat. In much the same way, as a queer theorist and scholar of gender studies, I find myself beckoned in by academic communities and pushed away at the same time — given interested glances because of my research but disapproving or apathetic looks because of my sexuality.[2] To be a student of popular culture is to be, after all, a little queer, a little strange, a little off-centre, or, as David Lavery affectionately calls *Buffy* scholars (lifting the quote from, of course, an episode of *Buffy*), a "high-functioning schizophrenic" (16). I am interested, then, in how the "family" of academia welcomes *Buffy* while being simultaneously repelled by it, and how, as a result of this disjunctive acceptance, scholars of popular culture must often create their own non-traditional communities within traditional academic spaces. Are these upstart families a reaction against the paternalizing and critical force of the academy, or are they entirely licensed *by* the academy as safe enclaves of resistance which can easily be reconstituted? What can the academy learn from the families on *Buffy*, and do those families, in fact, depend upon academics for their survival post-show?

Pauline Boss classifies family models by how they react to crisis situations, and states that "after a crisis, families can redefine themselves and their resources.... Crisis does not have to break the family structure ... [it] may, in fact, lead to an even higher level of functioning after recovery than before" (Boss, "Family Stress," 701). Open family models are more likely to respond positively to such crises, given that they place a premium on dialogue and inclusion, whereas closed family models, although they eliminate what Boss calls "boundary ambiguity," can also effectively eliminate communication in the process and leave themselves far more vulnerable to a crisis. David Cheale, building on Boss's ideas, suggests that "extremely closed and extremely open family systems are both identified with unhealthy forms of family life" (Cheale 69). Thus, the most durable family system is one that respects healthy boundaries while eliminating unhealthy ones — like impediments to communication — and which strikes, in a sense, a balance between inclusion and exclusion.

The question of how such a balance might be maintained, and how to know when it's only the negative that's being excluded through the construction of suitable boundaries, is a difficult one. The general criticism I have of this equilibrium model (and Boss never suggests that it is unproblematic) is that, regardless of context, it is impossible to create a boundary without practicing an exclusion of some kind.[3] If a family has no boundaries whatsoever, then it loses its very coherence as "family," and becomes something else — but if it maintains boundaries of power, authority and heredity, then it automatically creates a hierarchical model that depends for its very cogency on maintaining a center vs. a periphery.

Academic communities, if they indeed represent families, produce copious centers and peripheries in their desire to be inclusive and culturally responsible while still participating within the competitive guidelines laid out by late capitalism, which is the system that makes sustained scholarly analysis possible. We have already discussed, in turn, how *Buffy* and *Angel* are not always an "inclusapalooza," given the conspicuous and disturbing exclusions — primarily racial and ethnic — they practice in the name of universality. So neither of these families are particularly innocent, and neither represents a superior model. How, then, do they both rely upon each other? And what can they learn from each other?

Trinh T Minh-ha describes this atmosphere of late capitalism as a "maximal consumer society" which "operates with violent break-ins, always dividing and alienating at the same time ... and tolerating no single moment of undecisiveness, blankness or pause for fear of having to face its own void" (Minh-ha, 196). Given that post-secondary institutions are equally vulnerable to this divisive system that distributes wealth on the basis of "maximal" production, the policy decisions that they make around curricula have as much to do with enrollment numbers and funding decisions as they have to do with student interest and the possibilities for risky pedagogy. In this sense, popular culture–related course offerings tend to operate beneath the aegis of larger and more traditional departments, sneaking into English or History only as "special topics" courses, or as novelty offerings that provide a nice break for tenured faculty. Rarely are they treated as core courses, or as crucial discussions mobilized around popular concerns wherein the articulation and deconstruction of popular culture actually provides meaningful access to contemporary debates.

Academic interest in *Buffy* began as a kind of wry side-project within Sociology and English departments, a humorous gesture towards this show whose generic idiosyncrasies held a bit of deconstructive potential.[4] The first article I remember reading was Frances Early's "Staking Her Claim: Buffy the Vampire Slayer as Transgressive Woman Warrior," in the *Journal of Popular Culture* (35.3: 2001: 11–28). It belonged to the "*Buffy* as feminist-phenom" camp, citing the show's visible and implicit feminist commitments while, as most early *Buffy* scholarship did, ignoring its troubling invisibilities and exclusions. I remember being quite taken by the article, and marveling that an established scholar had taken the time to write it. This was, of course, before my introduction to *Slayage*—David Lavery and Rhonda Wilcox's online journal of Buffy Studies—which was like walking into the proverbial academic candy store. Even as someone who had written before on popular culture, I had still never made the connection that it was possible for a television show to produce an entire community of scholars engaged in vibrant debates with each other. I was still on the outside of this particular family, and much of what had kept me on the outside had to do with a sort of "pop-phobia" that I had internalized from working within the confines of traditional academic discourse as a graduate student.

Discussing Tolkien's *Lord of the Rings* in her book *In Defense of Fan-*

tasy, Anne Swinfen states that "Tolkien made fantasy 'respectable'" (Swinfen, 1).[5] In much the same way, I think, *Buffy* has made popular culture respectable. Treatment of the show has moved, over the course of only a few years, from scattered panels at pop-culture symposia to entire conferences organized around Buffy Studies. As an attendee of the Slayage International Conference on *Buffy the Vampire Slayer* (May 2004), I had the privilege of meeting over 400 scholars — some established, some emergent and many graduate students — from around the world, and each one of them, like myself, was excited beyond all reason that they were going to be talking about *Buffy* for the next three days. There was no veneer of academic decorum, no attempts to identify as people from History or Sociology departments who were simply moonlighting as pop-culture scholars for the time being. The majority of attendees were quite immediately vocal about what they loved, and what they hated, about *Buffy* and *Angel*, as well as the problems of translating that intense affectivity into the rigors of scholarly discourse.

Yet there was still a pervasive sense that this conference was somehow operating within the Buffyverse rather than in the "real" world. It was a highly structured event, quite generously funded, which attracted a great deal of media attention. All of the keynote speakers had either published books on *Buffy*, or had books in press, and their academic backgrounds were as diverse as their paper topics — everything from Spike and the Marquis de Sade to background music and narratology. But there was still a certain ethereal nature to the conference, a vague feeling that, although all academic conferences are essentially enclaves of "pure" scholarship that operate at a remove from the outside world, this conference in particular seemed off in another dimension somewhere. Most of us knew, I think, that when we returned to our respective departments, only a few people would ask us how Slayage 2004 had gone, or how our papers had been received. Generally, the response that I got as a result of attending the conference was "Wow, they really have whole conferences devoted to a television show?"[6] I might as well have attended a conference on the Moon, or a symposium on topiary, for all the good sense that it made to most of my colleagues.

There are all sorts of reasons why traditional and mono-disciplinary departments, such as English — my department — tend to take an amused attitude towards popular culture while generally excluding it as a category of serious analysis. Humanities departments, except at highly progressive or "experimental" institutions and liberal arts colleges, continue to operate through a foundational canon.[7] I can't think of an English department that doesn't employ one or two Shakespearean specialists, and these appointments are justified not only by adherence to the white literary canon, but more convincingly by renewable student interest. Students simply *like* to take classes on Shakespeare — the numbers aren't skewed on this. Shakespeare is a durable cultural icon, and the numerous filmic and literary adaptations of his work continue to represent an attractive imaginative arena for students from all disciplines.[8]

In this sense, the adaptability of this canonical staple is what allows it to remain canonical, but this adaptability is in general a non-threatening one, because, within the post-secondary system, it provides interesting spins on Shakespeare that can then be measured against superior source material. The more recent Shakespearean mutations, especially those geared towards youth, are thus reincorporated into the canon and ultimately deemed inferior to their original. This is the evolutionary power of the literary canon — to allow a playful space for potentially threatening copies of itself to exist, while simultaneously containing their transgressive energy by classifying them as deviations from a nostalgic and uncorrupted master-narrative.

Pop-culture remains different from *culture*, and the difference is more than a hyphen, although Jennifer Brody rightly acknowledges the epistemic workload of the hyphen as a device that "locate[s] intermediate, often invisible, and always shifting spaces between supposedly oppositional binary structures" (Brody, 149). Although culture is as much a contested idea as pop-culture, it is still overwhelmingly presented as a real and material artifact in danger of mutation or decline, rather than, like pop-culture, an improper copy or fabrication of the real whose various creative labors can never account for its mongrel origins. Global culture, as conceptualized by Arjun Appadurai, is really just a "successful hijacking of the twin Enlightenment ideals of the triumphantly universal and the resiliently particular" (Appadurai, 43). It is split along axes of nationality, ethnicity and geography, pulled between the global and the local, and does not serve as the bastion of Enlightenment certainty around conceptions of the human that it once did.

To call Shakespeare "culture" and *Buffy* "pop-culture" makes about as much sense, given this radical identity crisis within modernity, as calling Beethoven a great artist and Coldplay a pretty good one, or saying that Hemmingway is a great author and Michael Ondaatje is kind of all right. Canonization, like the ever-ubiquitous threat of terrorism, happens "close to home," and conferring the name of "culture" to a text is a tricky negotiation of popular opinion and scholarly legitimation, with each endorsement making the other possible.

But university English departments depend upon the marketability of Shakespeare as cultural rather than pop-cultural, because canonical literatures serve as a framework for departmental organization and hiring practices. Most departments employ hierarchical models that privilege certain literary periods while excluding or deferring other areas. You will often see, for instance, more than one American Studies professor within a major-university English department — sometimes as many as three or four, if you count professors who incorporate a lot of American literature into their research areas, even if they don't "exclusively" identify as American Studies scholars — but try to find several professors who specialize in queer theory, or literatures of the Black Atlantic, or Asian-American literatures.

These types of faculty appointments remain secondary to the centrist hirings within core canonical areas, and the majority of course offerings within most English departments will always focus on heterosexual and North American literatures, rather than on queer, or women-centered, or South Asian, or even Canadian (within Canada) perspectives. Yes — most universities in Canada still give only peripheral treatment to the foundational literatures of Canada within their syllabi, because they simply can't compete with the popularity of post-war American narratives of resilience, self-sufficiency and cultural relativism.

If pop-culture was given the same cloak of respectability as culture within post-secondary institutions, then we would see a wave of new hirings based on television, film and visual-arts specialties within traditional departments such as English and Sociology — not, as is the case today, a scattered community of pop-culture buffs who were hired to teach foundational subjects, and who are exhorted to publish within canonical areas while avidly, if constrainedly, producing pop-culture "asides" whenever they can find time to do so. Similarly, granting organizations would be distributing generous amounts of funding to critical research on the most popular and influential shows on television today—such as *The Sopranos*, *Sex and the City*, *Six Feet Under* and *Buffy*—as opposed to reserving their money for more legitimate academic debates that "fit" into classifiable, and therefore justifiable, research spaces. It is easy to begin a grant application when your project operates under the umbrella of Human Geography or Social Psychology, but much harder when your research is interdisciplinary, and your primary texts amount to a pile of VHS tapes.

But if academia is a family that rewards its classifiable members while excluding its less savory relatives, then why do pop-culture academics continue to belong to the latter category? I have previously characterized pop-culture as a threat to traditional academic discourses, and this threat arises from thc class-ambivalence that television scholarship in particular creates. In their study of television consumption within American households, Hoover et al. found that "the rules that parents make about the media tell us something about a family's taste ... people who are particularly worried about their class position might have greater motivation than others to police their tastes according to these naturalized middle-class norms" (Hoover, 44).

This grows out of Pierre Bordieu's theories on taste and class, and specifically his oft-quoted idea that "taste classifies, and it classifies the classifier. Social subjects, classified by their classifications, distinguish themselves by the distinctions they make, between the beautiful and the ugly, the distinguished and the vulgar, in which their position in the objective classifications is expressed or betrayed" (Bordieu, 6). But taste is never more complicated than when it is remediated through television, and the viewing "tastes" of audiences remain complex and overlapping expressions of national background and economic access, as well as gender and sexuality. It is not just a matter of what people are watching, but what they are *able*, given their economic, linguistic and cultural constraints, to watch. Viewing, then, becomes a measure of access, and access defines the parameters of cultural legibility.

There remains a financial—as well as an interpretive—gulf between "high art," including theater, opera and galleries, and "low art," including television, paperback novels and Hollywood films. When a single mother has to choose between renting a video and attending a dramatic production, the choice is not a matter of "taste," but a matter of financial accessibility. And, given the fact that, in Meg Luxton's view, "a high proportion of parents create their own informal child care arrangements" (Luxton, 174) due to lack of adequate daycare options, cultural displays within the home tend more towards *Sesame Street* than *M. Butterfly*—unless a yearly theater pass happens to be lying around somewhere. Television, in this sense, is relegated by cultural critics into the categories "working class" and "domestic," thereby becoming a feminized and class-bound discourse that can — in high art's opinion — only ever reflect, not equal, the cultural achievements of established literary and theatrical traditions. With prohibitive pricing, limited venues and child-unfriendly atmospheres, the theater and highbrow cinema — in other words, legitimate culture — continue to attract the urban affluent while discouraging those who are financially struggling, or those whose lives are connected more tightly to the home.

This leaves shows like *Buffy* confined to a domestic space that prohibits it from garnering the public accolades of a successful novel, or a celebrated work of art, because it is figured upon a ground that is structurally the opposite of "high" culture. Although most cultural critics employ euphemisms like "mass culture" and "lowbrow" when discussing television, what they are really suggesting is that televisual discourses will never be as culturally viable as literary or theatrical offerings because, unlike these traditions, television is accessible to poorer audiences, and is therefore guilty of poorer standards of writing and production. If poor families[9] are watching, and enjoying, a TV show, then what possible value could it hold for established academics who are publishing articles on avant-garde poetics and modernist trends?

The real threat here is that something crossing class boundaries, something affordable to families who might not be able to send their children to university, something that at first glance may not be "complex" enough to warrant scholarly analysis, is looming on the edges of academic writing. This brings us back to our discussion in the introduction about pop-culture as a threatening dispersal of scholarly complexity, with the attendant "all or nothing" belief: essentially, *if we let in* these *texts, we have to let in* everything. And what happens then?[10]

I am deliberately structuring my language here to reflect the traditional language of immigration policy, of inclusion vs. exclusion, because I believe that inclusive/exclusive protocols for family systems, academic systems and nation-states all share similar linguistic, as well as ideological, imperatives. Just as, in Saskia Sassen's argument, "immigration policy is shaped by an understanding of immigration as the consequence of the individual actions of emigrants ... [with] the receiving country [being] taken as a passive agent" (Sassen, 7), so are academic exclusions shaped by the idea that certain texts whose composition make them harmful to "real" culture are trying to get "in," and that, in order for the academy to maintain its coherency as an apparatus for locating and measuring culture[11], those texts need to be kept "out." There is no contrary realization that, rather than being, in Sassen's words, a "passive agent," academic communities actually influence trends within popular culture, and instrumentalize popular culture for its scholarly value while firmly disavowing any long-standing connections to it.

Families, like borders, are sites of social anxiety where leakages between classes, between cultures and between ethical frameworks can occur in unpredictable ways. As such, they are policed just like borders, with the understanding that state-policy shapes family-policy, and that, to paraphrase Lynn Haney, "the state reorganiz[es] familial bodies for non-familial purposes" (Haney, 4). If we conceptualize televisual discourses as belonging to an open-system family, a family that, as Reuben Hill describes it, is "an equilibrium-seeking and adaptive organization" (Hill, 12), then "openness" here denotes financial accessibility. Academic discourses, on the contrary, would have to remain within a closed-system family that draws visible boundaries around its members, and that defines itself primarily in opposition to everything outside of those boundaries.

A traditional nuclear family is a perfect example of this closed system, in that there are no step-siblings, no ambiguous parent figures, no queer parents or shared parenting duties or surrogate moms—just two biological parents. As a family, the academy continues to operate within the sort of relentlessly analytical systems-theory that dominated family studies after the second World War, and that assumed "a universal core to family life" (Shapiro, 8), with that "core" being the departmental structure that is organized around canonical sites of writing. Television Studies is not part of that core, and exists often as a specialized research center, or as an adjunct department that depends upon the patronage-umbrella of traditional faculties for its survival.

Like the polymorphous "Humanities" departments within universities that have no Classics or Medieval Studies departments, it is often a pastiche of interdisciplinary scholars who have to shuttle between multiple academic spaces in order to maintain full-time employment, often with little or no coordinated dialogue between those spaces. The very word "interdisciplinary" is a loaded term within post-secondary institutions, with people on the mono-disciplinary side conceptualizing anyone not classifiable within a department as being too disorganized, and people on the inter-disciplinary side criticizing "single-department" scholars for being too traditional and monologic in their thinking. Either way, to be interdisciplinary is often to feel a bit rootless, to resign oneself to commuting between departments, and to resemble, at times, the confused and embattled step child wandering from room to room in the house that academia built.

This brings us to the binary argument that keeps television in general, and *fantasy*-related television like *Buffy* in particular, outside of academic communities. It is a question of complexity. If, as Timothy Brennan suggests in the quote used at the beginning of this chapter, academics are necessarily "complex" people who locate and decipher "complex" cultural phenomena, then it stands to reason that complexity, as a measure of intellectual viability, emanates from within the academy — it is produced under the same "world-system of twentieth century capitalism" (Wallerstein, 107), as Immanuel Wallerstein would call it, that produces the ivory tower itself. This valorization of complexity has historically given rise to a lot of necessary self-criticism, a fantastic array of deconstructionist critiques and challenges to monolithic structures, and, perhaps more esoterically, the willingness to keep *looking* at things, to query the multiple inequalities that the academy was built on (and continues to recapitulate). But it has also set up a system of inquiry that privileges abstraction over positioning, de-centered suggestions over ethical frameworks, and ironic inflections over political alignments.

Television has been made to signify, within this model, everything that is not complex — everything that is aimed at the lowest common denominator, with that measurement being, essentially, anyone who is not a cultural critic, a writer or a social sciences researcher of some kind. Television is for the "masses," which is a sentiment dangerously close to the "unwashed masses" that Napoleon couldn't be bothered with in the eighteenth century. Television is for people *without* culture, rather than being a uniquely powerful and incredibly pervasive culture-form in its own right.

To privilege television programming with academic analysis would be to admit, on some level, that a TV show was as culturally viable as a novel, and that research around television was as socially significant as research around birth rates and international policy. For university professors, specifically, this would be tantamount to admitting that their student who has watched seven consecutive seasons of *Buffy* back to back has cultural knowledge as valuable, as analytical and as hard-won as a doctorate spent reading Proust and Stendhal. And that prospect, for most literary critics, is unimaginable.

Buffy is, without a doubt, a show about research and scholarship — academics play a crucial role in the lives of the Scoobies — but it draws an important distinction between opposing models of learning. On *Buffy*, research only has power when it is aligned with some kind of emotional core, when it actually takes a stance, makes a choice, defends someone or directly affects a person's lived reality. Buffy herself first makes this clear when she is arguing with Kendra, the Vampire Slayer sent to replace her, about individual vs. communitarian approaches to "slayage." When Kendra discounts Buffy's emotional liabilities in favor of rigorous training and research, Buffy protests that "my emotions give me power. They're total assets" ("What's My Line II," 12.10).

Later, we discover that there is actually a "handbook" for Slayers, but that Giles threw it out shortly after meeting Buffy, because he knew that he wouldn't need it. Buffy, in a sense, provides a flexible and living language for being the Slayer, and only privileges research when she knows that it's going to get something done. This distinction quickly becomes clear for Giles when he discovers that his impressive academic training as a Watcher has, in fact, left him completely devoid of fighting skills, interpersonal finesse or any of the various improvisations necessary for fighting evil alongside Buffy.[12]

In *Buffy*, research is a participatory affair, with the gang all sitting around a table and supporting each other, instead of a solitary person sitting in a library with a stack of books. Academics are intercut with dialogue about personal relationships, sarcastic quips, emotional support and, when it is deemed necessary, the moment of defeat when the books get closed something is *done*. Even Willow, who describes university rather appropriately as a "penetrating force" ("Freshman," 4.01), and who is the only member of the Scooby Gang, aside from Giles, to ever research independently, still knows when it's time to put the books away and drag out the weapons. It is this balance between analytical reasoning, emotional support and necessary physical action that creates the communitarian space necessary for the Scoobies to operate, and which ensures that every possible option for dealing with "evil" is explored before Buffy actually has to slay something. Research, then, is a family affair, and this brings us back to the open and inclusive nature of families on both *Buffy* and *Angel*.

The majority of this book has been devoted to outlining the multiple and convincing reasons why chosen families on *Buffy* represent flexible alternatives to biological families. *Buffy* is not alone in its privileging of open family systems, given the popularity of shows like *Friends*, *Sex and the City*, *Dawson's Creek* and *Six Feet Under*—all of which showcase either remarkably flexible, non-nuclear biological families, or which maintain their narrative focus on "urban" families of friends whose biological families are invisible or inconsequential. *Buffy* and *Angel* present families that are full of "boundary ambiguity," that accept strays and newcomers without judgment, and that continually revise and reconceptualize their own borders.

You can be a werewolf, a vampire, an ex-vengeance-demon, a witch, a covert government agent—you can even be queer, which is still a stumbling block for most primetime offerings. Heredity, biology, genetics, appearance, class, gender, sexuality ... none of these signifiers are crucially definitive within the Buffyverse. Your access to the Scooby Gang is based on your commitment to its mission, and your inherent sense of loyalty. Once you're in, you're loved—it's that simple. As illustrated in the episode "Family" (15.06), "blood kin" will never be as powerful as "family" here, and family is a measure of emotional attachment, not of heredity.

When Willow is surprised at Tara for never having mentioned her biological family, Tara protests, "I was just afraid if you saw the kind of people I came from, you wouldn't wanna be anywhere near me." Willow's reply is typical of critical Buffyverse wisdom: "See, that's where you're a dummy." As Buffy proves in this episode, it is possible to reorder the definition of family, to extend it in all directions so that it encompasses members based on compassion rather than genetics. The Scoobies, up to this point, have spent the past five seasons constructing a nurturing and supportive extended family that is completely removed from their respective biological families, and that remains more or less beneath the notice of their parents. Given Buffy's deadbeat dad, Willow's critical and academic mom (a gesture towards the ivory tower, for certain) and Xander's loud, adversarial parents, they are forced to rely on each other for stability, and discover that, contrary to the perceived moral efficacy of the nuclear family, this chosen family is actually more inclusive, flexible and durable than the corrupted nuclear families that they have all emerged from.

Obviously, this open-system family seems inviting to audiences, especially young audiences, who are disillusioned with their biological families. The idea of belonging to a space where your voice might be heard, where your embattled humanity — not your superpowers — make you special, and where you have a network of loving friends to support and protect you, is essentially the dream of every teenager struggling alone through the hell of high school. *Buffy*, as Joss Whedon has suggested in numerous interviews, conveys the impression that high school itself is the real challenge, far more difficult to slay than vampires or demons. To simply be a teenager, to get through each day, to graduate and step into your life, is a task far more daunting than patrolling graveyards or gathering exotic spell ingredients. And audiences connect with the Scooby Gang because, despite their peculiar adventures, all of their most difficult trials are ones based squarely in real life — maintaining relationships, chafing against parental authority, having one's heart broken, living away from home for the first time, going to college and, most poignantly, dealing with *natural* death.

This radical family system is not perfect. We have already discussed, at length, the racial, economic and cultural exclusions practiced by both shows. It is a sad fact that, to be a member of *Buffy's* chosen family, you need not have a particular economic or political background, but you do, apparently, need to be white. While *Angel* does have Gunn as a non-white character (unless we count Lorne, who is green), his presence on the show veers dangerously close to tokenization, and his inner-city background, although it emerges as a significant point of character development, ends up, I think, as merely a stereotypical indicator that white, middle-class audiences can recognize: the televisual trope of the black man from an impoverished economic background who is street-smart rather than book-smart (read: uneducated). Gunn's blackness remains something that his white friends can mimic — especially through the appropriation of slang — but Gunn's corporate "whitening" at the hands of Wolfram & Hart appears, from the start, to be an illegible and incomplete performance that must ultimately fail.[13]

What do audiences see when they look at these radical chosen families? I have argued in previous chapters that they see a firmly white, middle-class framework of social commitments, as well as an ideal of physical beauty — personified by Sarah Michelle Gellar — that remains unattainable for the vast majority of teenage girls who aren't equipped with personal trainers, organic chefs and platinum credit cards to spend at Bloomingdale's. But they also see a great deal of diversity, even if it operates within a fantastic register. They see Oz "come out" as a werewolf— a revelation to which Willow sagely replies that "three days out of the month I'm not much fun to be around either" ("Phases," 2.15). They see the gang's unconditional acceptance of Xander, who earns miserable grades in high school, skips college and holds a series of odd jobs before settling on working as a carpenter. They see Tara calmly accept the fact that Buffy has been using Spike for sex, even as she sobs "please don't ... please don't forgive me" ("Dead Things," 16.12). They see Willow's coming out process as one without consequences, where her friends come closer together rather than driving her away.

I was first attracted to *Buffy* not because of its novel packaging as a gothic fantasy, but because of the amazing durability of its inclusive family model. I will admit that I am no more immune to this desire for a utopian chosen-family than any other audience member, and that when I first saw the Scooby Gang researching with Giles in the library, I wanted to be part of the group. I wanted to wisecrack with Xander, and share Willow's social awkwardness, and swap book titles with Giles, and marvel at Buffy's strength and resilience. And, most of all, I wanted to possess that feeling of unqualified belonging, of being accepted within a circle of friends who absolutely watch out for you. I wanted to have a warm, inviting house where extended family members could lounge on the couch, make sandwiches in the huge kitchen, "funny shape" pancakes like Tara preferred, or Dawn's experimental peanut butter fajitas. Most of all, I wanted to believe that it was possible to maintain crucial human connections in a world that seemed so full of penetrating uncertainty, so shadowed with monsters both psychological and material, and, at times, so vampiric in its desire to drain every last drop of fortitude from you until, like Buffy, you had to admit that "I don't know how to live in the world if these are the choices" ("The Gift," 5.22).

I have found, to some extent, a version of this extended family within academic communities, and not just ones interested in *Buffy*. Like most, I entered graduate studies as a terrified and ill-prepared undergrad, totally uncertain of what awaited me or what I would be expected to do.[14] The first thing I did was identify those who were equally terrified, if not more so, and proceeded to hold onto them for dear life. Most of the friends that I made in those first few weeks are still my friends. We sought each other out because, like the Scoobies, we shared certain visual characteristics — an exilic quality, an outsiderness, an infatuation with fringe discourses and cultural works generally excluded from traditional academic discourse. We were all a bit queer, some metaphorically, some (like me) quite literally, and we gravitated to each other because everyone else seemed too unbearably normal. Like the Scoobies, we were looking for companions who would allow us to justify our own weirdness, our own sense of disjunction with our environments.

Given that academic spaces remain fraught with competition, friendships that emerge within them are always tenuous. One of the reasons that academia continues to underestimate popular shows like *Buffy* and *Angel* is because they place a premium on non-competitive models of acceptance and inclusion, whereas academic performance is entirely predicated on literary, as well as performative, competition. As an example of this, consider the fact that most intellectuals concerned with social justice end up working in an interdisciplinary department, like Women's Studies, or devote themselves wholly to grassroots organizations, front-line advocacy and the non-profit sector. The "pure" academics, however, find their lives increasingly structured by grant applications, publishing contracts, curriculum expectations, committee meetings and teaching obligations. There is little, if any, room for the vulnerability necessary to establish meaningful friendships, let alone the creation of intimate familial enclaves within proscribed academic spaces. Thus, family is functionally the opposite of the academic environment — unless, of course, you advocate for its inclusion, and go to the trouble of creating it yourself.

My advice to all students beginning their post-secondary studies, graduate and undergraduate alike, is first and foremost to make friends. For undergrads, the prospect of a friendless four-year stint at university is quite unbearable. For graduate students, and emergent scholars, the need for personal connections is even more pressing. Let's be honest: Life as an academic is punishing, and not just intellectually. The time spent reading and writing, the sleepless nights, the financial and geographic instability, the sense of placelessness, the constant competition and, finally, the drive for occupational security through an outmoded tenure system — all of these factors make professional scholarship a potentially isolating and traumatizing endeavor. And, embedded within these material concerns is the more abstract, but nevertheless omnipresent, questioning of one's own scholarly commitments: *What do I study, what area do I belong to, what is politically important to me, how do I classify myself as a researcher, what do I want my work to say — and what* does *it say — about me?*

If I have had any success as an emergent scholar working within what I often find to be the confining spaces of academia, then I credit it to the tremendous emotional, and intellectual support that I receive daily from my friends. This includes the friends who are also scholars — who I can call when I'm having a postmodern crisis — and the friends who are not scholars, who I can call when I just want a couch to sleep on, or a kind soul to watch a movie with, or a patient listener who can sit through my endless and sometimes ridiculous complaints about being a privileged scholar. I am well aware that I work within a system that rewards me for things that I can't control, like my masculinity and my whiteness, and which also punishes me for things that I can't control, like my sexuality and my passionate commitments. Without these friends, I would quite literally have no sounding board for ideas, no laughing messages on my answering machine, no invitations to drink a pot of tea while watching reruns of *Buffy*, and no worried e-mails sent to me when I've been too absorbed in writing to return phone calls. These people represent my lifeline, and, without them, I simply wouldn't have the emotional foundation necessary for embarking upon any sort of research, let alone an academic career that makes me financially, as well as metaphysically, uncertain.

Academic environments aren't necessarily conducive to these sorts of durable friendships, but they need to be cultivated precisely *because* academia militates against vulnerability and intimacy. It is, in my mind, impossible to be a responsible scholar without having a network of loved ones as a kind of free-floating conscience, a continual reminder of one's ethical frameworks, political dedications and passionate responses. If we aren't accountable to our friends, peers and families — be they biological or extended — then who *are* we accountable to? And is our drive to write as powerful, as enjoyable, without the knowledge that someone we care about will read the finished product? Despite all of our best political intentions, all of our passions for social justice and equality, are we not also writing, at times, to a few loved and cherished people who represent the audience that we measure ourselves against? Without this framework of accountability, our work as scholars would be just a calling out into the dark. And, even when we *are* calling out into the dark, when we are stretching bravely, perhaps stupidly, across some precipice of tradition, or flinging our ideas into the void — it still helps to know that a sympathetic ear will be listening, that someone will care, even if it happens to be a friend, colleague or parent.

I write about *Buffy* because I love the show, and because I am troubled by it. In fact, I write about most things, academically or otherwise, as a result of being both drawn to and repelled by them. Like most fans of *Buffy* and *Angel*, I see fragments of my own chosen families, as well as my biological ones, within the Scooby Gang and Angel Investigations. The radical theories of kinship that these family models offer — admission and acceptance based on love rather than blood — are theories that I try to apply to my own families, even, and especially, when it seems as if I'm laboring against centuries of hegemonic organization around just what "the family" is.

If current debates within family studies have any common thread, it is their almost unanimous disavowal of a "core" to the family that is locatable through systems-theory analysis, or through evolutionary principles, or through conflict/resolution models. If anything, as "family" expands to encompass same-sex parents, surrogate parents, step-families, foster children, single and dual and triple-parent households, the notion that a core family could exist, and that the nuclear family is the only appropriate model given the confines of late capitalism, needs to be stripped down and rebuilt. Notice I don't advocate for it to be thrown out as an ideology. It is difficult, if not impossible, to simply do away with centuries of rhetorical, sociological and state-interventionist policymaking around what constitutes a family.

But we do need to admit the new families that are emerging, and to reconceptualize patriarchal ideations of the family — especially those focused on exploiting female domestic labor while refusing to factor in its contributions to national economic growth — as more inclusive and gender-positive systems of family-belonging. I mentioned a Deleuzian family-rhizome in the introduction, but that's absurdly abstract. What we need is a conception of family that acknowledges domestic labor, that accords single mothers the same financial benefits and social security as married women, that tries to equalize the disorienting clash of gendered perspectives within the home — reinscribing the household as not just a masculine space of relaxation, and not just a feminine space for unpaid work.

University departments would benefit enormously from adopting a more inclusive and gender-positive model such as this one. Instructors could set aside some of their research to concentrate more on inventive and engaging pedagogy, as well as on actually counseling students and designing curricula that addressed their individual realities and backgrounds. Departments could offer more flexibility in their expectations of graduate students, allowing them to design more interdisciplinary coursework and fieldwork rather than confining them to certain proscribed areas that mostly serve to strengthen and reformulate the canonical foundations of the department itself. Scholars could actually have civilized and supportive conversations with each other at conferences, rather than anonymously criticizing each other's work, as well as intensely competing with each other. University presses could be given the support and funding needed to make riskier choices for their publication lists, rather than remaining prone to chronic understaffing and underfinancing. Academic grants could target exciting interdisciplinary and genre-bending research, instead of remaining with "safe bet" applications that are easily classifiable within legitimate and bounded areas of the Social Sciences umbrella.

And, most importantly, scholars could share their research with each other, rely on each other for editorial suggestions — as well as emotional support — instead of jealously guarding their work and keeping their developing projects under lock and key. Departmental meetings might actually contain some supportive and engaging conversation, rather than the noncommittal murmurings of a room full of academics all waiting to get back to their pressing book deals and articles-in-progress. It sounds trite, I know, but scholars could learn a lot from family models in general, and from the non-traditional families presented on *Buffy* and *Angel* in particular.

The three most important lessons that I've taken, from both the Scooby Gang and Angel Investigations, are as follows: 1) it's okay to grieve, as long as you don't try to destroy the world, 2) don't dismiss someone's obligations in comparison to your own, because they might actually be a vampire slayer (or a vampire with a soul) in disguise, 3) even when family seems futile and pointless and completely incapable of pulling you back from the edge, sometimes all it takes is a simple "I love you," and the memory of crayons.

This all sounds very utopian from a cynical perspective, but I find that, increasingly, my motivations as a scholar have to find their roots in optimism. I have to believe in the possibility for a better world, the kind of world that Angel describes to Connor when he says that heroes "live as though the world were as it should be, to show it what it can be" ("Deep Down," 4.01). Both Buffy and Angel refuse the inequalities that the world presents them with, and decide instead to create a new world in much the same way that marginalized individuals, along with communities, create what Michel de Certeau calls "the space of the tactic [which] ... is the space of the other ... it must vigilantly make use of the cracks that particular conjunctions open in the surveillance of proprietary powers" (de Certeau, 35). They both employ tactics that allow them to renegotiate the world, to carve out safe spaces where they can exist as diverse and unclassifiable human subjects without giving in to the pressures of representation, of taxonomy, of the protocols for measuring humanity which, in their sweeping generalizations, are likely to overlook both Buffy and Angel as appropriate humans.

My extended families aren't comprised of werewolves, or queer witches, or ex-demons, or even carpenters. We don't live on a Hellmouth, and we aren't being regularly assaulted by vampires, or any other supernatural phenomenon. But, as I hope that I have outlined throughout this book, fantastic particularities often translate into very ordinary and human universalities. The desire to respect the planet, and to access inner reserves of fortitude that may seem magical, doesn't have to be confined to witchcraft. The passion to spearhead justice, to protect your loved ones from various material (as well as psychological threats), to fight oppression in all its forms, doesn't have to embodied by a vampire slayer. And the quieter, but no less tricky, art of holding your family together, of seeing everyone's best self, of being an archive for your friends' hopes, peculiarities and memories, doesn't have to be practiced solely by a carpenter. All of these seemingly "supernatural" tasks have their own real-world corollaries, and all require a superhuman and lifelong effort — although the benefits of maintaining them are well worth the risks, the vulnerabilities and the potential missteps.

Family, whatever it means to each of us — whether it's two queer parents, one single parent, multiple parents spread across different households, or droves of step-siblings clamoring for attention — remains our most powerful and enduring means of living in this world. If the outrageous inequalities, exclusions and agonizing moments of our individual lives represent our own private Hellmouth, then our families, both the ones we're born into and the ones we choose for ourselves, represent our own personal Slayer, with an endless reservoir of strength that we can draw from again and again. As Buffy herself explains to Tara, "family" simply means whoever says "we're family"— it is a category that gains more power through enunciation than it does through biology.

Both *Buffy* and *Angel* present us with radical new models of family, just as they exhort us to appreciate and respect our own extended families — even when we don't want to, and even when the Scoobies seem infinitely better. For, as most fans of *Buffy* know, *who* you watch the show with is as important as the show itself, and having friends who share your passion, family members who can match your enthusiasm, and academic colleagues willing to join you in your deconstructive endeavors, is precious. *Buffy* and *Angel* are shows about family, and should be watched *with* family — whichever family you choose, and whichever family chooses you.

AFTERWORD

Families Beyond *Buffy* (or *Firefly*, and Everything After)

"How profoundly inclined we are by what Nietzsche calls 'the seduction of grammar' to read in a linear way."
—Judith Butler, *Interview* (732)

"I need that in Captain-Dummy-Talk, Kaylee."
— Malcolm Reynolds (*Firefly*, *Out of Gas*, 1.05)

It's done! What a relief! Now that the argumentative section of the book is over, we can really get down to the speculation. This is not exactly a conclusion, and not exactly an epilogue. It is more along the lines of what Terry Goldie, in his book *Pink Snow*, calls an *envoi*— referencing Stephen Leacock's famous *Sunshine Sketches of a Little Town*. Goldie characterizes this last chapter as less analysis and more "homage," or "a gentle recognition that the preceding volume was a realm of nostalgia; it is time to come back to the oppressive present" (Goldie, 236). I am not trying to suggest that the preceding chapters have been entirely nostalgic, and that we now need to return to an "oppressive present." But I do think that, after being immersed in the Buffyverse for a few hundred pages, we should surface for a few moments and address other shows, texts and ideas having to do with family. There is, after all, a world outside of *Buffy*. A lot of fans would disagree, but, alas, I know that it's true.

For all of the discussion on *Buffy* and *Angel* that's already taken place within this volume, there are still dozens more chapters that could be written, hundreds of pages worth of dialogue that could be analyzed. An ideal treatise on the show would have to include almost every exchange between the characters, since so much of what they say is significant, and so much of the joy of watching the show comes from latching onto casual dialogue. Simple Buffy-isms like "guestage," "wiggins" and "repeato-girl" could all spawn detailed discussions, and, luckily, have been given suitable treatment within Michael Adams' *Slayer Slang* dictionary (Oxford: 2003). For every scene that I've analyzed, there were dozens of scenes I had to leave out, for fear of my argument spiraling wildly beyond the constraints of this book. Any *Buffy* scholar can tell you that, when sitting down to write on the show, it isn't lack of ideas that becomes problematic — it's the complete surplus of theoretical material. Every episode delivers a postmodern grab-bag of fantastic one-liners, and, after writing each chapter, I would often come across a forgotten snippet of text and think *damn, why didn't I include that*? The temptation to cite all seven seasons is powerful.

More than one colleague has told me that *Buffy* is, essentially, just "too great" to subject to scholarly analysis. There is always the fear that treating something academically — especially a show that you love — will actually destroy your fixation on it, thereby transforming it into just another text. But, if anything, writing this book has only deepened my love of it. Each chapter has an emotional core to it, a climactic moment of narration wherein, as I was writing, I thought: *yes, I* really *do care about this*. I could see the characters in my mind, hear their voices and feel the emotional resonance of each episode coming back to me as I discussed it. Scholarship isn't always about flogging a text until something falls out of it. Sustained scholarly analysis can also be a kind of homage, a memorialization of a text that holds it up for inspection without necessarily canonizing it. I have to believe that, in some way, such love can translate into academic language, that it can survive the process of textualization and gleam through, somehow, sparsely visible but still there. If much of the discussion that has come before this is nostalgic, in the sense that it imagines *Buffy* and *Angel* as beloved texts, then this "conclusion" is a self-reflexive gesture towards that. Not standing on the outside, but, through some peculiarity of the page, standing at a slant.

I have, throughout this text, discussed a growing trend within televisual narratives to privilege chosen families over biological ones. *Buffy* and *Angel* are probably the most visually exotic examples of this, but they are certainly not alone. A show like HBO's *Sex and the City* revolves entirely around an "urban family" of friends, (four women) who meet in the same New York coffee shop every day to talk, complain, laugh and essentially narrate their own lives. Interestingly, it is one of the only shows I know of to actually incorporate female narration, with the character of Carrie (Sarah Jessica Parker) often interrupting the action with sarcastic voiceovers. It is also Carrie's job to "introduce" each episode by broaching a particular topic, and then close the episode by providing some type of conclusion. In this sense, the show is more like a novel than most, with each episode standing in as an enclosed chapter. There is a reason why Kim Akass and Janet McCabe's edited collection, *Reading Sex and the City* (IB Tauris: 2004), received so many submissions. What academic wouldn't want to analyze a show that presents each episode in terms of arguments and conclusions?

None of the characters in *Sex and the City* appear to have biological families. Charlotte York, who curates an art gallery on the Upper East Side and dreams of a pedigreed marriage, talks constantly about starting her own family without ever addressing any existing parents. She does have one sibling, a brother, who appears only for one episode. Similarly, we only hear about Miranda's mother once she has died, and the episode is about her death, not her life. Anyone who enters and leaves the series is coded in opposition to the four central characters. Romances and sexual relationships are always fleeting, but friendship lasts, and each episode — usually beginning with the characters' traditional breakfast in their favorite restaurant — reasserts the narrative supremacy of their friendship. Memorable conversations between the women include Charlotte's anxieties about having anal sex, Samantha's fear that her boyfriend's penis is much too small, Miranda's conviction that her ovaries are drying up, and Carrie's ongoing flirtations with the love of her life — a character known only as "Mr. Big."

Beneath this veneer of seemingly absurd topics, real, pressing questions about female paid labor, shifting definitions of feminism, sexual mores, fidelity, illness, death and urban solidarity are all addressed. Like *Buffy* and *Angel*, *Sex and the City* often manipulates some of its more ridiculous premises in order to explore critical issues, given the license that fantasy provides for social commentary. Unlike *Friends*, wherein nothing substantially negative that can't be solved within 22 minutes ever happens to the characters, *Sex and the City* allows for series-spanning problems and issues that don't always get resolved. All four women fight regularly but, like most dependable circles of friends, they always reconvene at crisis moments to support each other. Their relationship is more intimate, and more durable, than any romantic entanglement that gets parodied within the show, or even the long-lasting romances that actually get treated with some sensitivity. These friends are each other's ultimate critics, and ultimate supporters — they have virtually no need of a biological family, because they have created a more flexible substitute.

Another similar family system is presented in the Showtime offering *Queer as Folk*, whose complicated history of adaptation and network switching has equaled *Buffy*'s. It began as a miniseries in the UK, and transitioned to an American melodrama (now approaching its fifth season) that is actually filmed in Canada. Some of the characters from the British version were dropped, or came to be radically repositioned within the American version. The plot of the original miniseries — which basically showcased the sexcapades and nightlife of four queer men in Manchester — was transformed into a character-driven serial about an enduring group of queer friends, including two lesbians married to each other, and their various attempts to negotiate life in urban Pittsburgh.

Queer as Folk is a little different, in that some of the characters' biological families are actually present. Michael Navotney, a comic book–loving department store clerk who falls in love with an academic (oh, what a fantasy!), is quite intimately involved in the life of his mother, Debbie. In fact, Debbie is such a supportive, queer-friendly, PFLAG mom that she actually gets on everyone's nerves. Like *Sex and the City*, however, on *Queer as Folk* all of the characters meet daily at the same restaurant (where Debbie happens to work) to discuss their lives, commiserate and generally interact with each other. Debbie serves as an acting-mom to all of them, not just Michael, since she seems to be the only parent in attendance. And the overriding suggestion is that these characters have created a family for themselves, and that any endorsement or celebration of their lives and relationships emanates from inside that group rather than from an outside authority.

And, of course, where would a discussion of chosen families be without citing Joss Whedon's "other" show, *Firefly*? The idea of choosing a support system rather than relying on a biological family is, I think, more apparent from the beginning in *Firefly* than it ever was in *Buffy* and *Angel*. The very first episode introduces us to an ensemble cast of nine characters, rather than the more manageable "core" Scoobies (Buffy, Xander, Willow, Giles) or the principle characters opening *Angel* (Cordelia, Doyle and Angel himself). Being a captain, it seems at first that the character Mal (short for Malcolm Reynolds) is the head of this particular family. But, as with *Buffy*, it soon becomes clear that authority is shifting within the *Firefly* crew, and that each family member makes a unique and cohesive contribution to the group. Even the quietest and least physically imposing member, Kaylee, provides an essential service: She literally keeps their ship flying, and is a brilliantly intuitive engineer.

Like *Buffy* and *Angel*, *Firefly* is explicitly a show about battling oppression in various forms. The refrain in the title song, "You can't take the sky from me," suggests an indomitable settler spirit that can't ever be fully subsumed, and just the sort of rugged individualism that we've talked about in previous chapters. The "monster" in *Firefly*, however, is a very human system of authority — the Alliance, a governing body that controls and monitors newly terraformed planets, and which suspiciously resembles a sort of futuristic Watcher's Council. Two of the characters on Mal's ship, *Serenity*, are fugitives running from the Alliance, and thus the whole narrative structure of *Firefly* is a kind of perpetual motion. The characters are always running somewhere, always on the move, continually struggling to eke out a bare existence among the "outer planets" while helping people along the way. Their version of Angel's hotel or the Summers' home is *Serenity* itself, a ship that is constantly moving. It is the ultimate gesture towards a constructed family: a home that you can take anywhere.

Like Buffy and Angel, Mal does everything in his power to ensure the cohesion of his extended family. The characters gather every night in the *Serenity*'s dining area to talk, strategize or just tell bawdy stories. Mal is fiercely protective of his crew, even the fugitives Simon and River, who retain their essential outsiderness while still managing to find a place among the others. When he discovers that Jayne has attempted to sell them both to the authorities, he locks his friend — whom he has known a lot longer than Simon and River — outside of the cargo bay and threatens to drop him into the atmosphere. "You turn on any of my crew," he says to Jayne, "you turn on me" ("Ariel," 1.08). His relationship with Kaylee resembles that of an older brother, and he often teases her, calling her "little Kaylee" and accusing her of chattering too much, when in fact it is clear that he wouldn't think twice about killing anyone who tried to harm her. This is a sentiment that most big brothers share.

Although *Firefly* only aired 13 episodes (the remaining two can be seen on the DVD set), each was nuanced and amazingly well-written. On the DVD commentary for the Season 1 set, Joss Whedon describes the pressure of having to write a series that was constantly in danger of being cancelled, and describes how it adds an element of urgency to the narrative. Each episode, then, is written as if it might be the last, and each could very well stand on its own as a contained and engaging story. Two scenes stand out for me in their presentation chosen families: one in the episode "Out of Gas" (1.05), the other in "Objects in Space" (1.10).

In "Out of Gas," the *Serenity* literally runs out of gas — the engine seizes, the life support system fails and the ship is left floating. But this event isn't really the narrative thrust of the episode. The true action occurs in a series of flashbacks and recollections, which piece together Mal's relationships with his friends. We see Mal trying to convince Zoe, a friend and former soldier like him, that the ship is actually space-worthy rather than the piece of junk that it once resembled. He insists that the *Serenity* will allow them to "live like real people. Small crew, them as feel the need to be free … never be under the heel of nobody again." Later, we see him meeting Kaylee for the first time, who he discovers in a heavy make-out session with the previous engineer. It becomes clear to him, however, that Kaylee — despite her lack of life experience — is a much better engineer than the one he originally hired, and he gives her a job on the spot. "I just gotta ask my folks!" she replies excitedly, running off, and this is the last significant mention of anyone's biological family, for the surrogate family on the ship becomes a flexible and enduring replacement.

Through a variety of events that I can't summarize, Mal ends up in the ship's sick bay, heavily drugged and being tended to by Simon (the doctor). Like Xander, Mal's body is often displayed as a parodic spectacle — he ends up naked in one episode, and this time he is stripped to the waist, looking exposed and incredibly vulnerable to everyone watching. Drifting out of consciousness, he asks, suddenly concerned, "You all gonna be here when I wake up?" They all reply in the affirmative, and Mal's last mumbled words before peacefully passing out are "'kay ... that's good." He falls asleep with a smile on his face, entirely childlike in his pleasure at having a family to wake up to. Kaylee only reinforces this by calling him a "good boy" for managing to fix the ship, and, just this once, everyone seems to be watching out for Mal, rather than the other way around.

"Objects in Space" addresses family by way of a very different idea. River, Simon's sister, is perhaps the most peripheral character in *Firefly*, yet her presence is also what drives the narrative action. In his efforts to keep her away from the corrupt scientists of the Alliance, Simon has turned both of them into fugitives. But River remains the ultimate exile. Her language is halting and somewhat schizophrenic, she is afraid of most people, and she appears to be able to read minds. It all seems a little hackneyed, but, as with most projects written by Joss Whedon, the cliché is only present as a ground from which to start. The rest of the show is about complicating and expanding that cliché, exposing the gray areas that exist within it, and challenging the very idea that we, as an audience, can predict what a character might do because he or she falls into a particular televisual type.

River's telepathic abilities manifest themselves in this episode as disorienting moments of prescience and understanding. As she listens to her friends talk, she experiences moments of narrative fracture, wherein the characters suddenly address her directly — that is, they leave their external conversations for a moment and speak to her, cruelly, brutally, and with unsparing honesty. Whether they tell her exactly what they are thinking, or what she *assumes* they are thinking, is difficult to discern. When River stumbles into a late-night conversation between Simon and Kaylee about his medical days, she seems momentarily happy at seeing Simon so relaxed. Then, abruptly, he turns to her and says, "I would be there right now," intimating that, if not for River, he would still be enjoying his old life as a top surgeon. River's subsequent "reading" of Book, the ship's onboard preacher, is even more disturbing, when he snarls at her: "I don't give half a hump if you're innocent or not." All of these impressions are abstract and evocative, not exactly decoded thoughts so much as scattered feelings that the characters seem to emanate. Their very illegibility points not only to the commonly held idea that we wouldn't *really* want to hear what other people are thinking about us, but to the fundamental impossibility of "reading" another's mind, given that, in all probability, our reading wouldn't make any sense.

Much of what River hears convinces her that she doesn't belong on the ship, and that it will be simpler for everyone if she goes along with a bounty hunter, Jubal Early, who's been sent to collect her. Speaking through *Serenity*'s loudspeaker, she tells the crew that, if she left, "everyone could just go on without me, and not have to worry. People could be what they wanted to be ... live simple." Mal does not accept this, of course. There is a scene that occurs immediately after this, a wonderful scene, when Mal, clad in a spacesuit, goes to retrieve River from Jubal's ship. River floats through space towards him, arms outstretched, and Mal catches her. "Permission to come aboard?" she asks, but it is clear that Mal has already admitted her into the family, already taken her under his protective wing. "Give your brother a thrashing for messing up your plan," Mal insists, and River rolls her eyes, saying only, "He takes so much looking after." It is the sole biological relationship here, between River and Simon, that seems to require maintenance — not the extended family on board *Serenity*.

Yet this relationship between River and Simon also deserves some attention. It has no correlation in any other Joss Whedon show, and represents his sole positive depiction of a biological brother/sister connection, as opposed to the copious chosen-family connections that *Buffy* and *Angel* convey. Their connection is often a silent one, but their love for each other is clearly visualized in almost every scene that they share. One that stands out for me is a moment at the end of the two-part episode "Serenity" (1.11, 1.12), when both characters have only just been introduced as fugitives and accepted onboard the ship. River, seeing a cut on Simon's lip from trying to defend her, reaches up and gently touches just the tips of her fingers to his mouth. "I didn't think you'd come for me," she says.

Simon's reply is perfect, in that it echoes exactly the sentiment shared between Willow and Tara in the episode "Family." "Well, you're a dummy!" (1.12), he says. River accepts this. It is clear that their connection is equal to that shared by the rest of the crew, and thus they are a family within a family. *Firefly* is unique in this way, because, rather than rejecting biological families, it incorporates hereditary kinship into a radical extended family, suggesting that both emotional connections can build and inform each other. Simon and River's sibling relationship is not a "pure" example of family in comparison to the diluted version of the *Serenity* crew — it is, instead, a more traditional family system that only strengthens the non-traditional system of which it has become a part. Both families shape each other, and both learn from each other. This is part of what makes *Firefly* an even more progressive show than *Buffy* or *Angel*, and also, most likely, the reason why it was cancelled. Too much emotion — not enough action.

Being part of a family, these shows tell us, is like being part of an unbalanced equation. There is never a sense of total completion, never a certainty that everything is operating as it should. But, somehow, things seem to go right. As Mal observes, the prospect of being in constant motion, of flying across hostile space, "ain't much ... [but] it's enough" (1.12). Finding a place within these families doesn't always mean finding a place in the outside world, and, often, insecurities and threatening forces persist. It is possible, like River, to feel exiled while belonging to a family, or, like Willow, to know that you can destroy your family with the barest of thoughts. But if family wasn't assailable within these narratives, if it wasn't a system that *could* be threatened, if it didn't have permeable boundaries, then it wouldn't actually mean a lot. The fallibility of family is what *Buffy*, *Angel* and *Firefly* all suggest, along with the conviction that it is better to participate within something fallible then to throw it away altogether, because its flaws are what make it precious.

The trick is to keep going. Keep flying. When Buffy is asked "Now what?" in the final episode of Season 7 ("Chosen," 7.22), she seems relieved, even though she has no idea what to do next. She knows, as do the rest of the Scoobies, that their family is powerful enough to survive just about anything, and that, despite uncertainties around how to put their lives back together after closing the Hellmouth, whatever happens next will be something that they face together. Geography and circumstance don't matter. Robert Frost, in his oft-quoted verse "Death of the Hired Man," wrote that "home is the place where, when you have to go there, they have to take you in." The Scoobies, the crew of Angel Investigations, and the family on board *Serenity* all take home with them, constructing it as they go along, bending it when they have to, and enlarging it to encompass the various radical theories of kinship that sustain them as family members. They don't ever have to go home because, as long as they're with each other, they *are* home. Their citation of "family" is what makes it real, and their continual re-creation and renegotiation of "home" is what allows the concept to emanate between them.

These radical chosen families are, as I have mentioned before, not perfect. They are not superior copies of biological families, and it is impossible for audiences to wholly identify with them while discarding their actual families. Whether they are at the forefront of a trend to replace the biological family on television with a radical substitute, or simply fantastic imaginings of families that could be, the fact remains that these systems of kinship are complex, enduring and full of hope. They offer new constellations of belonging, and new ways of living in the world. Their imagination exceeds the scope of Family Studies, producing bizarrely and wonderfully intertwined models of solidarity and emotional resonance. They suggest that weird, queer, exotic, indescribable and even undead families can be better than traditional ones. And that, no matter what your family looks like, the goal is to maintain it, to strengthen it, to trim the edges, batten down, keep flying.

Chapter Notes

Introduction

1. Roland, Barthes. *Pleasure of the Text*, trans. Richard Miller (NY: Hill and Wang, 1975).

2. Jacques, Derrida. "Living On: Border Lines," in *Deconstruction and Criticism*, ed. Harold Bloom (NY: Seabury Press, 1979).

3. Authorization in the sense that, as Trinh T. Minh-ha characterizes it, "authorized voices authorize themselves to be heard ... authorizing at times to de-authorize." *When the Moon Waxes Red* (NY: Routledge, 1991, 188).

4. Shelley Jackson. *Patchwork Girl* CD-ROM (Eastgate Systems, 1995).

5. Arwen Spicer "'Love's Bitch, but Man Enough to Admit it': Spike's Hybridized Gender" *Slayage* 8 (December, 2002).

6. Gertrude Stein. *Lectures in America* (NY: Random House, 1935).

7. Deleuze Gilles, and Félix Guatari, *A Thousand Plateaus: Capitalism and Schizophrenia* (Minneapolis: University of Minnesota Press, 1987).

Chapter One

1. I base my use of the term "grotesque" on Bakhtin's discussion of it in *Rabelais and His World*, in which he characterizes the grotesque as a display of threatening physicality, intimately tied to notions of social anarchy and *carnivàle*. The grotesque can be a body that terrifies us, that makes us cringe, but that also inexplicably attracts us. It almost always manifests itself in an overabundance of the physical, an hyper-corporeal body that demands to be looked at. In the case of *Buffy*, Spike's body often falls within these terms. He spends a lot of his time in various states of undress, and his body is made to be looked at, to be desired. Yet it is also an abject body, dead, pale and vampiric.

2. Names and naming are significant within the series "Buffy" with its immature and "Californian" associations; "Xander" as a diminutive of the more appropriate "Alexander," further shortened to "Xan"; and of course "Willow," with its ties to the natural world. The materiality of Willow's name is interesting: Willows are supple, bending but seldom breaking.

3. I have no idea what happens to this kitten in later episodes. She seems to vanish.

4. She is the only character capable of using a computer, which, in Sunnydale, can effortlessly decrypt all manner of civic and governmental databases. In the Buffyverse, technology often seems less real than magic. Warren, Andrew and Jonathan, for instance, are often comically seen using technology in an effort to appear more Bond-like, whereas Willow's magic is always discussed in terms of ethics and responsibility.

5. This "hijacking" of Willow's body is a common occurrence within the show, gener-

ally associated with the most powerful magic. It remains disturbing, however, that when Willow is at her most powerful, she also seems to be possessed by magic itself. There is the suggestion here that Willow is somehow not responsible for some of these spells—that magic is actually working through her, rather than her controlling the magic, which sets up basically all Wiccan power within the dangerous parameters of addiction.

6. "I *killed* Angel," she tells Xander. "Do you even remember that?" And, indeed, this reality is rarely touched upon after the third season. This theme of sacrifice, however, will come to dominate Season 7, as the Slayer's struggle between personal happiness and prophesied duty are explored to a greater extent. I was disturbed at how the Slayer's "mission" began to be rearticulated in military terms within this Season, becoming increasingly known as "the cause," and discussed in terms of insiders vs. outsiders. The Slayer potentials seemed, like draftees, to be forced to fight, and there was really only one proper side. Whether this recapitulated North American dialogues on the fight against terrorism, or whether the First Evil represented a specular version of "global terror," is a debate beyond the parameters of this text.

7. Spike's attempted rape of Buffy in the episode "Entropy" (6.18) also occurs without any vampiric transformation—that is, even when Spike's desire completely controls him, he still appears human. Much discussion has centered on this event, which seems to have been meant by Joss Whedon to "remind" the audience that Spike was still, in fact, a morally ambivalent character, rather than the cheerful babysitter who watches Dawn and hangs around the Summers' front yard.

8. The Bronze is one of those incongruous safe places within the Buffyverse—clearly meant to be a "hip" hangout in Sunnydale, but never quite escaping its own improbability. Like most dance club/bar/hangout spots in television shows aimed at twentysomething audiences (like The Peach Pit in *Beverly Hills 90210*, or Babylon in *Queer As Folk*), the Bronze is a convenient space, within which the principle characters can always have extended conversations (because the music is only loud when nobody is talking). Nobody ever really goes on dates at the Bronze—it mostly serves as another meeting place for the Scoobies, and thus gets interestingly recoded as an intimate space for friends rather than a sexy space for dating. It is also, like most places in Sunnydale, located immediately adjacent to a vampire-infested alley.

9. It is also worth noting that Buffy's transformation into the hybrid–Slayer is similarly coded to (but visually the opposite of) Willow's transformation into dark or "über-Willow." Buffy's eyes become golden and radiant, whereas Willow's become black and devouring. Buffy transforms bullets into doves, whereas Willow freezes them—both actions most keenly representing the containment and displacement of technology by mystical power.

10. It seems clear that Spike wants his soul back for selfish reasons—that is, he wants Buffy to love him, and figures that having a soul will make this possible. But it ends up being a lot more than he bargained for, and also, in his own words, "a bit worse for lack of use" ("Beneath You," 7.02). Angel's soul almost always manifests itself in terms of guilt, regret and general "brooding." But Spike's soul seems like a more profound fracture, actually driving him insane for a period, and wreaking havoc on his normally clever language practices. Like Illyria, Spike spends a few episodes not being a character at all, but rather a sort of mystery—partly the old Spike, and partly someone new. This is, I think, when Spike is at his most intriguing.

11. Buffy seems, for the most part, incapable of indulging any of her fantasies in a healthy or positive way. Her dreams of being "normal again" translate into a frightening psychotic episode, wherein she believes that she is trapped in an institution ("Normal Again," 6.17). When she gets to act out her fantasies of being invisible, she ends up merely feeling empty and unwanted ("Gone," 6.11). When she indulges in violent and self-annihilating sexplay with Spike, she only feels ashamed at having used him to fill the void that her resurrection left behind. In this sense, Buffy is meant to be the Slayer, because being the Slayer is the only reality that she can actually fathom.

12. Audiences can't help noticing that Willow, even at her most addicted, still appears remarkably attractive and well-rested. The character of Amy is the one visibly coded as

an addict, showing up at Buffy's house to steal spell ingredients, and then getting violently ill when Buffy interrogates her ("Wrecked," 6.10). But Willow, despite her grossly enlarged pupils, doesn't seem to change all that much physically. It is this visual nuance that allows her character to maintain coherence, and that keeps her well within the parameters of audience acceptance.

13. The notion of the "costume" is further explored in the "The Body" (5.16), when Willow interrogates her own dependence on childish dress: "Why can't I just dress like a grown-up? Can't I *be* a grownup?" At this point her language dissolves, and she must turn to Tara, whose kiss — both comforting and traced with erotic power — serves here as a silencing technique (Willow stops talking) and as a force of embodiment (she is then strengthened, and supported, by Tara's presence). Interestingly enough, this entire scene is touched off by Willow's search for "the blue," a sweater that Joyce (who is now herself "the body") always liked. Willow's vacillations regarding what to wear to the hospital (an uncertainty usually reserved for social events) underscores her slippage between identities: purple is too "royal," yellow too "happy, lala, look at me," and every article of clothing thus becomes unsatisfactory.

14. This is, I think, also a premonition of things to come for Willow. Just as she inscribes Tara's body with text about pain and suffering, so is Willow's own body literally inscribed by magic, absorbing the text from hundreds of black arts books so that Willow, herself, actually "becomes the magic."

15. Willow's attempt to magically alter Tara's memory — the "tabula rasa" spell — is the ultimate repositioning of identity. To maintain her lover's (and her family's) expectations, Willow feels that she must eradicate any hint of transgression and start anew. As illustrated in the episode itself (6.08), this "new" position is entirely illegible — although Willow does, interestingly enough, 'decode' her sexuality once more, despite everyone's assumption that she must be straight.

Chapter Two

1. One of the texts on *Buffy* and family that I found particularly helpful was Viv Burr's "Friends are the family we choose for ourselves," a conference paper presented at the *Slayage* International Conference on *Buffy the Vampire Slayer* (May 28–30, 2004, Nashville TN). As this is still a relatively new critical "look" into the Buffyverse, there is not yet a base of scholarship to point to — although a great deal of articles already written on *Buffy* include inevitable, if peripheral, treatments of family. There is also Peg Aloi's "My art belongs to daddy: Rupert Giles as magical mentor," also presented at the 2004 conference.

2. For a valuable treatment of the relationship between visibility/invisibility and whiteness, see Sally Robinson's book *Marked Men* (2000), wherein she argues that white masculinity creates symbolic crises within its own structure, then paradoxically manages those crises in order to continually maintain its status as an overriding cultural category. These crises emerge, Robinson contends, primarily when the white body rewrites itself as wounded or victimized, thereby appropriating the politics of victimization from other marginalized cultural categories, and speaking "from" the space of marginality and victimization that it has traditionally enforced on *other* groups.

3. Xander also states in this episode that "they'll never know how hard it is," thereby suggesting that his status as "seer," whatever privileges it might entail, is also a position of profound dislocation, loss and confusion.

4. Cordelia is chosen by the "Powers That Be" to become a higher being in the episode "Tomorrow" (3.22), which seems to be an extension of her earlier transformation into a hybrid Demon/Human. This job description remains suitably vague.

5. Texts dealing with the relationship between masculinity and whiteness that I found to be most helpful in assembling this discussion — besides Robinson's *Marked Men* — were Hazel Carby's *Race Men* (1998) and Kaja Silverman's *Male Subjectivity at the Margins* (1992). Carby and Silverman discuss the extent to which the Black male body has historically been a site for the inscription of white male anxiety around issues of physical power, sexual virility and cultural hegemony.

6. Judith Halberstam discusses this at length in her book *Female Masculinity* (1998), and her characterization of the "femme pre-

tender" (see Chapter 7, "Drag Kings: Masculinity and Performance") will become an important signpost of performed masculinity within this treatment of Xander.

7. For article-length works that discuss this racial absence (or "absent presence"), see Lynn Edwards' "Slaying in Black and White" (2002) and Kent Ono's "To Be a Vampire on *Buffy the Vampire Slayer*" (2000). Most of the other works that treat this topic are conference papers, and thus difficult to access. For a detailed list, see the online *Slayage* "Buffy Studies Bibliography" (http://www.slayage.tv).

8. Obviously, magic and physical force occur within the realm of the symbolic as well on *Buffy*. Magic comes to be a signifier for addiction in regards to Willow, just as physical strength comes to signify emotional distance and "coldness" for Buffy in later episodes.

9. When I was giving a paper on Xander at the *Slayage* International Conference on *Buffy the Vampire Slayer*, my panel got into a debate around Xander's flirtation with queer sexualities, and a colleague asked what it might mean if Xander were actually queer. We concluded that the show's handling of a visible queer relationship between Xander and another man (Riley, perhaps?) would have been impossible within the current televisual climate. Although prime-time shows have aired same-sex kisses before (most notably *Ellen, Will and Grace, Party of Five* and *ER*), there has yet to be an un-comedic, clearly sexual kiss between two queer-identifying men on any of the basic cable networks.

10. See, among other sources, Andy Mangels' "Lesbian Sex = Death?" in *The Advocate* (Issue 869, 8/20/2002: 1–3)

11. Spike is a perfect example of a character whose erotic potential emerges from his flirtation with male masochism, and whose various feminizations at the hands of Buffy herself are continually recast as a kind of obsessive heterosexual devotion rather than a gesture towards possible queerness.

12. See Wilcox, Rhonda. "T. S. Eliot Comes to Television: Buffy's 'Restless.'" *Slayage: The Online International Journal of Buffy Studies* 7 (2002). http://www.slayage.tv/*essays/slayage7/Wilcox.htm.*

13. See Jean Baudrillard's *Simulation and Simulacra* (1995), wherein chains of desert-imagery proliferate, including his oft-quoted assessment of hyperreality as "the desert of the real."

14. Kristeva elaborates on this notion specifically in her book *Powers of Horror* (1982).

Chapter Three

1. The adjacent apartments that the *Friends* characters share, located in central Manhattan (probably on the edge of the Upper East Side, given their proximity to Central Park), would cost several thousand dollars per month to rent — a clearly prohibitive sum for a generally unemployed actor (Joey), a data processor (Chandler), a masseuse who works in the "informal" sector (Phoebe) or a chef (Monica). Even Rachel, who appears to be some sort of buyer for Macy's, would have little money left for her multiple trips to popular cafes and restaurants. Similarly, the reality of five orphans (only three of whom are employed) maintaining a three-story house in San Francisco — as the characters do in *Party of Five*— seems equally absurd.

2. Midway through Season 1 and sporadically throughout Season 2, Fisher and Sons is approached by a funeral megacorp, "Kroener," whose ominously Germanic name portends exactly the divide-and-conquer strategy that a North American audience is expecting. Kroener's C.E.O. and media spokeswoman, Mitzy, whose ambition has clearly been gender-pathologized here as greed, tries multiple times to cajole David into selling the business. She is, of course, continually rebuffed by Nate and his transparently ethical masculinity — which often translates into a specifically middle-class framework for what is "right."

3. I should clarify this bit of philosophical indulgence. I am paraphrasing here Kant's ideas in *Metaphysics of Morals* around utilitarian ethics — that is, the suggestion that, in order to conceptualize an action as inherently "moral," we must first recast it as being universally applicable. To tell a "moral" lie, for example, we must imagine a universe where everyone lied. This condensation of Kantian ethics is probably unforgivable, but I employ it here simply to point to Buffy's

relatively simple moral compass — that killing a human is wrong, that apocalypse is bad, and that people need to be saved.

4. By "pre-oedipal," I am referring to the stage of maternal connection that occurs before Freud's oedipal stage — a phase wherein mother and child are physiologically, as well as psychically, undifferentiated. Julia Kristeva, in works such as *Powers of Horror*, discusses at great length the extent to which language as a patriarchal project is threatened by this lack of differentiation or "mother tongue."

5. It is unclear whether or not Mr. Summers pays any form of child support. He makes only a few appearances throughout the run of the show, the last being in "Normal Again" (6.17) as a figment of Buffy's imagination — making him seem as disconnected from Buffy herself as Joyce, who has actually died.

6. This state most resembles Bakhtin's notion of *heteroglossia*, which "permits a multiplicity of social voices and [a] wide variety of their links and interrelationships (always more or less *dialogized*)" (Bakhtin, *Dialogic*, 269). He discusses this at length in *The Dialogic Imagination* (1981).

7. It is the "boring" deaths which seem to stick in *Buffy*, including Tara's death by an errant bullet (meant for Buffy herself). Darla's suicide, in many ways, also seems almost quotidian, given that it is accomplished through an ordinary wooden stake. The "staking" of vampires on both *Buffy* and *Angel* is such a daily routine, such a non-event, that the reality of a central character — Darla — actually perishing from a wooden stake seems like a terrible inversion of the ordinary.

8. In the Season 6 DVD commentary for The Body, Joss Whedon discusses the many long takes and "oners" — single shots without cutting away — that he utilized to most approximate the experiential "entrapment" of dealing with death. He lauds Sarah Michelle Gellar in particular for having to perform over and over again, pushing herself to raw and emotional point over the course of several days worth of shooting.

9. "Death is your gift," Buffy is told by her spirit-guide in the episode "Intervention" (5.18), and by the end of "The Gift" (5.22) she seems to fully understand what this means — both for her and for Dawn. But, as remaining seasons of *Buffy* show, dying is actually the easy part. The excruciating complexities of living are what continue to confuse Buffy, especially with her mother gone.

10. When I originally discussed some of my financial criticisms of *Buffy* with friends and colleagues, I was surprised by their immediate willingness to defend the show. Most were willing to accept the fact that Giles had an unqualified sum of money saved up from his days as a Watcher, or that Buffy would still be able to keep her house in suburban California on a shift worker's salary. Everyone seemed to agree that, with all programs like *Buffy*, there was a crucial point at which willing suspension of disbelief had to "kick in" so that one could actually *enjoy* the show without criticizing it. What interested me was that, for most viewers, that "cut-off" point for analysis of *Buffy* seemed to be finance, with nobody really interested in just what sorts of economic peculiarities were operating within the show.

11. Despite its fantastic milieu, *Buffy* is still a show about the *realities* of growing up — of experiencing high school, of undertaking responsibility, and of developing an identity separate from parental and other authority figures. With that guiding principle in mind, it seems paradoxical to suggest that we should celebrate *Buffy* as a show that "really gets adolescence right," yet refrain from criticizing it as a show that also makes a lot of sweeping and fantastic generalizations regarding race and economic access.

12. I should say that I am mostly treating humanities scholars here, since they comprise the bulk of scholarship around *specific shows* (as opposed to audience research, and spectatorship studies, which generally take place within media and cultural studies). Television Studies as a discipline emerged from the British cultural studies tradition, which in turn came out of Birmingham University in the 1970s. In general, though, "television studies" points to critical research around media theory, participatory studies and the like, whereas scholarly treatment of particular shows — such as articles on *Buffy* — have mostly been isolated to the humanities field, and especially concentrated within English.

13. Timothy Brennan sums up the American cultural saturation of the Third World

by reminding us that "Puerto Ricans and Liberians field a larger knowledge of the United States than North Americans do of Puerto Rico and Liberia" (Brennan, 3). In *Hybrid Cultures* (1995) and *Consumers and Citizens* (2001), Nestor Garcia Canclini discusses this cultural invasion in terms of competing audio visual spaces and the breakdown of regional culture in favor of a global "pastiche."

14. For a detailed analysis of Latin-American representation within a variety of media, focusing especially on hybridity and biraciality, see Gloria Anzaldua's *Borderlands / La Frontera* (1999), as well as her edited collection, *Making Face, Making Soul* (1990), which explores a variety of critical perspectives by women of color.

15. Financial independence is, in fact, a staple of fantasy/sci-fi television dramas. The characters in the Canadian thriller-drama *Nikita* all work for a paramilitary organization that is independently funded (and affords them with housing). *Stargate-SG1* also employs a military organization that funds its members' various expeditions to increasingly exotic dimensions (although *Stargate*, at least, attempts to criticize many of the imperialist ethics that inform its plot). The characters in *Charmed* managed to inherit an enormous house (not unlike Buffy's), and, although they all have jobs, they are also able to spend an unusual amount of time at home crafting rhyme-poor spells.

16. In *Forever*, immediately after Joyce's funeral, Buffy admits to Angel, "Mom was the strong one in real life. She always knew how to make things better" (5.17). The interesting thing about this is that, after Joyce's death, very little mention is made of her character's legacy for the duration of the show. She appears once as a ghost, but this seems to be a ploy of the First Evil rather than an actual spirit manifestation. Joyce's discursive absence from the fabric of the show suggests that Buffy really has taken on her duties as mother.

Chapter Four

1. This fathering relationship also extends to the Giles-Willow relationship, and finds its most troubling expression in Season 6, immediately after Willow has raised Buffy from the dead. Giles is clearly incensed at Willow, not just for failing to "respect the forces of nature" ("Flooded," 5.04), but for exhibiting the arrogance that will, in part, lead her towards addiction. In *Grave*, Willow criticizes Giles for "butting in on things that don't concern you," and it becomes clear, especially in the later episode "Lessons" (7.01), that Giles's paternal and pedagogical relationship includes Willow as well as Buffy.

2. Here I am referring to Angel's mystical manipulation of Connor's memories, in order to give him a "normal" life — which Connor eventually accepts, although not without a few interruptions for the sake of protecting his father (see the Season 4 episode "Home" [4.22]).

3. Middle-aged white men, such as Quentin Travers and Roger Wyndam-Price, are not generally presented as positive characters within *Buffy* or *Angel*. Giles is probably the only exception to this rule, and this has mostly to do with his construction as an anti–Watcher in opposition to the politics of the Council. It would be worthwhile, I think, to conduct a critical treatment of middle-aged white men in both shows, especially comparing their power and privileging with that of adolescent white women.

4. Mr. Summers and Roger Wyndam-Price are absent/negligent fathers; D'Hoffryn, the patron-demon in charge of vengeance demons, is a sort of demon-father to Anya, although their relationship is coded with disturbingly erotic overtones; Corbin Fries transforms his own son into a chemical bomb in the Angel episode "Conviction" (5.01); and we have all, of course, feared that our father might really be a cyborg, as is the case with Wesley in the episode "Lineage" (5.07).

5. The historical persistence of the nuclear family, especially in visual media, is made possible by what Michael Shapiro calls a "willed forgetting" on a global scale, in that it is continually presented as a "historically stable, noncontingent result of natural inclinations and morally appropriate choices" (Shapiro, 2), rather than as a flexible site that varies depending upon geographic, political and historical context.

6. It seems likely that Cordelia has a trou-

bling relationship with her parents, although this is only hinted at within both *Buffy* and *Angel.* Janet Halyfard, in an unpublished conference paper on Cordelia, suggests that she has clearly been spoilt in material terms, but there are considerable hints that she has been neglected emotionally, and more or less abandoned by her family after her parents' falling out with the IRS" (2004).

7. I base this information on the 2002 (released July 2003) Current Population Report on *Children's Living Arrangements and Characteristics,* U.S. Census Data, compiled by Fields et al. This is available online at the U.S. Census Bureau Homepage (http://www.census.gov).

8. Canadian Census Data, although available online through *Statistics Canada* (http:// www.statcan.ca), is organized around free vs. pay content, with only the most rudimentary data available for free viewing. I have based my research on the 2001 *Family and Household Living Arrangements* data.

9. For a critical treatment of Giles' background (as well as a fascinating look at consumption and "suckage" within the show), see McNeilly, Fisher and Silka's article "Kiss the Librarian, But Close the Hellmouth," *Slayage* 2 (2001). See also Matthew Pateman's article "'You say tomato': Englishness in *Buffy the Vampire Slayer,*" *Cercle* 8 (2003): 103–113, *www.cercles.com/n8/pateman.pdf,* for an extended treatment of British tropes within the show.

10. I am indebted here to Peggy Davis' unpublished conference paper, "'I'm a Rogue Demon-Hunter'": Wesley's Transformation from Fop to Hero on *Buffy the Vampire Slayer* and *Angel,*" which was presented at the *Slayage* 2004 conference. She traces Wesley's evolution from a comical character on *Buffy* to a fully formed and morally ambivalent character on *Angel.*

11. Although I could have easily written a chapter on Lorne's queer mothering techniques, I found myself content with the idea of mothering/fathering being spread amongst Angel, Giles, Wesley, Buffy, Fred and Cordelia, and thought in the end that including Lorne would be stretching the point. He does, however, deserve a separate article or chapter, given the wonderful complexities of his character. His general avoidance of physical struggle, love of the divas, powers of empathy and penchant for silk bathrobes all code him playfully as a queer character, although he appears, for the most part, to be asexual. Like Warren, Lorne's sexuality is a site of comic ambiguity rather than a serious lived reality, which, in some sense, is vaguely insulting to queer communities while being post-structurally interesting to gender theorists. Several contributors to Stacey Abbott's *Investigating Angel* book (forthcoming) touch upon Lorne, and Stan Beeler's chapter ("Outing Lorne: Performance for the Performers") treats him as a representation entertainment culture within L.A.

12. In this episode (Provider), money is actually associated with extradimensional aliens who seem to communicate through a series of clicks and whistles; in *Buffy*'s episode (Flooded), it is associated with a bounty hunter–demon. Either way, the issue of money gets hijacked by fantasy here, being redeployed as something strange and fantastic, rather than as a necessary commodity for the characters.

13. I base my rudimentary understanding of the ethics of care on Grace Clement's work *Care, Autonomy, and Justice* (Westview: 1996), in which she argues that the social division between dialogues of care and justice is false, given that care underlies much responsible public policy, and that juridical scripts inform private, as well as public, relationships (Clement, 69–75). Daniel Engster writes critically and insightfully on Clement's work, as well as care ethics from a global perspective, in his article "Care Ethics and Natural Law Theory: Toward an Institutional Political Theory of Caring," *Journal of Politics,* Volume 66 Issue 1 (February 2004). For a recent book-length treatment of care ethics, see also Ruth Groenhout's *Connected Lives: Human Nature and an Ethics of Care* (Rowman and Littlefield, 2004).

14. Douglas Petrie, who wrote this episode, clearly knows the comic value of a Jabba the Hutt–type monster. Balthazar is visually exotic while remaining essentially nonthreatening (generally, he just waves his arms around). This somewhat resembles Wesley himself, who carries his Watcher's pedigree with him, but has very little else to recommend him as either a leader or a fighter.

15. Foucault defines the idea of govern-

mentality, as opposed to "government," as the "conduct of conduct," or "the way in which the conduct of a whole of individuals is found implicated, in an ever more marked fashion, in the exercise of sovereign power" (Foucault, *On Governmentality*, 101). In this sense, governmentality represents any invasion of the private sphere by governmental policy as an attempt to shape daily life. It is not power *over* citizens, but rather an instrumentalizing of citizens' own power that forces them to monitor and police themselves. I will discuss this idea further in Chapters Five and Six.

16. William James actually popularized the idea of "rugged individualism," a particularly early-American philosophy of masculine self-sufficiency and capitalist mobility, in his 1896 essay "The Will to Believe." He describes the ideal man as a "tough-minded accepter of facts," and states that proper Democracy must "'continue the manliness to which the military mind clings." Herbert Hoover recapitulated these ideals in what came to be known as his "Rugged Individualism" campaign speech, delivered to a New York audience in 1928.

17. For a critical treatment of Spike's ambiguous soul, see Gwyn Symonds' conference paper "A Little More Soul Than Is Written": Acting 'Spike' and the Ambiguity of Evil in Sunnydale," presented at *Slayage* 2004.

Chapter Five

1. Cordelia sleeps with Connor in the episode "Slouching Towards Bethlehem" (4.04), thereby completing the circuit of erotic incest within *Buffy* and *Angel* by becoming a mother who sleeps with her "son." I am aware of the outrageously visible oedipal connections here just begging to be discussed, but will avoid that particular psychoanalytic road, given my preoccupation with sociological and family-based criticism (rather than psychoanalytic theorizing).

2. Kristeva describes her own career-long project as a bridging of psychiatric practices and literary discourses, describing how, initially, she wanted to "analyze the acquisition of language and psychotic language as critical discourses. For neutral description or observation is not enough: I had to involve myself in order to understand how the people I hear are contributing to the transformation of a relationship" (Kristeva, *Interviews*, 147). For her, the psychiatrist who is also a linguist represents the ultimate conjunction of analytical techniques, and psychoanalysis remains the necessary ground from which all literary analysis must emerge.

3. Fred's exposure to, and subsequent enslavement within, a hostile dimension represents a parallel of Illyria's experience, for both are rendered "slaves" of a sort, stripped of their essential subjectivity and marooned within a world that disdains or threatens them. And, just as Fred was duped by a professor (see the episode "Supersymmetry," 4.05) who she trusted and used as part of his science experiment (which results in her being transported to Pylea), so was Illyria, in a sense, violently resurrected by her last surviving follower (the character Knox) and transported into a world that has no place for her.

4. This is based on a Sears advertising campaign that ran in 1997, and was designed, one presumes, to highlight the mega-department store as a fashionable clothing outlet rather than simply a place for buying VCRs and riding mowers. As a bizarre conjunction of *Buffy*, advertising and family, I should admit that my mother works for Sears and that she remembers this ad campaign well, given how much her family ridiculed it. "Seen the softer side of Sears lately, mom?" I often asked her, to which she would roll her eyes and insist that she didn't write the advertising copy.

5. Xander is the poorest member of the Scoobies, although he still lives in a modest house and gets an entire basement to himself before moving into what looks suspiciously like a luxury apartment. Faith's economic background is uncertain, but her speech resembles a kind of Boston working-class vocabulary, and her aggressive characteristics, I think, are discomfortingly linked here with her speculative poverty. Either way, *Buffy* clearly demonstrates that characters who aren't middle-class, or who are living somewhere on the borders of middle-class economic security, have far less stable family atmospheres and backgrounds.

6. Jean Swanson's book *Poor Bashing*

describes the extent to which people living in poverty internalize critiques leveled at them by various media sources. This leads them to feel ashamed about their living situation, rather than realizing that it is an unequal capitalist economy — which encourages competition among the poorest of the poor — that creates this situation, not the poor themselves (Swanson, 1–10).

7. This book treats the character of Gunn only peripherally, and I hope that forthcoming scholarly articles and book chapters by writers of color will discuss him in greater depth. As a white scholar, I feel myself coming up against the limits of experience when trying to discuss Gunn's blackness. I have thus opted to create a space of criticism around his character, without fully trying to explore his multiple perspectives as the sole recurring person of color within either *Angel* or *Buffy*. For a more detailed discussion of Gunn, see "From Rogue in the Hood to Suave in a Suit: Black Masculinity and the Transformation of Charles Gunn," Michaela Meyer's troublingly titled chapter in Stacey Abbott's forthcoming *Investigating Angel* collection (IB Tauris).

8. We should bear in mind that Fred actually leaves her supportive family (who find her after years of searching) because she feels more at home with Angel and company ("Fredless," 3.05). Cordelia doesn't appear to have much of a family to go home to, and her choice to stay in L.A. is originally a career decision — she wants to become an actress — rather than a result of feeling "at home" in the city.

9. Robinson and Skill point out that, even as late as 1995, the percentage of white families on television was 80.5 percent, and that, while Hispanic and African-American families had an extremely peripheral presence, "Asian or American Indian families were less likely to be found in a series featuring a family than was a family with an alien boarder from the planet Melmac" (148; 158).

10. As with *Buffy*'s "matter-of-fact" queer relationship between Tara and Willow, wherein the characters experienced no real homophobia or discomfort among their friends, Gunn and Fred's interracial relationship is de-politicized by *Angel* and presented as merely a quirky romance. I am not suggesting that a televisual romance, because it is interracial, must deliberately make reference to the historical criticisms from white audiences that such relationships have received, both on television and in film. But I do think that, in their attempts to maintain narrative rather than political coherence, both *Buffy* and *Angel* often sidestep critical issues around race, gender and sexuality that ought to be addressed, unless we are willing to accept that these characters live in a utopian world without violence, homophobia, racism, sexism and poverty (which they clearly do not, given that these material, as well as discursive, inequalities, find their way into both shows through various channels).

11. Lilah's entrepreneurial individualism, her intense ambition and her subsequent disconnection from any coherent group of family and friends makes her a troubling and fascinating character. Her death codes her, in a way, as a failed New Woman, whose greed and ambition end up destroying her, while her only redeeming characteristic seems to be her emotional connection with Wesley. I don't think that *Angel* intends to construct Lilah as an irredeemable super-bitch who "just once" experiences something close to love with a heterosexual man, but the stereotype does stick. For a more nuanced reading of the Lilah-Wesley relationship, along with a discussion of "female agents" in *Angel*, see Jennifer Stoy's chapter "'And Her Tears Flowed Like Wine': Wesley/Lilah and the Complicated(?) Role of the Female Agent on *Angel*" in Stacey Abbott's *Investigating Angel* collection.

12. Amy Acker's performance in this death scene is tremendous, and also critically interesting because her character seems to hover between a child and adult state. She insists that her death be as painless as possible for both her biological and extended families, even choosing to die in her bedroom, with Wesley, rather than in a hospital. But her final words, "Please, Wesley, why can't I stay?" ("A Hole in the World," 5.15) are the plea of a terrified child. Wesley is both her partner and her caretaker here, and thus fulfills his ultimate role as Watcher by being the only witness to Fred's death and Illyria's subsequent birth.

13. I attended a panel at the *Slayage* conference on racial representation within *Buffy*, and was more than a little anxious to discover

that it was a room full of white scholars. I was made even more anxious when *nobody* mentioned this fact, and found myself sinking into an uncomfortable silence during the presentations, angry at myself for not being able to say anything — and, furthermore, not being quite sure what I *wanted* to say. The whole situation rose all sorts of uncomfortable questions about white scholarly investment in racial representation. Ewan Kirkland delivered a self-critical paper on the cultural entitlements of whiteness within the series, and was careful to mention the potentially ridiculous idea of a white scholar talking about whiteness to a room full of white people at a panel on *race*. Jeffrey Middents, who identified as Mexican-American, gave a paper discussing themes of minstrelsy and racial stereotyping within the *Once More With Feeling* musical episode, and included demographic information on the racial breakdown of California, pointing to the fact that Hispanic audiences, given the size of the Hispanic community within California, were severely underrepresented in *Buffy*. At one point, the sole woman of color in the audience, who never introduced herself, criticized Jasmine's depiction as a tyrannical ruler because the idea of a black woman controlling the world seemed frankly unrealistic. I was extremely relieved when I heard her speak, but I also knew that part of this relief stemmed from my own white guilt around the voyeuristic nature of discussing non-white representation in a room full of white people. Much, much more work on *Buffy*, *Angel* and race needs to be done in scholarly and popular media.

14. Despite *Angel*'s careful reinscription of its narratives as action-based in Season 5, the show was still cancelled, which leads us to believe that sometimes a cultural vehicle can "have it all" and still not satisfy the networks. As a reminder of this, Joss Whedon's *Firefly*, which now has a huge and devoted cult fan base, was cancelled because, in its first (and only) season, it seemed to be more a show about character development and emotional connections than a show about space ships, train heists and explosions.

15. Given that Cordelia gets to be both saint and mother as a result of this storyline, I wonder if the creation of Illyria is not, after all, some kind of exchange for *Cordelia's* specialness, rather than a punishment of Fred's ambivalence. As Spike reminds Willow and Xander after Buffy has been resurrected, "That's the thing about magic. There's always consequences" ("Afterlife," 6.03), and perhaps Illyria is a kind of consequence.

16. Kristeva, describing the insider/outsider binary within academic communities, says, "I think it's a question of an individual fighting spirit — almost animal-like — for someone to remain vigilant while being on the inside" (*Interviews* 125). In much the same way, I think, Illyria becomes an "animal-like" vigilance on the inside of Angel Investigations, maintaining her essential outsiderness while criticizing the human relations that she sees as damaged, flawed or inexplicable.

17. On a more abstract level (could I possibly *be* more abstract?), Illyria also represents the theme of exile and outsiderness that pervades the narratives of both *Buffy* and *Angel*, the feeling of not belonging anywhere. Dawn is similar to Illyria, in that she is not quite human, yet wants to be part of human intimacy and interaction. Willow is the same, knowing that she has the power to destroy the world, yet wanting desperately to fit in and be loved by the people who knew her when she was an awkward and inarticulate nerd. I don't think the message here is as reductive as *nobody fits in anywhere*, but I do think that certain characters in *Buffy* and *Angel* operate at a fundamental remove from everyday society for very specific reasons having to do with gender, sexuality and cultural background, which I have attempted to discuss throughout this book.

18. For another troubling example of maternity producing a hybrid child, and resulting in the death of the mother, see the character "Blade" — a vampire hunter who is part-vampire himself. Blade began as a comic book character, created by Marv Wolfman and Gene Colan, and was adapted into a hit series of films beginning with 1998's *Blade* (Stephen Norrington, director; David S. Goyer, writer), and culminating *Blade: Trinity* (written and directed by Goyer). Fascinating intersections of race (Blade's/Wesley Snipe's eroticized and hyper-masculinized black body), technology and inventive vampire traditions (such as the "corporatization" of vampire families) have produced a lot of

interest within academic communities. For a critical exploration of mysticism vs. technology within *Blade*, see John J. Jordan's article "Vampire Cyborgs and Scientific Imperialism: a Reading of the Science-Mysticism Polemic in *Blade*" in the *Journal of Popular Film and Television*, vol. 27, no. 2, Summer 1999: 4–15.

Chapter Six

1. David Lavery drove this point home for me when he described the initially lukewarm response of publishers to his *Twin Peaks* collection *Full of Secrets* (Wayne State University Press, 1995). He wrote in an e-mail that it "was rejected by a score of publishers, all of whom thought it wouldn't sell 500 copies. It has now sold 12,000" (November 26, 2003). Pop culture texts clearly sell well, but their production is often hampered by an academic caginess on the part of publishers — an uncertainty around the legitimacy of the text and, by extension, the legitimacy of fan interest.

2. In *Bodies That Matter*, Judith Butler insists that "it is important to resist that theoretical gesture of pathos in which exclusions are simply affirmed as sad necessities of signification" (53). In my experience, visible and unjustifiable exclusions in lectures, on syllabi, in scholarly articles — exclusions within graduate curricula, that is — get overlooked as the "sad necessities" of composing "universal" courses that are actually speaking to no one because they address no specific bodies, no specific histories and no problematic sexualities. I can't count how many times I've been the "queer" voice in a classroom, the one asking the "queer" questions, just as I have colleagues who feel as if they are the "Black" voice or the "Asian" voice within classroom discussions, trying to advocate for particularity while feeling as if they are hijacking the "universal" conversation. It is often the case that being an academic means getting to write peripherally about your own lived experience while sacrificing any meaningful personal dialogue around that experience in order to become a "well-rounded" scholar, which is a prospect that I don't accept.

3. Families, like all communities, produce what Zoe Newman calls a "desired 'safety' ... [that] will always require us to find and expel some new enemy within the group" (Newman, 132). Any family that coheres around certain moral principles will define itself primarily by what it leaves out, what it rejects.

4. I should not attempt to exempt myself from being part of this "humorous gesture." When I first wrote on *Buffy* for Lavery and Wilcox's journal *Slayage*, it was more a cathartic exercise than a scholarly project. I had been watching a lot of *Buffy* reruns over Christmas holidays, and thought that it might be interesting to write something academic on the series — especially on the Willow-Xander relationship that intrigued me so much. I submitted the article mostly because I was interested in talking to David and Rhonda, and I wouldn't have even known about *Slayage* if my office-mate at the time, Glen Stosic, hadn't mentioned it to me in passing. It all seemed very fun and low-stakes, until the article was accepted (after a variety of revisions), and suddenly the prospect of writing academically on *Buffy* was quite real. This book actually began as my doctoral dissertation — I subsequently changed my doctoral research and kept working on the book as an entirely separate project, but when I first presented it to my supervisor, Dr. Peter Dickinson, as a proposal, I thought for sure he would reject it. Again, I was amazed that he liked the project, and this says a lot about internalized "pop-phobia" among academics. Even those who love pop culture, and who write on it critically, still often fear that their work isn't legitimate.

5. I should add that it often takes a change of medium to make a cultural artifact "respectable" once again. Jay David Boulter and Richard Grusin call this media-change "remediation," a centuries-old phenomenon suggesting that "no medium today, and certainly no media event, seems to do its cultural work in isolation from other media, any more than it works in isolation from other social and economic forces" (Boulter and Grusin, 15). *Lord of the Rings* is a perfect example of this, given that any sort of academic criticism around Tolkien's work — excluding the journal *Mythlore*, which is exclusively dedicated to Tolkien and publishes shorter work — had been at a stand-

point since the late 1970s until the advent of Peter Jackson's film trilogy. Now we have books like *The Lord of the Rings and Philosophy* (Open Court, 2003), as well as a forthcoming special issue of *Modern Fiction Studies* on Tolkien's work.

6. My mother's response remains the best. When I found out that my essay on Willow had won a "Mr. Pointy" award—which is fabulous, and actually shaped like a stake, and sitting on my desk right now—I phoned my mom from the hotel in Nashville to tell her. "Mom," I said, "I got a Mr. Pointy!" There was a polite pause on the telephone, and then she replied, "Honey, I don't think your mother needs to know that." I won't even talk about the adventure of trying to cross the Canadian–U.S. border with a sharpened stake in my suitcase.

7. Columbia University's English graduate studies program is called "Comparative Literature," which at first seems more progressive and accurate than "English." But its guidelines stipulate that each student must choose a geographic concentration for her literary area, and thus choose, in effect, a national literature to study. "I study British post-war literature" is an easier statement for most hiring committees to digest than "I study media, popular culture, queer literatures and Canadian poetry." Trust me.

8. Part of this adaptive durability comes from the fact that, as Richard Burt describes it in his book *Unspeakable ShaXXXspeares* (St. Martin's, 1998), "Shakespeare is cited in a popular culture that is now co-extensive with youth culture [and] Shakespeare films have been directed at a youth market at least since Franco Zeffirelli's *Romeo and Juliet* [1968]" (Burt, 2–3).

9. It remains troubling, however, that many poor families are captive audiences to television—given their limited financial ability to access more expensive cultural displays like theaters, art galleries and even feature films—yet television addresses primarily middle-class rather than poverty-line viewers, and continues to valorize the type of conspicuous consumption that poor audiences are exactly unable to partake in. The result is almost evangelical, in that poor audiences are being addressed, via the only media that they consistently have access to, with messages that make them feel completely disconnected from a televised world that is itself a middle-class fantasy.

10. The next frontier, I think, beyond critical study of television shows remains the analysis of video games. Although there is already a growing number of academic publications looking at gaming culture, there are few, if any, university courses that treat computer games, and as yet no collections devoted to querying a specific game. Can an edited volume on Square's *Final Fantasy* series for the Sony Playstation, or Sierra's *King's Quest* series for PC, be far behind? For survey-treatments of PC and console games, see James Newman's book *Videogames* (Routledge: 2004), and Mark Wolf and Bernard Perron's *The Video Game Theory Reader* (Routledge, 2003). The general consensus within traditional academic circles is that, once Routledge grabs hold of something, it must be legitimate. So hopefully this will encourage independent scholars to write on more specific gaming titles.

11. This location, and in effect "maintenance," of culture by western academics is often predicated on the erasure of particularity in favor of what Homi Bhabha calls the "museumification" of culture. "Western connoisseurship," he states in an interview, "is the capacity to understand and locate cultures within a universal timeframe that acknowledges their various ... contexts ... only to eventually transcend them and render them transparent" (Bhabha, *Third Space*, 209).

12. More than one *Buffy* critic has pointed out the vital role of language as a weapon in the show, and especially how sarcasm and irony act as discursive tools for Buffy as she fights vampires. She needs to *insult* her enemies rather than simply slaying them, and, really, their defeat occurs first at the level of language; it is this initial defeat that leads to their ultimate physical demise.

13. Again, Gunn, as a character, deserves more detailed critical analysis than I can offer in this book. Also, my euphemisms about "limits of experience" when talking about Gunn do, after all, add up to the inescapable fact that I am white and Gunn is not. I feel uncomfortable, as a white scholar, talking too extensively about a black character, especially when my background is not in critical race studies. This discomfort is worth exploring—

indeed, it is something I strive to address in all of my work, and I think that more white scholars need to admit that they share such discomfort rather than offering patronizing attempts to critically treat non-white characters. But, in terms of *this* text, such analysis is beyond my scope. I invite others to take up these questions, and to criticize my avoidance of them where such criticism is necessary.

14. I have heard this experience called by many names, but all are variations of "The Imposter Syndrome" — that is, the belief that all of your peers (and friends) are much better scholars, and that they intuitively understand what it means to be a grad student in a way that you never will. It can extend to the belief that everyone is a better writer than you, everyone understands Foucault more than you, and everyone is a much better teacher-facilitator than you. This belief is widespread, and present in virtually every grad student I've ever met, which leads one to believe that it is basically impossible. If everyone thinks that everyone else is incompetent, then nobody is really incompetent. The belief is just a psychological defense mechanism that shields one from criticism, leading one to believe that, *since I'm stupid, then I can't be held to the same standards as everyone else.* Even tenured faculty I've spoken to still experience this from time to time. So, it doesn't necessarily pass — but it does, over time, get more manageable.

Bibliography

Abbott, Stacey, ed. *Reading* Angel. August 2005, London: IB Tauris, forthcoming.

Adams, Michael. *Slayer Slang:* A Buffy the Vampire Slayer *Lexicon.* Oxford: Oxford University Press, 2003.

Aitken, Stuart. *Family Fantasies and Community Space.* New Brunswick, N.J.: Rutgers University Press, 1998.

Akass, Kim, and Janet McCabe, eds. *Reading* Sex and the City. London: IB Tauris, 2003.

Albada, Kelly F. "The Public and Private Dialogue About the American Family on Television." *Journal of Communication* vol. 50, no. 4 (autumn 2000).

Aloi, Peg. "My Art Belongs to Daddy: Rupert Giles as Magical Mentor, Indulgent Father, Book Man." Paper given at *Slayage* conference on *Buffy the Vampire Slayer* (2004).

Anzaldua, Gloria. *Borderlands* (La frontera). San Francisco: Aunt Lute Books, 1999.

_____, ed. *Making Face, Making Soul: Creative and Critical Perspectives by Women of Color.* San Francisco: Aunt Lute Foundation Books, 1990.

Bakhtin, Mikhail. *The Dialogic Imagination.* Trans. Michael Emerson and Caryl Holquist. Austin: University of Texas Press, 1981.

_____. *Rabelais and His World.* Trans. Helen Iswolsky. Bloomington: Indiana University Press, 1984.

Barthes, Roland. *Pleasure of the Text.* Trans. Richard Miller. New York: Hill and Wang, 1975.

Bassham, Gregory, and Eric Bronson, eds. The Lord of the Rings *and Philosophy: One Book to Rule Them All.* Chicago: Open Court, 2003.

Baudrillard, Jean. *Simulacra and Simulation.* Trans. Sheila Glaser. Ann Arbor: University of Michigan Press, 1994.

Beeler, Stan. "Outing Lorne: Performance for the Performers." Ed. Stacey Abbott. *Investigating Angel.* London: IB Tauris, forthcoming.

Bernard, Jessie. *The Future of Marriage.* New York: World Publishing, 1972.

Bhabha, Homi K. *The Location of Culture.* New York: Routledge, 1994.

_____. "The Third Space: An Interview with Homi Bhabha." Interview by David Bennet and Terry Collits. *Literary India.* Eds. Patrick Colm Hogan and Lalita Pandit. New Delhi: Rawat Publications, 1997.

Boss, Pauline. "Family Stress." Eds. Marvin B. Sussman and Suzanne K. Steinmetz. *Handbook of Marriage and the Family.* New York: Plenum, 1987.

_____, and Greenberg. "Family Boundary Ambiguity." *Family Process,* pg. 23, 1984.

Boulter, Jay David, and Richard Grusin. *Remediation: Understanding New Media.* Cambridge, Mass.: MIT Press, 1999.

Bourdieu, Pierre. *Photography: A Middle Brow Art.* Trans. Shawn Whiteside. Stanford: Stanford University Press, 1990.

Bowman, Laurel. "*Buffy the Vampire Slayer*: The Greek Hero Revisited." Faculty Webpage: http://web.uvic.ca/~lbowman/buffy/buffythehero.html.

Brantley, Cynthia. "Colonial Africa: Transforming Families for Their Own Benefit (and Ours)." Eds. Lynne Haney and Lisa Pollard. *Families of a New World.* New York: Routledge, 2003: 138–55.

Brennan, Timothy. *At Home in the World.* Cambridge, Mass.: Harvard University Press, 1997.

Burr, Viv, and Christine Jarvis. "'Friends Are the Family We Choose for Ourselves': Young People and Families in *Buffy the Vampire Slayer.*" Paper given at *Slayage* conference on *Buffy the Vampire Slayer* (2004).

_____. "Scholar/shippers and Spikeaholics: Academic and fan identities at SC*BtVS.*" *European Journal of Cultural Studies,* August 2005.

Burt, Richard. *Unspeakable ShaXXXspeares: Queer Theory and American Kiddie Culture.* New York: St. Martin's, 1998.

Butler, Judith. *Bodies That Matter.* New York: Routledge, 1993.

_____. "Changing the Subject: Judith Butler's Politics of Radical Resignification." Eds. Gary A. Olsen and Lynn Worsham. *JAC.* 20.4 (2000): 727–63.

_____. "Doing Justice to Someone." *GLQ.* 7.4 (2001): 621–36.

Canadian Census Data, 2001: "Families and Household Living Arrangements." http://www.statcan.ca.

Canclini, Néstor Garcia. *Consumers and Citizens.* Trans. George Yudice. Minneapolis: University of Minnesota Press, 2001.

_____. *Hybrid Cultures.* Trans. Christopher L. Chiappari and Silvia L. Lopez. Minneapolis: Minnesota University Press, 1995.

Cannon, Martin. "The Regulation of First Nations Sexuality." *Canadian Journal of Native Studies,* vol. 18, no. 1, (1998): 1–18.

Carby, Hazel. *Race Men.* Cambridge, Mass.: Harvard University Press, 1998.

Carson, Anne. *Eros the Bittersweet.* Normal, Ill.: Dalkey Archive, 2000.

Cheale, David. *Family and the State of Theory.* Toronto: University of Toronto Press, 1991.

Clement, Grace. *Care, Autonomy, and Justice: Feminism and the Ethics of Care.* Boulder: Westview, 1996.

Conrad, Joseph. *Heart of Darkness.* Ed. D.C.R.A. Goonetilleke (1899), 2d ed. Peterborough, Ontario: Broadview, 1999.

Davis, Kingsley. *Human Society.* New York: Macmillan, 1949.

Davis, Peggy. "'I'm a Rogue Demon-Hunter: Wesley's Transformation from Fop to Hero on Buffy the Vampire Slayer and *Angel.*" Conference paper, *Slayage* 2004.

de Certeau, Michel. *The Practice of Everyday Life.* Berkeley: University of California Press, 1984: 35–37.

Deleuze, Gilles, and Félix Guatari. *A Thousand Plateaus: Capitalism and Schizophrenia.* Minneapolis: University of Minnesota Press, 1987.

Derrida, Jacques. "Living On: Border Lines." In *Deconstruction and Criticism.* Ed. Harold Bloom. New York: Seabury Press, 1979.
Douglas, William. *Television Families: Is Something Wrong in Suburbia?* Mahwah, N.J.: Lawrence Erlbaum, 2003.
Eco, Umberto. *Apocalypse Postponed.* Bloomington: Indiana University Press, 1994.
_____. *Limits of Interpretation.* Bloomington: Indiana University Press, 1990.
Edwards, Lynne. "Slaying in Black and White: Kendra as Tragic Mulatto in *Buffy the Vampire Slayer.*" Eds. Rhonda Wilcox and David Lavery. *Fighting the Forces.* Lanham, Md.: Rowman and Littlefield, 2002: 85–96.
Engster, David. "Care Ethics and Natural Law Theory: Toward an Institutional Political Theory of Caring." *Journal of Politics,* Volume 66, Issue 1 (February 2004).
Feldman, Shelley, and Lourdes Beneria, eds. *Unequal Burden.* Boulder: Westview, 1992.
Fields, Jason, et al. "Children's Living Arrangements and Characteristics." Current Population Report, U.S. Census Bureau: http://www.census.gov.
Foucault, Michel. *The History of Sexuality v.1.* Trans. R. Hurley. London: Allen Lane, 1979.
_____. "On Govermentality." *I&C* 6: 5–22. 1979.
Frost, Robert. "Death of the Hired Man." *The Poetry of Robert Frost.* Ed. Edward Connery Latham. New York: Holt, Rinehart and Winston, 1969.
Gavigan, Shelley. "Feminism, Familial Ideology, and Family Law." Ed. Meg Luxton. *Feminism and Families.* Halifax: Fernwood, 1997: 98–123.
Gilder, George. *Life After Television.* New York: W.W. Norton, 1992: 22.
Goldie, Terry. *Pink Snow.* Toronto: Broadview, 2003.
Groenhout, Ruth. *Connected Lives: Human Nature and an Ethics of Care.* Lanham, Md.: Rowman and Littlefield, 2004.
Halberstam, Judith. *Female Masculinity.* Durham, N.C.: Duke University Press, 1998.
Halfyard, Janet K. "The Greatest Love of All: Cordelia's Journey of Self Discovery." Paper presented at *Slayage Conference on Buffy the Vampire Slayer,* May 28, 2004.
_____. "Love, Death, Curses and Reverses." *Slayage* 1.4 (2001): 1–8.
Haney, Lynne. "In a Family Way: Theorizing the State and Familial Relations." Eds. Lynne Haney and Lisa Pollard. *Families of a New World.* New York: Routledge, 2003: 1–14
Hartmann, Heidi. "The Family as the Locus of Gender, Class, and Political Struggle." *Signs* No. 6, (1981).
Hegel, GWF. *Phenomenology of Spirit.* Trans. A.V. Miller. Oxford: Clarendon Press, 1977: 288.
Hill, Reuben. "Modern Systems Theory and the Family." *Social Science Information* no. 10 (1971).
Hobbes, Thomas. *Leviathan* [1651]. Oxford: Clarendon, 1909.
Hochschild, Arlie. *The Second Shift.* New York: Viking, 1989.
Hoover, Stewart, et al. *Media, Home, and Family.* New York: Routledge, 2004.
Jackson, Shelley. *Patchwork Girl.* CD-ROM. Eastgate Systems, 1995.
James, William. "*The Will to Believe" and Other Essays in Popular Philosophy, and Human Immorality.* New York: Dover, 1956.
Jordan, John J. " Vampire Cyborgs and Scientific Imperialism: A Reading of the Science-Mysticism Polemic in *Blade.*" *Journal of Popular Film and Television* vol. 27, no. 2 (summer 1999): 4–15.
Jowett, Lorna. *Sex and the Slayer.* Middletown, Conn.: Wesleyan University Press, 2005.

_____. "The Summers' House as Domestic Space in *Buffy the Vampire Slayer.*" *Slayage* Issue 13, (2004).

Kaveney, Roz. *Reading the Vampire Slayer.* London: IB Tauris, 2002.

Kincheloe, Joe, and Peter McLaren. "Rethinking Critical Theory and Qualitative Research." Eds. Norman Denizen and Yvonne Lincoln. *The Handbook of Qualitative Methods.* Newbury Park, Calif.: Sage, 1994.

Kirkland, Ewan. "*Buffy the Vampire Slayer* and Constructions of Whiteness." Paper given at *Slayage* conference, 2004.

Kristeva, Julia. *Julia Kristeva, Interviews.* Edited and translated by Ross Mitchel Guberman. New York: Columbia University Press, 1996.

_____. *Powers of Horror.* Trans. Leon S. Roudiez. New York: Columbia University Press, 1982.

Krzywinska, Tanya. "Hubble-Bubble, Herbs and Grimoires." Eds. Rhonda Wilcox and David Lavery. *Fighting the Forces.* Lanham, Md.: Rowman and Littlefield, 2002.

Lacan, Jacques. *Écrits.* Trans. Alan Sheridan. London: Routledge, 2001.

Lavery, David. *Full of Secrets: Critical Approaches to* Twin Peaks. Detroit: Wayne State University Press, 1995.

_____. "I Wrote My Thesis on You: *Buffy* Studies as an Academic Cult." Keynote Address given at *Slayage* 2004.

_____, and Rhonda Wilcox. *What's at Stake in* Buffy the Vampire Slayer. Lanham, Md.: Rowman and Littlefield, 2002.

Lehr, Valerie. *Queer Family Values.* Philadelphia: Temple University Press, 1999.

Levi, Primo. *If This Is a Man; and, The Truce.* London: Abacus, 1987.

Locke, John. *The Locke Reader.* Ed. John W. Yolton. New York: Cambridge University Press, 1977.

Luxton, Meg. "Nothing Natural About It: The Contradictions of Parenting." Ed. Meg Luxton. *Feminism and Families.* Halifax: Fernwood, 1997: 162–81.

Mangels, Andy. "Lesbian Sex = Death?" *The Advocate,* Issue 869, 8/20/2002: 1–3.

McLuhan, Marshall. *Essential McLuhan.* Ed. Eric McLuhan. Ontario: Anansi, 1995.

McNeilly, Fisher, Silka. "Kiss the Librarian, but Close the Hellmouth." *Slayage,* 2: 2001.

Mendlesohn, Farah. "Surpassing the Love of Vampires." Eds. Rhonda Wilcox and David Lavery. *Fighting the Forces.* Lanham, Md.: Rowman and Littlefield, 2002.

Meyer, Michaela D.E. "From Rogue in the Hood to Suave in a Suit: Black Masculinity and the Transformation of Charles Gunn." Ed. Stacey Abbott. *Reading* Angel. London: IB Tauris, forthcoming.

Middents, Jeffrey R. "A Sweet Vamp: Critiquing the Treatment of Race in *Buffy* and the American Musical: 'Once More, With Feeling.'" Paper given at *Slayage* conference, 2004.

Minh-ha, Trinh. *When the Moon Waxes Red.* New York: Routledge, 1991.

Moen, P., and A. Schorr. "Families and Social Policy." Eds. Sussman and Steinmetz. *Handbook of Marriage and the Family.* New York: Plenum, 1987.

Mulvey, Laura. "Visual Pleasure in Narrative Cinema." Ed. Patricia Evans. *Issues in Feminist Film Criticism.* Indiana: Indiana University Press, 1990: 483–94. Originally published 1975.

Newman, James. *Videogames.* New York: Routledge, 2004.

Newman, Zoe. "The Bisexuality Wars." Ed. Terry Goldie. *In a Queer Country.* Vancouver: Arsenal Pulp, 2001.

Ono, Kent. "To Be a Vampire on *Buffy the Vampire Slayer*: Race and ('Other') Socially Marginalizing Positions on Horror TV." *Fantasy Girls: Gender in the New Universe of*

Science Fiction and Fantasy Television. Ed. Elyce Rae Helford. Lanham, Md.: Rowman and Littlefield, 2000.

Parsons, Talcot. *The Social System*. New York: Free Press, 1964.

Pateman, Matthew. "'You Say Tomato': Englishness in *Buffy the Vampire Slayer*." *Cercle* 8 (2003): 103–13. www.cercles.com/n8/pateman.pdf.

Peters, Suzanne. "Feminist Strategies for Policy Research." Ed. Meg Luxton. *Feminism and Families*. Halifax: Fernwood, 1997: 48–59.

Plato. *The Republic*. Trans. A.D. Lindsay. London: Dent, 1976.

Robinson, James, and Thomas Skill. "Five Decades of Families on Television." Eds. Jennings Bryant and Alison Bryant. *Television and the American Family* (2d ed). Mahwah, N.J.: Lawrence Erlbaum Associates, 2001: 139–62.

Robinson, Sally. *Marked Men*. New York: Columbia University Press, 2000.

Rose, Nikolas. *Powers of Freedom*. New York: Cambridge University Press, 1999.

Rosemblatt, Karin Alejandra. "Forging Families: Gender, Reform, and the Popular Front State in Chile." Eds. Lynne Haney and Lisa Pollard. *Families of a New World*. New York: Routledge, 2003: 119–38.

Said, Edward. *Culture and Imperialism*. New York: Knopf, 1993.

Sappho. "Throned in Splendor, Deathless, O Aphrodite." Trans. Richard Lattimore. *The Norton Anthology of World Masterpieces: The Western Tradition*. Vol. 1, 7th Edited by Sarah Lawall. New York: Norton, 1999.

Shapiro, Michael. *For Moral Ambiguity: National Culture and the Politics of the Family*. Minneapolis: Minnesota University Press, 2001

Silverman, Kaja. *Male Subjectivity at the Margins*. New York: Routledge, 1992.

Simkin, Stevie. "'You Hold Your Gun Like a Sissy Girl': Firearms and Anxious Masculinity in *BtVS*." *Slayage* 11/12 (2004).

Smith, Dorothy. "Women, the Family, and Corporate Capitalism." Ed. M. Stephenson. *Women in Canada*. Toronto: New Press, 1973: 14.

South, James B., ed. Buffy the Vampire Slayer *and Philosophy*. Chicago: Open Court, 2003.

Spicer, Arwen. "'Love's Bitch, but Man Enough to Admit It': Spike's Hybridized Gender." *Slayage* (8): December, 2002.

Spivak, Gayatri Chakravorty. "Can the Subaltern Speak?" from *Marxism and the Interpretation of Culture*. Ed. G.C. Spivak. Chicago: University of Illinois Press, 1988.

Stein, Gertrude. *Lectures in America*. New York: Random House, 1935.

Stoy, Jennifer. "'And Her Tears Flowed Like Wine': Wesley/Lilah and the Complicated(?) Role of the Female Agent on *Angel*." Ed. Stacey Abbott. *Reading* Angel. London: IB Tauris, forthcoming.

Symonds, Gwyn. "A Little More Soul Than Is Written": Acting 'Spike' and the Ambiguity of Evil in Sunnydale," presented at *Slayage* 2004.

Taylor, Ella. *Prime-Time Families: Television Culture in Postwar America*. Berkeley: California University Press, 1989: 3. Wallerstein, Immanuel. *Geopolitics and Geoculture*. Cambridge, Mass.: Cambridge University Press, 1991.

Wilcox, Rhonda. "T. S. Eliot Comes to Television: Buffy's 'Restless.'" *Slayage: The Online International Journal of Buffy Studies* 7 (2002): www.slayage.tv/essays/slayage7/Wilcox.htm.

Winslade, Lawton J. "Teen Witches, Wiccans And 'Wanna-Blessed-Be's.'" *Slayage* (2001): 1–11.

Wolf, Mark J.P., and Bernard Perron, eds. *The Video Game Theory Reader*. New York: Routledge, 2003.

Index